B

A MISSION
DIVIDED

RACE, CULTURE & COLONIALISM
IN FIJI'S METHODIST MISSION

A MISSION
DIVIDED

RACE, CULTURE & COLONIALISM
IN FIJI'S METHODIST MISSION

KIRSTIE CLOSE-BARRY

Australian
National
University

PRESS

Published by ANU Press
The Australian National University
Acton ACT 2601, Australia
Email: anupress@anu.edu.au
This title is also available online at press.anu.edu.au

National Library of Australia Cataloguing-in-Publication entry

Creator: Close-Barry, Kirstie, author.

Title: A mission divided : race, culture and colonialism in Fiji's
                 Methodist Mission / Kirstie Close-Barry.

ISBN: 9781925022858 (paperback) 9781925022865 (ebook)

Subjects: Methodist Church--Missions--Fiji.
                 Methodist Church of Australasia. Department of Overseas
                 Missions.
                 Methodist Mission (Fiji)--History.
                 Religion and politics--Fiji--History.
                 Christianity and culture--Fiji--History.
                 Missions--Political aspects--Fiji--History.
                 Fiji--Politics and government--19th century.

Dewey Number: 266.02399409611

Cover design and layout by ANU Press.

Cover photograph by R H Rickard and others for the Methodist Church of Australasia, Department of Overseas Missions, 'Series 01: Photographic prints of missionaries and Indigenous people in the Northern Territory, Papua New Guinea, Fiji, Samoa and India, ca 1885–1938', PXA 1137, 490-535, pic acc 7061, neg 46, Mitchell Library, State Library of New South Wales. Published with permission of Uniting Church of Australia.

Contents

List of Maps and Figures

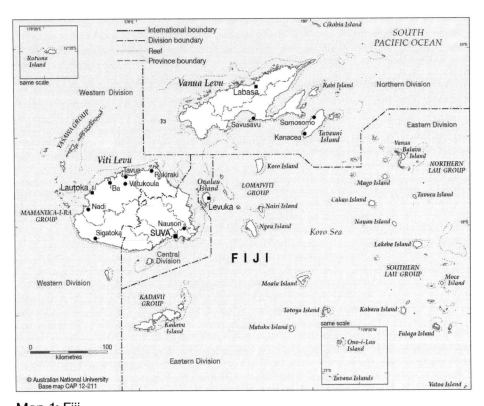

Map 1: Fiji.

Source: CartoGIS, College of Asia and the Pacific, The Australian National University.

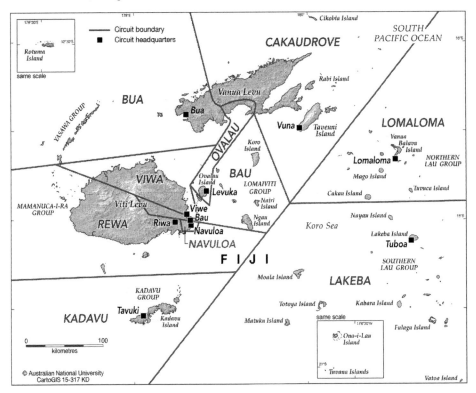

Map 2: Fiji Methodist Mission Circuits, 1874.

Source: CartoGIS, College of Asia and the Pacific, The Australian National University.

Units of Currency

1 penny (d) = 1 cent

1 shilling (s) = 12 pence (d) = 10 cents

1 pound (£) = 20 shillings = 2 dollars (when the Australian pound was converted to the dollar in 1966, the rate of conversion for the new decimal currency was two dollars per Australian pound)

Acknowledgements

There are many people who I need to thank for their help in bringing this book into being. Firstly, I thank the three people who supervised my thesis. My primary supervisor was Helen Gardner, who helped me wrangle my ideas into logical prose. My associate supervisors, Joanna Cruickshank and David Wetherell, also provided thoughtful feedback at crucial moments. All continue to be great sources of support.

I am deeply indebted to the generosity of people in Fiji such as Deaconess Una Matawalu, Tauga Vulaono and Save Nacanaitaba, as well as the families who accommodated Una and me on our fieldwork in the north-west of Viti Levu in 2010. I was greeted warmly by the descendants of Ratu Nacanieli and Apolosi Rawaidranu at various stages of my research and it has been amazing to share our histories.

Scholars from the University of the South Pacific have also welcomed and cared for me during my field work. I note especially Max Quanchi, Morgan Tuimalealiifano and Christine Weir. I also want to note the kind guidance and hospitality of Carolyn and Andrew Thornley during my trips to the Mitchell Library in Sydney.

Thank you to willing interviewees, the Reverend Cyril Germon, Wendy and Peceli Ratawa, as well as the descendants of Robert Green and Doug Telfer for lending me material from their archives. I would also like to make special mention of Talatala Josateki Koroi, who I interviewed for my thesis and who passed away while I made the final edits for this book. He was an exceptional person and I am blessed to have known him.

I have also been aided immensely by the employees at the various archives I have worked in. Not only have they assisted my research in finding documents, but also in providing biscuits and cups of tea (Monte Carlos at the Uniting Church Archives in Elsternwick hit the spot), conversation and company, and even thread and needle when I ripped my pants on a filing cabinet in the National Archives of Fiji reading room. Thank you to all of the archivists and librarians at the National Archives of Fiji, Queen's College Library, Uniting Church Archives in Elsternwick, the St Marks National Theological Centre archives (where the Tippett Collection is housed), the State Library of Victoria, and the Mitchell Library in the State Library of New South Wales. I am also very grateful to Kylie Moloney and Ewan Maidment from the Pacific Manuscripts Bureau for facilitating my access to Methodist records, and thank you to the leaders of the Fijian Methodist Church too.

Thank you also to Tiffany Shellam, Christopher Waters, Sophie Loy-Wilson, Victoria Stead and the other staff at Deakin University, the Australian Catholic University and more recently the Pacific Adventist University with whom I have worked with throughout my years of study. I would like to acknowledge my friends from the Professional Historian's Association, Way Back When and the Pacific History Association for the moral support and shared passion for the past. These have been some of the more quirky, creative, and unashamedly enthusiastic historians I have ever known.

This book is dedicated to my kind, wise family who constitute the best bunch of fruitcakes I know: to James and Hamish; Mum, Dad and Andy; my brilliant uncles, aunts and cousins. They are always with me, through thick and thin. I'm grateful to all of my great aunts and uncles and all of my grandparents who shared their own stories with me and fostered my interest in the past. This book is particularly for Gran, though, who introduced me to Fiji through her childhood stories, and the generations of our family whose paths I have followed back to Fiji. Were it not for my family, I would not be who I am. While I know that my ancestors' place in the colonial past is fraught, I do believe we can learn from their stories and those with whom they shared their lives to build histories that can inform the building of better societies today.

Preface

In 2010, when I conducted fieldwork at Nailaga, a small village in the north-west of Fiji's main island of Viti Levu, the *lali* (drum) was one of the significant sounds that marked time in the village, signalling the start of church-based events, including Bible studies and women's groups.

Figure 1: 'The *lali*'.

Source: Photo by R H Rickard and others for the Methodist Church of Australasia, Department of Overseas Missions, 'Series 01: Photographic prints of missionaries and Indigenous people in the Northern Territory, Papua New Guinea, Fiji, Samoa and India, ca 1885-1938', PXA 1137, 327-535, pic acc 7061, neg 79, Mitchell Library, State Library of New South Wales. Published with permission of Uniting Church of Australia.

Nailaga has a special place for my family, so I felt at ease there. It was my Granny's stories that first took me to Nailaga. Members of my family had lived there for years at a time, working as missionaries for the Methodist Church of Australasia. In fact, my family was, for generations before Granny came along, part of the processes of colonisation in the Pacific. Leaving England for Hobart in 1839, my great-great-great-great-great-grandfather John Waterhouse took up the position of General Superintendent for the Methodist Mission of Australasia, overseeing the Pacific Island mission sites. Several of his sons subsequently travelled to Fiji in later decades to spread the Word. Most notable among them was Joseph Waterhouse, who lived at Viwa throughout crucial years of deliberation for Ratu Epinisa Cakobau, who in 1874 negotiated the cession of the islands to Britain. Joseph Waterhouse was the brother of my great-great-great-great-grandfather, Roland. A few decades later, the first of my ancestors arrived in the north-west of Viti Levu. This was Roland's grandson, Charles Oswald Lelean. Nailaga was Uncle Charlie's first port of call after arriving in Fiji fresh from theological training at Queens College in Melbourne. His first wife died and was buried there. Approximately 30 years after Charlie had started working in Fiji, his nephew Arthur Drew Lelean followed. This was my great-grandfather. My grandmother, Alison, was born in Suva while her father worked on Taveuni. Arthur took over the superintendency of Ba district in 1923, when Granny was only two years old, and Nailaga became the place where she ran amok with her brothers and enjoyed cakes and cucumber sandwiches with her Nanna.

Here I was, just over 80 years since Arthur Lelean and his family had left Fiji, with a different purpose. I am not a missionary, but I wanted to understand the work my family had done in Fiji. I did not want to write a hagiography, nor did I want to be a glorified genealogist. I was prepared to be critical. However, I was learning that my great-grandfather Arthur had supported a grassroots Fijian nationalist movement through the 1920s and '30s, and with my interest in indigenous efforts to assert autonomy in the face of European colonial control, I could not ignore what he had done during his time in Ra province.

Hearing the *lali*, Arthur did not seem so far away. I was reminded of the question that other scholars have posed about missionaries' role as imperialists, or as the harbingers of modernity.[1] Many have queried the extent to which missionaries acted as cultural imperialists, or whether they were beneficiaries

---

1   J H Darch, *Missionary Imperialists? Missionaries, Government and the Growth of the British Empire in the Tropics, 1860–1885*, Colorado Springs, Paternoster, 2009, p. xix. It has been asked of many colonial contexts, not just Fiji: see G Nanni, *The Colonization of Time: Ritual, Routine and Resistance in the British Empire*, Manchester, Manchester University Press, 2012, p. 16. See Nanni's discussion on Victoria, p. 86. Nanni applies this argument to settler colonies such as Victoria and the Cape colony in South Africa, hence there are bound to be alternative perspectives in non-settler colonies. P Grimshaw, 'Missions, Colonialism and the Politics of Gender', in *Evangelists of Empire: Missionaries in Colonial History*, Melbourne, University of Melbourne Press, 2008, p. 6.

of the processes of colonialism.[2] The *lali* — a mark of Fiji's 'ancient' culture — was still being used to communicate, to mark time, to call people together. The *lali* had either defied the rhythm of colonialism, or somehow beat alongside it. It symbolised a continuation of indigenous culture where I had presumed that, like in Australia, European norms would have been enforced throughout the nineteenth and twentieth centuries.

While walking in the footsteps of my ancestors, I learned that the Methodist mission was very much a part of the colonial landscape, and has played a large role in fostering the divisions between the indigenous and Indo-Fijian communities we see in Fijian society today. Not only were indigenous and Indo-Fijian church members kept out of the highest positions of authority in the mission for as long as possible, but the mission was organised in a way that can be described as racial segregation. This book examines closely the processes through which the Methodist mission was organised on ideas about race and culture. In particular, it looks at the Methodist mission's response to the challenge of catering to two large ethnic populations in Fiji during the twentieth century — the indigenous community, and the Indian diaspora community. Missionaries tried to build two 'national' Methodist churches: one 'Fijian' and one 'Indo-Fijian'.[3]

---

2   A Porter, *Religion Versus Empire? British Protestant Missionaries and Overseas Expansion, 1700–1914*, Manchester, Manchester University Press, 2004, pp. 61, 316.
3   J Comaroff and J Comaroff, *Of Revelation and Revolution: The Dialectics of Modernity on a South African Frontier*, vol. 2, Chicago, University of Chicago Press, 1997, p. 5.

Introduction

This book examines the modes of colonial governance adopted by the Methodist Overseas Missions of Australasia's mission in Fiji, which included the development of categories that defined ethnic divisions and hierarchies. It looks specifically at the mission's operations in Fiji during the late nineteenth and early twentieth centuries. Concepts of race and culture were used to position people within the mission's structure, through economic and social stratification. Missionaries adopted this separatist, hierarchical organisational technique with the belief that it would ensure the creation of two separate churches — Fijian and Indo-Fijian — that would hold relevance for its members. Overall, this book identifies the processes of inclusion and exclusion that operated in a church within a colonial context, and elucidates some of the implications that arose. Europeans fractured their own hegemony, as did non-European modes of resistance and disaffection with this structure. The paradoxical formation of a racial hierarchy placed indigenous peoples at the bottom, and yet missionaries often believed that the mission should display indigenous ascendancy. Indo-Fijians, while deemed one of the most crucial ethnic groups in the colony, were always marginalised within the mission. This book includes stories of those that were affected and disaffected with the mission throughout its history, how Europeans entrenched structures of inclusion and exclusion based on ideas around race and culture, and ways in which non-Europeans responded to ethnic difference. Separation of the communities was never complete — there were intimate moments of encounter and exchange, and ongoing relationships built between people. Yet the ways in which difference was demarcated through the structures of institutions have had a lasting impact on Fijian society.

The Methodist mission in Fiji was organised in a way that mirrored the systems of governance used in British colonies under indirect rule. Indirect rule, as Mahmood Mamdani has shown in his deliberations over British Africa, was adopted in Fiji, and this method of governance was used to promote leadership through chiefs or an educated elite, while developing ethnicised categories of organisation based on conceptualisations of custom.[1] Missionaries followed suit, shaping their structures around what they identified as custom. One example of this included attempts to identify a chiefly leadership that could work in the ministry. Yet while 'native' Christians were not excluded from the ministry outright, there were still moments where we can identify resistance to colonial rule, or at least disaffection, to draw on terms utilised and defined so well in studies of colonial Fiji by Martha Kaplan and John Kelly.[2] Despite the 'politics of affection' used to build alliances with the indigenous Fijian community, there were moments within the mission's history where disaffection was evident. Disaffection was not necessarily felt towards the individual mission workers (although this was certainly sometimes the case) but rather at the nature of colonialism within the colony. Disaffection with the design of colonialism that was reflected in the mission's structures fostered Fijian and Indo-Fijian engagement with politics and with nationalistic movements, and prompted efforts at the decolonisation of the mission. The story of the mission, therefore, fits within the same narratives of colonial rule and resistance that have been employed by postcolonial scholars interested in decolonisation.

The similarities between the ideas held by missionaries and colonial administrators were undoubtedly due in part to their shared exposure to the ideas flowing through the imperial networks that Alan Lester, Tony Ballantyne and Antoinette Burton have studied in the Pacific. As a result, the same humanitarian ideals that informed the colonial administration's implementation of indirect rule, responses to nationalist movements, and then decolonisation, were often also employed by missionaries.[3] Throughout the nineteenth century, the British Empire acquired Pacific territories. After the acquisition of Australia in 1778, its envoys travelled increasingly via Australia's east coast. Some of those who departed from Hobart, Melbourne, Sydney and Brisbane were humanitarians, intent on delivering Christianity to so-called 'primitive' peoples. While misfits and brutes from Europe, America and other British colonies sporadically washed up in Fiji, the first Methodist missionaries to establish a base in Fiji did so in 1835 via Tonga, and were isolated from European settlements.[4] They preceded the cession of the Island group by nearly 40 years. By 1853, when the Australian-based Methodists

1   M Mamdani, 'Historicising Power and Responses to Power: Indirect Rule and its Reform', *Social Research*, vol. 66, no. 3, 1999, p. 865.

2   M Kaplan and J Kelly, 'Rethinking Resistance: Dialogics of Disaffection in Colonial Fiji', *American Ethnologist*, vol. 21, no. 1, 1994, pp. 123–29.

3   Regarding imperial networks, see A Lester, 'Imperial Circuits and Networks: Geographies of the British Empire', *History Compass*, vol. 4, no. 1, 2006, pp. 124–41; T Ballantyne and A Burton (eds), *Moving Subjects: Gender, Mobility and Intimacy in an Age of Global Empire*, Illinois, University of Illinois, 2009. Regarding decolonisation of churches, see H Gardner, 'Praying for Independence', *Journal of Pacific History*, vol. 48, no. 3, 2013, pp. 123–4; J A Bennett, 'Meditation', *Journal of Pacific History*, vol. 48, no. 3, 2013, p. 323.

4   S B Degei, 'The Challenge to Fijian Methodism: The *vanua*, Identity, Ethnicity and Change', Masters thesis, University of Waikato, 2007, pp. 8–9.

acquired responsibility for Pacific missions, the cotton industry was changing the Fijian landscape, with crops established, and people, seeds and material resources moving with considerable speed thanks to the advent of steam ships.[5] With increasing pace, humanitarian workers and their ideas circulated between Pacific wharves, spreading throughout the islands. This only increased after annexation, when sugar planters rushed to the islands to establish crops, build mills and crush cane.

Australian Methodist missionaries were intrinsic to colonialism in Fiji, and this colonialism was divisive, creating a bifurcated system that demarcated people on the basis of race, and politicised indigeneity.[6] Australia's own indigenous peoples had experienced the most atrocious process of colonialism, and many coming out of that colony were keen not to see the process of widespread annihilation by disease and genocide perpetuated elsewhere. By the time Europeans reached Fiji, there were many who looked for different ways to secure indigenous rights despite colonial rule. Indigenous leadership was harnessed, with leadership training one of the important aspects of mission, both before and after annexation. Missionaries had relied on good relationships with chiefs to negotiate access to lands and peoples. By the 1860s, Fijian ministers were being trained in the islands, before returning to their villages to preach. In this way, native authority within the mission pre-dated the official commencement of British indirect rule, but came to operate according to the same principles.

Plans for a Fijian church were disrupted with the annexation to Britain in 1874, when the first governor, Sir Arthur Gordon, and subsequent governors oversaw the migration of 60,965 indentured labourers to Fiji between 1879 and 1916.[7] Gordon had adopted this system in an effort to preserve customary Fijian society, noting that indigenous engagement in plantation systems in the West Indies had been highly detrimental. He did not want to be responsible for the same degree of devastation in Fiji.[8] Missionaries had to respond to this increased diversity within the colonial society, taking part in the governing project of managing difference.[9] Missionaries debated the best practical responses to the presence of the Indian community, and through this we can trace their ideas about culture and race. Politicisation was achieved through political manoeuvres and economics as much as socialisation: the colonial administration,

---

5   P France, *The Charter of the Land: Custom and Colonization in Fiji*, Melbourne, Oxford University Press, 1969, p. 37.
6   M Mamdani, *When Victims Become Killers: Colonialism, Nativism, and the Genocide in Rwanda*, Princeton University Press, 2002, p. 33.
7   K L Gillion, 'The Sources of Indian Emigration to Fiji', *Population Studies*, vol. 10, no. 2, 1956, p. 139.
8   I M Cumpston, 'Sir Arthur Gordon and the Introduction of Indians into the Pacific: The West Indian System in Fiji', *Pacific Historical Review*, vol. 25, no. 4, 1956, p. 371.
9   M Mamdani, *Define and Rule: The Native as Political Identity*, Cambridge, Massachusetts, Harvard University Press, 2012, p. 2.

its industries and the mission were co-benefactors, each aiding the other to grow and develop. The issue of land was forever in the back of peoples' minds, especially as Indo-Fijians left their contracts and took up plots of land around the colony. In 1901, the Methodist Overseas Missions of Australasia was based in Melbourne, and Methodists from across the country were investing regularly in the mission and its projects, including training indigenous peoples for yeoman-type work. Encouraging indigenous Fijians to make the land financially productive, to engage in the capitalist economy, was seen as a way to protect their lands from the encroachment of Indo-Fijian settlement. This supported indigenous paramountcy, yet the mission hired both Fijians and Indo-Fijians and had to manage the tensions that this elicited. This workplace offers a fruitful site to analyse encounters, and this book weaves together the stories of many, but not all of the mission's workers, who were confronted by what they perceived to be a clash of cultures.

Both groups were categorised as 'native' and defined by their traditions.[10] Tradition, custom and culture have been discussed at length by Pacific historians and anthropologists. Historians and anthropologists alike have discussed the ways in which custom has been deployed in Pacific politics by indigenous peoples to create greater cohesion within island societies, and this book contributes to what has been a long, continuing discussion on the topic.[11] While writing this book I have been conscious of the post-independence era of Fiji, where culture, custom and indigeneity have been a mark for inclusion or exclusion from what constitutes Fijianness. As Jocelyn Linnekin described, cultural identities have formed the basis for political mobilisation and unity.[12] Examining the mission's history helps us to historicise this phenomena, through identifying missionary and ministerial engagement with ideas around land and labour.

Building on Elizabeth Elbourne's scholarship that links the peripheries of Empire to its heart, as well as the important work of Alan Lester and Tony Ballantyne that examined the trajectories of colonial administrators and the 'webs of empire' respectively, I considered the connections between missionaries in Fiji and international organisations, especially the broader international mission movement.[13] Brian Stanley suggested that the 'three selves' policy forced missionaries to consider their position in the colonial landscape, and it was true that in Fiji, this policy prompted missionaries to question the way in which they held and exerted authority, and answer to Fijian and Indo-Fijian ministers'

---

10   Ibid., p. 4.
11   Imperial Circuits and Networks: Geographies of the British Empire', *History Compass*, vol. 4, no. 1, 2006, pp. 124–41.
12   Linnekin, J, and L Poyer (eds), *Cultural Identity and Ethnicity in the Pacific*, Honolulu, University of Hawai'i Press, 1990, p. 150.
13   E Elbourne, *Blood Ground: Colonialism, Missions and the Contest for Christianity in the Cape Colony and Britain, 1799–1853*, Canada, McGill Queen's University Press, 2002, p. 13.

demands for greater responsibility and ownership of Methodism. The 'three selves' church policy necessitated transformation, and this provoked an early effort at decolonisation. Scholars of Fiji's decolonisation will notice similarities between the debates in the mission, those that occurred in the 1950s and 1960s within the colonial administration, and even debates that occurred elsewhere in the Pacific.[14] When the church decolonised in 1964, six years before the Fijian nation came into being in 1970, it became a testing ground for developing the Fijian nation. The transition of control from Europeans to non-Europeans in the Fijian Methodist Church therefore sits within the broader story of Pacific — and indeed global — decolonisation.

Everyone who worked for the mission either loosely or directly engaged with the idea of the 'three selves' church. It was a model for missions that promised to establish an independent indigenous church. It required that steps be taken to ensure the church was self-supporting, self-governing and self-propagating. The principles of self-support, self-governance and self-propagation form the axis for this book. The 'three selves' policy was developed originally by Henry Venn while he worked in Africa, and was subsequently adopted by other denominations, and refined by ecumenical groups in the twentieth century, particularly the International Missionary Council.[15] Missionaries in Fiji took part in these international forums, and frequently discussed their ideas about self-support, self-governance and self-propagation in the Fiji mission field in their internal correspondence, publications such as *The Spectator* and *The Missionary Review*, books, lectures for the Laymen's Missionary Movement, sermons, and in newspapers. The 'three selves' church policy was often discussed at the mission's annual synod meetings in Fiji, and by the mission board in Sydney: at all levels. Tracing the discussions relating to the 'three selves' church thus offers a study of discourses around colonial governance.

---

14   R Norton, 'Accommodating Indigenous privilege: Britain's Dilemma in Decolonising Fiji', *Journal of Pacific History*, vol. 37, no. 2, 2002, pp. 133–56; themes of indigenous agency, globalisation and neo-colonialism can be read in this text — particularly Chapters Eight and Nine — but are not the key themes, as these terms developed more in the post-colonial period. See H Gardner and C Waters, 'Decolonisation in Melanesia', *Journal of Pacific History*, vol. 48, no. 2, 2013, pp. 115–16. See also H Gardner's discussion on the independence of Vanuatu's church prior to the state's decolonisation, 'Praying for Independence', *Journal of Pacific History*, vol. 28, no. 2, 2013, pp. 122–43.

15   See copy of the original 'Plan for Establishing Missions in the Foulah Country in Africa' as cited in W T Smith, 'An Appraisal of Thomas Coke's Africa Mission, 1796–1811', *Church History*, vol. 40, no. 3, 1971, pp. 309–11; This was incorporated into the Methodist platform for missions in 1813, see C J Davey, *The March of Methodism: The Story of the Methodist Missionary Work Overseas*, London, Epworth Press, 1951, p. 21. For missionary James Calvert's involvement in debates at the Methodist Ecumenical Meeting about self-support in Fiji in 1881, see *Proceedings of the Ecumenical Methodist Conference Held in City Road Chapel, London, September 1881*, London, Wesleyan Conference Office, 1881, p. 482. See also J Zorn, 'Changes in the World of Mission and Ecumenism, 1947–1963', *International Review of Mission*, vol. 88, no. 350, 1999, pp. 279–90.

Concepts of race and culture were evident in missionaries' discussions about 'self-support', a term that generally referred to the financial matters of the mission. Ideally, the Methodist membership would contribute enough funds to cover the running costs of the mission and its projects. Some funds came from overseas donors, but in light of the 'three selves' policy objective of setting up a 'native' or 'indigenous' church — remembering that the Indo-Fijian branch was also considered 'native' — the aim was to establish a church that would survive without overseas aid. This idea extended to rationale for the payment of indigenous workers, as well as programs designed to train an indigenous yeomanry. Missionaries hoped that the minister's wages could be drawn solely from money provided by Fiji's congregations, which would be made easier through Fijian engagement in an agrarian system of land use. Ideas about custom and culture, and each ethnic groups' familiarity with finances and economic matters pervaded the discussions regarding Fijian self-support. Indo-Fijians were generally considered to be better with money, and engaged in agriculture as soon as they arrived in the colony under indenture, but the Indo-Fijian Methodist community was so small that they relied on international donations. It was not considered fair or appropriate to draw on funds raised by Fijians to build the Indo-Fijian church. There was thus an economic rationale behind the division of the mission that linked back to perceptions of culture and custom.

Missionaries were supposed to install non-European people to run the mission (this was 'self-governance'), requiring a full transition of authority from European missionaries to 'native' ministers. Self-representation, missionaries believed, would enhance the mission's legitimacy. The mission was required to train local ministers to a standard that would allow them to both administer, and minister, the Methodist community. The extent to which this training should be enacted was constantly deliberated. European missionaries rarely agreed on how much control non-European ministers should have within the mission, and both Fijian and Indo-Fijian ministers regularly contested their limited role in mission governance. This book considers the issue from both European and non-European perspectives. I have made a concerted effort in this book, where I can, to bring forward the voices of non-European ministers and laypeople.

The final of the three principles, self-propagation, referred to the acceptance of a 'true' form of Christianity that reflected the character of the peoples of what the missionaries referred to as the 'native' mission, and the subsequent ability of the 'native' church to evangelise and sustain a religious community: to propagate Christianity. European missionaries were often troubled by the extent to which the Fijian and Indo-Fijian communities had adopted Christianity. While the other two principles of self-support and governance were complex issues, this was perhaps the most difficult for missionaries to negotiate, as there was a lack of consensus about what signified 'self-propagation'. Again, this was tied to matters of custom and tradition: how much custom should be preserved, and which elements should be discarded. Missionaries constantly assessed the degree of genuine conversion to Christianity, the potential for the faith to be sustained, and for 'native' ministers to adequately deliver God's word to their congregations. Even more challenging was defining a 'Fijian' or 'Indo-Fijian' version of Christianity. Methodist missionaries had translated the Bible and Wesleyan literature into Fijian and Indo-Fijian languages, for example, and were often willing to permit culture to filter into Methodism in various ways, usually in the practice of faith, but this always had limitations. Missionaries in the field had to define the fine line between a Christianity that reflected a national culture through a process of acculturation, and one that was syncretistic.[16]

Ideally, an autonomous church would reflect the 'national' character of the people it housed, and could be described as 'native' or 'indigenous' to its location.[17] It demanded the devolution of the mission — the transition from European to indigenous ownership and authority. Historian John Garrett pointed to both international and grassroots efforts to speed up the process of devolution;[18] this book brings those local and transnational pressures into sharp relief. Looking at missionary engagement with these three concepts of self-support, self-governance and self-propagation allows us to examine missionary rationale for maintaining European control. It also allows us to identify moments when Fijian and Indian responsibility and autonomy escalated. It highlights moments where Fijian and Indo-Fijians recognised and rebelled against their exclusion in certain spheres of the mission, particularly their exclusion from leadership positions. Shining a light on those moments of protest, we get a sense of how boundaries between the three main ethnic groups in Fiji (European, Fijian and Indo-Fijian) shifted over time.

---

16 I have summarised the 'three selves' church principles by drawing on my archival research, as well as documents produced after ecumenical conferences, articles written in scholarly mission journals, as well as Brian Stanley's work. See for example, *Proceedings of the Ecumenical Methodist Conference Held in City Road Chapel, London, September 1881*, London, Wesleyan Conference Office, 1881, p. 466; B Stanley, *The World Missionary Conference, Edinburgh 1910*, Grand Rapids, Eerdmans, 2009; F Lenwood, 'The International Missionary Council at Lake Mohonk, October 1921', *International Review of Missions*, vol. 11, 1922, pp. 30–42; B Mathews, *Roads to the City of God: World Outlook from Jerusalem*, London, Edinburgh House Press, 1928; W R Hogg, *Ecumenical Foundations: A history of the International Missionary Council and its Nineteenth Century Background*, New York, Harper and Brothers, 1952, pp. 244–5.

17 B Stanley, 'The Church of the Three Selves: A Perspective from the World Missionary Conference, Edinburgh, 1910', *Journal of Imperial and Commonwealth History*, vol. 36, no. 3, 2008, pp. 435–51.

18 J Garrett, *Where Nets Were Cast: Christianity in Oceania since World War Two*, Suva, Institute of Pacific Studies, University of the South Pacific in association with the World Council of Churches, 1997.

In fact, because the mission was designed as a 'national' church, missionaries, Fijians and Indo-Fijians were constantly involved in the nationalist project of defining the national character of the colony.[19] As outsiders to these cultures, missionaries drew on their own local experiences in the mission field but also depended on anthropological concepts of 'culture'. Today we understand that 'culture' is something that people learn; it is abstract, can change, and is not attached to a person's ethnicity. This distinction was not always clearly made by missionaries at the turn of the twentieth century.[20] Missionaries understood 'culture' in various ways over time, either adopting rudimentary or more academic perspectives. Sometimes affronted by the realisation that race did not define a person's cultural practices, many missionaries reassessed their understandings about people's ability, need or desire for cultural change during or after their time working in the mission field. Missionaries were often drawn to theories and debates occurring in anthropology, which helped them to better understand, or at least feel better equipped to make sense of the world around them.[21] Often, though, missionary's interpretations of anthropology and the ideas being discussed within the discipline were rather vague. As a result, while the links between the discipline and the mission field are clearly there, they are somewhat amorphous. Where possible, I have defined the correlations between them.

Missionaries struggled not only to convert the lessons from anthropology into mission practice, but also to transition the ideal of the 'three selves' church from a principle on paper into a lived reality. The debates about the principle in ecumenical circles, such as the International Missionary Council, assumed that there was a binary relationship between indigenous peoples and Europeans in each mission field, rather than the multicultural or multi-racial society that existed in many colonies, including Fiji.[22] The term 'native' or 'indigenous' church was applied in the assumption that missionaries would be working with only one cultural group. There was, therefore, little clear guidance from the international mission movement on how to establish a multi-racial mission.

---

19   I am particularly influenced by the theories of B Anderson, *Imagined Communities: Reflections on the Origins and Spread of Nationalism*, London, Verso, 1991; E Hobsbawn, *Nations and Nationalism since 1780: Programme, Myth, Reality*, Cambridge, Cambridge University Press, 1990; H Bhabha, *Nation and Narration*, London, Routledge, 1990.

20   T H Eriksen, *Small Places, Large Issues: An Introduction to Social and Cultural Anthropology*, third edition, New York, Pluto Press, 2010, p. 3.

21   Stanley suggested that missionaries turned to pseudo-scientific theories of race. B Stanley, *The World Missionary Conference, Edinburgh 1910*, Grand Rapids, Eerdmans, 2009, p. 309; P Harries, 'From the Alps to Africa: Swiss Missionaries and Anthropology', in H Tilley and R J Gordon, *Ordering Africa: Anthropology, European Imperialism, and the Politics of Knowledge*, Manchester, Manchester University Press, 2007, p. 201; A Kuper, *The Reinvention of Primitive Society: Transformation of a Myth*, New York, Routledge, 2005, pp. 11, 93.

22   Malaysia was another good example, where Methodist missionaries tried to accommodate several cultural groups within the one mission structure. T R Doraisamy, *The March of Methodism in Singapore and Malaysia, 1885–1980*, Singapore, Stanford Press, 1982, pp. 14, 61, 80.

The result in Fiji was the creation of a segregated mission that catered to two 'national characters', one for 'Fijians' and another for 'Indo-Fijians'. There was another section again for the European community. The 'three selves' policy ideals were then adapted to the specific needs of each branch of this one mission. One of the difficulties encountered by missionaries was designing a mission for a community that was not indigenous to the land. Tensions developed because of the separation of the branches, exacerbated by racial and cultural hierarchies that were embedded in the mission's framework, including rates of pay. Despite being at the bottom of the pay scale hierarchy constructed within the mission, Fijian interests were often given precedence over those of the Indo-Fijian community. These complex tensions are explored throughout the book through the examination of the 'three selves' church policy.

The book opens with the mission's establishment of separate 'Fijian' and 'Indo-Fijian' branches in 1901, which formed the foundation for two separate, ethnicised Methodist identities in Fiji. It examines the reasons for the split, both practical and ideological. The justification for the separation was primarily the cultural differences between these communities. Missionaries drew on anthropological theories and their personal experiences to develop their understandings of difference. Chapter One focuses on the creation of the Indo-Fijian branch, and the subsequent social and geographical boundaries that emerged within the mission under the guidance of its chairman, the Reverend Arthur James Small, and the man who became a leader in the Indo-Fijian branch and later the mission board, the Reverend John Wear Burton. This chapter focuses on the challenges specific to the Indo-Fijian Methodist community.

Chapter Two examines the debates around the 'three selves' policies within the 'Fijian' branch from 1900 to 1920 in order to further explore the reasons for the mission's segregation. It identifies specific challenges that existed in the 'Fijian' branch that inhibited the full realisation of self-support, self-governance and self-propagation. It highlights the marked differences between the two branches of the mission. Having been established for much longer than the 'Indo-Fijian' mission, the 'Fijian' branch had already adopted a system for extracting funds from its membership and paying its 'native ministers'. Fijian ministers, known as *talatala*, were also already being ordained. The principles of self-support and self-governance in particular were addressed in vastly different ways to the Indo-Fijian branch, which was only just starting. While this was due to the length of time missionaries had worked in this branch, the specific cultural milieu they were adapting the 'three selves' model to brought a range of concerns unique to the Fijian branch to the fore.

The connection between mission and anthropology is drawn out in Chapter Three, specifically the adoption of a type of 'functional anthropology' which would promote what historian David Wetherell has referred to as 'tranquil colonialism'.[23] Anthropology was being used to respond to anti-colonial, nationalist ideas that had started to ferment in the colonies.[24] John W Burton was made General Secretary of Methodist Overseas Missions, and was one of the main people advocating changes to missionary training, which he did while based at the Methodist headquarters in Sydney. Burton encouraged the transnational flow of ideas, acting as a conduit not only for the mission board but also the International Missionary Council to the mission field. As they attempted to respond to anti-colonial movements, missionaries tended to rely increasingly on anthropology to better comprehend social change, and what they considered to be a transition towards modernity.

Chapter Four takes us beyond the debates of the mission's leadership to look at how the 'three selves' church principle was taken up at the grassroots village level during the 1920s and 1930s. This chapter focuses on the north-west of Viti Levu, and the Ra circuit, where Nailaga is situated. It was here that the Toko farmers organised throughout these decades a group that has come to be remembered for their efforts to establish a national Fijian church in the 1940s. Key figures in this chapter are Ratu Nacanieli Rawaidranu, who was the Toko farmers' chief, and several successive European missionaries: Charles Oswald Lelean, A Wesley Amos, and Arthur Drew Lelean. The farmers worked to ensure that they could create a self-supporting and self-governing church, but self-propagation was a constant theme in this region due to rumours of occult activities occurring at the mission site. This chapter contributes to Martha Kaplan's analysis of the Tuka cult of the nineteenth century, and studies of the notorious Fijian leader Apolosi Ranawai, by identifying signs of the presence of 'cults' in the Ra region.[25] The Toko farmers' project signified the consolidation of this ethno-nationalist movement, framing it within the mission's larger objectives of self-support, self-governance and self-propagation. This chapter outlines the connection between the *lotu* (church), labour and *vanua* (land) in new ways, and suggests that while missionaries were encouraging a turn to modernity, this was never disconnected from efforts to ensure indigenous rights to land.

Chapter Five looks more specifically at the principle of self-governance through the experiences of two men who were classified as 'native' (non-European) ministers, and who both expressed some disaffection with the mission's modes of exclusion. The first was the Reverend Aseri Robarobalevu, who was the first indigenous Fijian minister to assume the superintendency of a Methodist circuit

23 D Wetherell, *Charles Abel and the Kwato Mission of Papua New Guinea 1891–1975*, Melbourne, Melbourne University Press, 1996, p. 151.
24 Ibid.
25 M Kaplan, *Neither Cargo nor Cult: Ritual Politics and the Colonial Imagination in Fiji*, Durham, Duke University Press, 1995.

in 1930. The second was Indo-Fijian catechist Ramsey Deoki, who became deeply disaffected with colonialism and the limitations it placed upon him, and who campaigned throughout the 1930s to be ordained and to be treated as an equal. After a long struggle, he was finally ordained in 1939, which brought the Indo-Fijian branch of the mission much closer to realising the principles of the 'three selves' church. Both of these men pushed the existing boundaries of the mission, moving into areas that had previously been exclusively occupied by Europeans.

Chapter Six takes the reader into the 1940s. The Toko farmers featured in Chapter Four became spokespeople for autonomy, making an official request for a 'Fijian' church in 1941. The tensions between the mission's chairman, the Reverend William Green, and Burton, who remained the General Secretary of Methodist Overseas Missions until 1945, highlights tensions between the mission board in Sydney and the field related to approaches to the 'three selves' church principles. Set at the height of the Pacific War, missionaries monitored anti-colonial and racial consciousness in the mission and amongst their congregations. The continued missionary engagement with anthropology fostered an increasing focus on race and culture, and the impacts of colonialism on indigenous peoples.

Missionaries continued to monitor racial consciousness in the broader community while also considering the racialist nature of the mission into the post-war period, which is covered in Chapter Seven. The plans were laid during the years immediately after World War II for the full transfer of authority from European to Fijian and Indo-Fijian peoples. Missionaries continued to use anthropology to consider the social changes wrought by the war, and how they might manage them through processes of 'reconstruction'. Throughout the 1940s, the shift towards greater self-governance is evident through the increasingly vocal Fijian and Indo-Fijian leadership, especially Deoki's growing confidence in demanding a greater wage, autonomy and authority. There were definite signs of anti-colonial feeling amongst the mission's workers. In the years immediately after World War II, missionaries responded to anti-colonial feeling by continuing to abide by the 'three selves' policies, especially by supporting a growing Fijian and Indo-Fijian ministry and furthering the acculturation of Christianity.

It was not until the 1950s, however, that the mission's workers started to question the segregation between the 'Fijian' and 'Indo-Fijian' branches. The events of this decade are described in Chapter Eight. In the wake of the Toko farmer's request for a 'Fijian' church, and of course the ongoing demand that missionaries devolve the mission to become an autonomous church, the mission's leadership, now including the Reverend Cecil Gribble as general secretary, pushed forward with plans to ensure self-support, self-government, self-propagation and integration. Chapter Eight covers the debates related to segregation, and the impact of the shift in demographics after World War II. Indo-Fijians were now the colony's majority, and missionaries wondered what that would mean for their Methodist institution and its Fijian membership.

The ninth and final chapter of the book looks at efforts to unite the church after 60 years of segregation. Unity was discussed but only came into serious consideration at the eleventh hour. One of the main proponents of unity, the Reverend Setareki Tuilovoni, led debates in the final years before devolution, and this chapter traces his opinions and those of other mission leaders about unity and division before the autonomous church conference was established in 1964. Ultimately, the mission's leaders struggled to overcome the long-maintained boundaries between the Fijian and Indo-Fijian Methodist communities, leaving a divided church.

Careful explication of the role of missionaries in colonialism is necessary before I proceed. As Elizabeth Elbourne noted in the South African context, missionaries did not necessarily cause colonisation, but in many instances they facilitated it. To me, this almost amounts to the same thing. Missionaries were actively involved in the broader imperialist project, acting as intermediaries between indigenous peoples, merchants, plantation owners and colonial administrators. I endeavour to push beyond suggestions that missionaries were ambivalent individuals.[26] The arguments put forward by John and Jean Comaroff regarding European hegemony in the Cape Colony has been a useful framework that allowed me to consider the dialectics of culture in Fiji. Their contention that hegemony of the dominant culture is never complete is crucial in comprehending change over time. To deny potential for shifts and fractures in the hegemony would be to argue that societies are static, and this book demonstrates quite the opposite: Fiji's society was constantly transforming despite efforts to induce a static cultural state. There were efforts to create hegemony, which we can see through efforts amongst missionaries to preserve European control over certain spheres of the mission. The temptation may be to depict European culture as the hegemon, through the repetition of certain practices that depicted prestige and negated the position and privilege of non-European peoples. This is particularly true for this study, which focuses so closely on the commodification of 'native' labour through the mission. Indeed, Methodism put a price on a person's ability to conform to repetitious performances of culture and spirituality.

---

26 E Elbourne, *Blood Ground: Colonialism, Missions and the Contest for Christianity in the Cape Colony and Britain, 1799–1853*, Canada, McGill Queen's University Press, 2002, p. 13.

However, European missionaries constructed conflicting hegemons through their efforts to build the mission's divisions around certain cultural practices, signs and symbolisms.[27] I have endeavoured to demonstrate this through elucidating the extent of indigenous agency in the colonial setting. Heavily influenced by Lammin Sanneh's discussions about indigenising Christianity, and finding that what he has written correlates with what I found in the archives, I have tried to acknowledge the forces of colonialism and power wielded by Europeans, and indigenous peoples' subsequent push towards transformation and transition, while conceding that within that dynamic there remained space for indigenous agency. Indigenous peoples challenged European rule and actively fractured colonial control. There were some quiet, and not so quiet, manoeuvrings occurring within the mission throughout the 60 years under review in this book, through which indigenous and Indo-Fijians negotiated changes in the mission's structure. While it is fair to say that at times they benefited from the changing mindsets of Europeans, those changes were often the result of their modes of resistance and expressions of disaffection. Mamdani's work on indirect rule has aided my thinking on this question of colonial authority and indigenous agency. The work of John Kelly and Martha Kaplan has also informed my discussions about agency and resistance in colonial Fiji. Their scholarship has helped to push forward discussions beyond Gramscian understandings of power to consider resistance through expressions of sentiments of affection and disaffection amongst non-Europeans who were caught within the colonial systems of categorisation.

Ideas about colonial modes of categorisation and control have underpinned the scholarship of many postcolonial historians in recent decades. This was true for Ann Laura Stoler's work on the creation of colonial categories around race and gender in 'Rethinking Colonial Categories', published in 1989. While this was published nearly 30 years ago, the colonial methods for governance that Stoler described — that societies were governed through the creation of boundaries around race and gender — were so relevant and so strongly reflected in the Fijian colonial archives that I felt it necessary to draw on her concepts to arrange the material.[28] Other scholars, focusing more firmly within the Pacific region, have also made similar arguments about the racialised structures of colonial rule. In 'Land, Labour and Difference: Elementary Structures of Race', Patrick Wolfe contributed to studies of colonial governance when he identified land and labour as the foundation of relationships between colonisers and the colonised

---

27   J Comaroff and J Comaroff, *Of Revelation and Revolution: Christianity, Colonialism, and Consciousness in South Africa*, vol. 1, Chicago, The University of Chicago Press, 1991, p. 25.

28   A L Stoler, 'Rethinking Colonial Categories', *Comparative Studies in Society and History*, vol. 31, no. 1, January 1989, pp. 134–61.

in settler and slave colonial societies.[29] He has suggested that the expropriation of indigenous peoples from land has been the more prominent factor in the Australian settler colonial experience, with the utility of indigenous labour being of negligible or lesser importance.[30] I examined this idea in my Master's thesis, and argued that both land and labour were central sites where colonial relationships were forged. I also took historian Lynette Russell's comments about the rapid mobility of physical and social borders and boundaries in settler society through time into consideration.[31] Though Fiji was not a settler colony, I have drawn on these theoretical discussions about colonialism and power to examine the mission as a site that drew on 'native' labour, I further the contention that labour has been a crucial point of contact between the colonisers and the colonised in Fiji, and that this was often linked to concerns about protecting indigenous lands and paramountcy. This simultaneously provoked and reinforced the creation of boundaries.[32] Examining an institution that had operated in the Pacific for nearly 130 years allowed some greater understanding of the processes through which it reinforced colonial protocols of creating ethnicised categories, and due to the ways in which it did this — through the establishment of hierarchies and reinforcing nationalist identities — we can also examine structural inequalities in the colonial setting.

It is this examination of boundaries that sets this book apart from previous scholarship on the Methodist history in Fiji. The study of boundaries and separate nationalisms explored throughout the book offers a foreground to the development of ethno-nationalist sentiment and indigenous paramountcy that many scholars of Fiji have addressed in recent historical and anthropological scholarship. Anthropologists Matthew Tomlinson and Christina Toren have written in recent decades of the continuing place of indigenous culture in the Fijian Methodist Church.[33] Yet, true to much literature on Fiji, those scholars who focused on one community have usually excluded the other. The anthropological studies of the Fijian Methodist Church have made little to no mention of the Indian community, enhancing perceptions that it is a

---

29   P Wolfe, 'Land, Labour, and Difference: Elementary Structures of Race', *The American Historical Review*, vol. 106, no. 3, 2001, pp. 866–905.

30   Ibid., p. 867.

31   L Russell, *Colonial Frontiers: Indigenous-European Encounters in Settler Societies*, Manchester, Manchester University Press, 2001, pp. 1–2; K Close, 'Invisible Labourers: Cape Bedford Mission and the Paradox of Aboriginal Labourers in World War Two', Masters thesis, University of Melbourne, 2009.

32   Ibid., p. 5.

33   M Tomlinson, 'Sacred Soil in Kadavu, Fiji', *Oceania*, vol. 72, no. 4, 2002, pp. 237–57; M Tomlinson, *In God's Image*; M Tomlinson, 'Passports to Eternity: Whale's Teeth and Transcendence in Fijian Methodism', in L Manderson, W Smith and M Tomlinson (eds), *Flows of Faith: Religious Reach and Community in Asia and the Pacific*, Melbourne, Springer, 2012, pp. 215–31; C Toren, 'Making the present, revealing the past: The mutability and continuity of tradition as process', *Man*, New Series, vol. 23, no. 4, 1988, pp. 696–717; C Toren, 'Becoming a Christian in Fiji: An Ethnographic Study of Ontology', *Journal of the Royal Anthropological Institute*, vol. 10, no. 1, 2003, pp. 709–27.

Fijian institution. Jacqueline Ryle has noted this tendency and examined racial tensions in her recent work, *My God, My Land*.[34] Through identifying tensions between the Fijian and Indo-Fijian communities, particularly where it has been most acute concerning land, this book adds historical context to the anxieties that anthropologists have recorded in the present day.

While racial and cultural constructs are examined most frequently in this text, I also elucidate, where possible, where class was defined. Class was one of the key ways in which European ministers classified the non-European ministry, and their systems of wage distribution challenged conventional customary hierarchies while constructing a class system based on education and access to commodities and enhanced mobility. This is a slight diversion from John Kelly's argument, constructed in reference to Frantz Fanon, that race *replaced* class as an organising principle in Fiji.[35] Rather, within the mission, race and class were both important, alongside cultural considerations. There were thus multiple organising principles in operation at any one time within the mission's structure, all of which needed to be constantly checked and rechecked by those who worked within it. This was, to draw on Lorenzo Veracini's discussion about the transformative nature of colonialism in Fiji, one of the factors that drove alterations within the Fijian social fabric.[36]

Mission historians, the Reverend A Harold Wood and Andrew Thornley, pointed to the racial cleavage of the mission by writing separate histories for its 'Indo-Fijian' and 'Fijian' branches, but neither discussed the reason for segregation and how these debates changed or continued over time.[37] John Garrett's expansive work alerted us to the impact of ecumenical mission movements in the Pacific, and particularly to the importance of the International Missionary Council. It was not long before I was able to connect the dots between the Fijian Methodist Mission's archival record and Brian Stanley's more recent historical study of the International Missionary Council and the 'three selves'

---

34   J Ryle, *My God, My Land: Interwoven Paths of Christianity and Tradition in Fiji*, Farnham, Surrey, Ashgate, 2010; J Ryle, 'Roots of Land and Church: The Christian State Debate in Fiji', *International Journal for the Study of the Christian Church*, vol. 5, no. 1, 2005, pp. 58–75.

35   J Kelly, 'Fear of Culture: British Regulation of Indian Marriage in Post-indenture Fiji', *Ethnohistory*, vol. 36, no. 4, 1989, p. 383.

36   L Veracini, '"Emphatically not a white man's colony": Settler Colonialism and the Construction of Colonial Fiji', *Journal of Pacific History*, vol. 43, no. 2, 2008, p. 196.

37   A Thornley, 'The Methodist Mission and the Indians in Fiji, 1900 to 1920', Masters thesis, University of Auckland, 1973; A Thornley, 'The Methodist Mission and Fiji's Indians: 1879–1920', *The New Zealand Journal of History*, vol. 8, no. 1, 1974, pp. 137–53; A Thornley, 'Fijian Methodism: 1874–1945: The Emergence of a National Church', PhD thesis, The Australian National University, 1979; A H Wood, *Overseas Missions of the Australian Methodist Church: Fiji*, vol. 2, Melbourne, Aldersgate Press, 1978; A H Wood, *Overseas Missions of the Australian Methodist Church: Fiji-Indian and Rotuma*, vol. 3, Aldersgate Press, Melbourne, 1978.

church principle.[38] The 'three selves' concept was important to missions throughout the world, and I will leave it to scholars better acquainted with other mission fields to comment on how it was adopted and adapted elsewhere and by other denominational groups.

---

38   B Stanley, 'The Church of the Three Selves: A Perspective from the World Missionary Conference, Edinburgh, 1910', *Journal of Imperial and Commonwealth History*, vol. 36, no. 3, 2008; J Garrett, *Where Nets Were Cast: Christianity in Oceania since World War Two, Suva, Institute of Pacific Studies,* University of the South Pacific in association with the World Council of Churches, 1997, pp. 240, 400.

CHAPTER ONE

Foundations for an Indo-Fijian Methodist Church in Fiji

On 10 October 1901, European missionaries and Fijian ministers gathered on Fiji's Bau Island for the annual Synod of the Australasian Methodist Overseas Missions. At this meeting, symbolically held on the island that was the home of Fiji's supreme chiefly Cakobau family, attendees addressed the challenge created by the growing Indo-Fijian community by establishing an Indo-Fijian branch. While Methodists had already been working to evangelise Indian indentured labourers, this had formerly taken place under the umbrella of the Rewa circuit of the mission. The creation of the Indo-Fijian branch established a systemic segregation based on the perceived cultural differences between the two predominant non-European populations in the colony. This chapter traces the development of the institution's structure through mission policies: the creation of separate administrative systems that categorised Methodists according to race, akin to the observations that John Kelly has made about the structure of Fiji's secular government that simultaneously entrenched European authority.[1] While the decision to split the institution resulted from practical difficulties associated with ministering to communities that spoke different languages, it was also informed by internationally accepted mission policy around acculturating economics and leadership models. The overarching goal was to establish a self-supporting, self-governing and self-propagating 'native church': the 'three selves' church policy supported by international ecumenical movements. Missionaries believed that creating a 'native' Methodist church that included both Fijian and Indo-Fijian converts would be too problematic. This chapter describes how European missionaries addressed the presence

---

1   J Kelly, 'Threats to Difference in Colonial Fiji', *Cultural Anthropology*, vol. 10, no. 1, 1995, p. 64.

of the Indo-Fijian community in the first two decades of the twentieth century, the practical and theological imperatives, and theories about race and culture that informed them. Ultimately, it was through the convergence of international and local policies that missionaries devised a scheme to separate the 'natives' in a bid to keep order and peace.

Indian labourers arrived in Fiji from 1879 onwards to work in the sugar industry. Under the British administration's indenture scheme, 45,000 workers came from Uttar Pradesh (including Basti, Gonda, Faizabad, Sultanpur, Azamgarh and Gorakhpur), and 15,000 from the southern areas of Madras, Arcot, Tanjore, Krishna, Goavari, Vizakhapatnam, Coimbatore and Malabar.[2] Workers came from an array of classes, castes and religious backgrounds, but were mainly Hindu or Muslim.[3] Fiji's first census in 1881 counted 588 Indian labourers, whose numbers swelled as the colony's sugar industry grew. Many remained in Fiji when their contracts expired, either because they were unable to return to India, or because they chose to renew their contracts. Others settled on farms or in the colony's growing townships.[4] By 1901 there were 17,105 Indians in Fiji, accounting for 14.2 per cent of the colony's population.[5] Despite being away from their homeland, the labourers transported their cultures, and then altered and adapted them, across the *kala pani*.[6] As the Indo-Fijian community grew, missionaries began to reimagine the mission and its needs, and tried to do this in a way that suited the community as they saw it.

It took 22 years from the start of indenture for the missionaries to create this official strategy for evangelisation in the Indo-Fijian community. The potential for a mission to the Indo-Fijian population in Fiji was first spoken about at mission board meetings in Sydney in 1884, but until the 1901 synod, the mission's efforts were haphazard, and a dedicated mission to the Indian community proved difficult to implement with only limited funds and resources available. The discussions followed a similar pattern to those described by John Kelly, when he outlined the British project of categorisation in Fiji and the desire to keep the Indian communities separate from the colony's indigenous peoples.

---

2   B V Lal, (ed.), *Crossing the Kala Pani: A Documentary History of Indian Indenture in Fiji*, Canberra, Division of Pacific and Asian History, Research School of Pacific and Asian Studies, The Australian National University, Suva, Fiji, Fiji Museum, 1998, p. 1.

3   Ibid., p. 2.

4   Fiji Bureau of Statistics – Key Statistics: June 2012, Population, 1.2A Census Population of Fiji by Ethnicity, www.statsfiji.gov.fj/Key%20Stats/Population/1.2%20pop%20by%20ethnicity.pdf, accessed 22 March 2013; B V Lal, *Chalo Jahaji: A Journey Through Indenture in Fiji*, Division of Pacific and Asian History, The Australian National University and Fiji Museum, 2000, p. 27.

5   Fiji Bureau of Statistics – Key Statistics: June 2012, Population, 1.2A Census Population of Fiji by Ethnicity, www.statsfiji.gov.fj/Key%20Stats/Population/1.2%20pop%20by%20ethnicity.pdf, accessed 22 March 2013.

6   B V Lal, (ed.), *Crossing the Kala Pani: A Documentary History of Indian Indenture in Fiji*, Canberra, Division of Pacific and Asian History, Research School of Pacific and Asian Studies, The Australian National University, Suva, Fiji, Fiji Museum, 1998, p. 2.

This 'modality of colonial practice' was incorporated into the mission's systems, and was displayed in the way in which they recruited workers for each branch.[7] The mission tried to source both Europeans and Indians to evangelise the Indo-Fijian community. An untrained Indian catechist named John Williams arrived in 1892 from Faizabad, and though the mission board did not appoint him to any official position, Williams worked alongside European missionary the Reverend Henry Worrall in the Rewa circuit.[8]

Another Australian, Hannah Dudley, arrived in 1897 and was the first to be appointed by the board to work exclusively with the Indo-Fijian community, having been inspired by a speech given that year by Worrall.[9] She was also the first female missionary to be formally appointed to work in Fiji, though many missionary wives had served alongside their husbands in an unofficial capacity before her. Dudley brought a wealth of experience from her time as a missionary to women with the Zenana mission movement in India.[10] By the time Dudley was recruited to the Indo-Fijian mission, the board had plans to establish a 'Fiji Coolie Mission', and hoped that Dudley would take the lead.[11] Yet Dudley worked fairly independently during her first few years in the colony, with minimal direction from the mission's chairman.[12] With limited resources, Dudley worked to her own plans and devoted most of her energies to building an orphanage.[13] Her efforts with children attracted some converts, but conversion rates remained small.

The Indo-Fijian community was generally ambivalent or resistant to Christianity. Conversion placed Indo-Fijians in a complex position. When considering this we might go back to Stoler's ideas about 'cultural criteria' and how they can be prescribed and attended to both in the home and in public spaces.[14] Dudley noted something to this effect in a report she made in 1898:

---

7   A H Wood, *Overseas Missions of the Australian Methodist Church: Fiji*, vol. 2, Melbourne, Aldersgate Press, 1978, p. 9; J Kelly, 'Threats to Difference in Colonial Fiji', *Cultural Anthropology*, vol. 10, no. 1, 1995, p. 65.
8   A H Wood, *Overseas Missions of the Australian Methodist Church: Fiji-Indian and Rotuma*, vol. 3, Aldersgate Press, Melbourne, p. 10.
9   Ibid., pp. 10, 13.
10   For more information on the Zenana movement, see R Howe, 'The Australian Christian Movement and Women's Activism in the Asia-Pacific Region, 1890–1920s', *Australian Feminist Studies*, vol. 16, no. 36, 2001, p. 312
11   M Sidal, *Hannah Dudley: Hamari Maa: Honoured Mother, Educator, and Missioner to the Indentured Indians in Fiji, 1864–1931*, Suva, Fiji, Pacific Theological College Press, 1997, pp. 18–19.
12   Ibid., pp. 17–18.
13   A H Wood, *Overseas Missions of the Australian Methodist Church: Fiji-Indian and Rotuma*, vol. 3, Aldersgate Press, Melbourne, 1978, p. 16.
14   A L Stoler, *Carnal Knowledge and Imperial Power: Race and the Intimate in Colonial Rule*, Berkeley and Los Angeles, University of California Press, 2002, p. 18.

An Indian in becoming a Christian, they believe, ceases to be an Indian; he eats meat willingly, drinks water others have been drinking, and breaks other Hindu religious laws, the doing of which is considered by them far more heinous than any violation of the moral code. They believe that Christianity is the religion for Europeans and Hinduism is for the Indians.[15]

Dudley had observed the deeply personal implications for Indians as they adopted their new faith. There was a widely held perception that Indians who converted to Christianity would leave their old cultural practices behind. This led to exclusion from the Indo-Fijian community, where conversion to another faith was viewed as 'apostacy': a regression from Islam or Hinduism. To build on Stoler's argument, the ways in which Indo-Fijians who converted to Christianity engaged in certain practices that were attached to their national or cultural identity maintained their difference from other Christians in Fiji, but similarly their adoption of new practices set them apart from others of their ethnic background. A national identity was being carved out at the most intimate levels, both in practical ways and through spiritual engagement.

Indo-Fijian converts were not necessarily warmly embraced into the Methodist community, being simultaneously excluded from European or Fijian spaces. Divisions were created early on. There were separate churches, schools and meetings created for Indo-Fijian Methodists. Shortly after her arrival in 1897, Dudley established the first school exclusively for Indo-Fijian children in Suva.[16] While in the early days of her work she conducted Christian teachings in the shared space of the Jubilee Church in Suva, an Indo-Fijian mission hall was opened on 19 December 1901 at Nausori, specifically for Indo-Fijian Methodist worship.[17] Christianity might have been seen to negate Indo-Fijian culture by those who practiced Hinduism or Islam, but it did not make converts 'less Indo-Fijian' in the Methodist community. This adds to the argument, put forward by John Kelly, that 'categories of difference based on custom, culture, or level of civilisation, and based on "race", mixed with and eventually contended with, the distinction of religion in definition and maintenance of boundaries between categories of people'.[18] Race, along with these other features that distinguished Fiji's peoples as different from one another, which were often broadly defined as 'custom', operated as a means of defining boundaries. Indian converts acquired a new category, a liminal position between the Indian community

15   H Dudley, Circuit reports, October 1898, Ref M/94/(b), NAF, cited in M Sidal, *Hannah Dudley: Hamari Maa: Honoured Mother, Educator, and Missioner to the Indentured Indians in Fiji, 1864–1931*, Suva, Fiji, Pacific Theological College Press, 1997, p. 38; A H Wood, *Overseas Missions of the Australian Methodist Church: Fiji-Indian and Rotuma*, vol. 3, Aldersgate Press, Melbourne, 1978, p. 30.
16   A H Wood, *Overseas Missions of the Australian Methodist Church: Fiji-Indian and Rotuma*, vol. 3, Aldersgate Press, Melbourne, 1978, p. 13.
17   Ibid., p. 15.
18   J Kelly, 'Threats to Difference in Colonial Fiji', *Cultural Anthropology*, vol. 10, no. 1, 1995, pp. 66–67.

and the larger Fijian Methodist community in the new spaces created for Indo-Fijian Methodists.[19] While excluded from Fijian and European worship and educational spaces run by the Methodists, a new social space was defined for Indo-Fijian Methodists.

The man who oversaw the racial separation of the mission was the Chairman of the Fiji District, the Reverend Arthur J Small. The mission's leadership during the late nineteenth and early twentieth centuries came from England or the nearby British settler colonies of Australia and New Zealand. Many mission leaders had little or no previous contact with Indian peoples or cultures before arriving in Fiji. Small was born in 1854 and had immigrated to Australia from Camden, England, in 1862 as an eight-year-old.[20] He arrived in Fiji in 1879, at the age of 25, in the same year that the first indentured Indian labourers disembarked from the ship the *Leonidas* in Levuka, the colony's administrative capital. Despite his limited engagement with non-European peoples, like other humanitarians and colonial administrators, Small brought his understandings of race from the Empire's metropole to its peripheries. Small's transnational interactions proved crucial to shaping his approach to governing the mission.[21] As Stoler suggested of other colonial administrators, Small's knowledge of difference travelled with him.[22]

Without pause, Small launched straight into his work with the Fijian community.[23] Stationed on the chiefly island of Bau, he was geographically removed from plantations and the colony's trading centres. Small therefore had only limited contact with Indian indentured workers during his early days in the colony. He chatted with traders and gradually learned more about Indian peoples from them and his colleagues. During the 1880s, he conducted a few baptisms for Indo-Fijian Methodists, but it was not until he became chairman of the mission in 1900 and was charged with responsibility for the Indo-Fijian circuit that he engaged more consistently and directly with Indo-Fijians.[24] He was charged with visiting Indo-Fijian inmates at the Suva prison as part of his regular ministerial duties.[25] He was then also responsible for managing

19   A Thornley, 'The Methodist Mission and Fiji's Indians: 1879–1920', *The New Zealand Journal of History*, vol. 8, no. 1, 1974, p. 141; B V Lal, 'Odyssey of Indenture: Fragmentation and Reconstruction in the Indian Diaspora', *Diaspora: A Journal of Transnational Studies*, vol. 5, no. 2, 1996 , p. 170; J Kelly, 'Threats to Difference in Colonial Fiji', *Cultural Anthropology*, vol. 10, no. 1, 1995, pp. 66–67.
20   Memories of Winifred McHugh, PMB 156, p. 1.
21   R Skinner and A Lester, 'Humanitarianism and Empire: New Research Agendas', *The Journal of Imperial and Commonwealth History*, vol. 40, no. 5, 2012, p. 734.
22   A L Stoler, *Carnal Knowledge and Imperial Power: Race and the Intimate in Colonial Rule*, Berkeley and Los Angeles, University of California Press, p. 16; H Gardner, *Gathering for God: George Brown in Oceania*, Dunedin, Otago University Press, 2006, p. 149.
23   Memories of Winifred McHugh, PMB 156, p. 17.
24   A J Small, diary, 29 June – 19 July 1885, MSS 3267/1, Item 1, ML; A H Wood, *Overseas Missions of the Australian Methodist Church: Fiji-Indian and Rotuma*, vol. 3, Aldersgate Press, Melbourne, 1978, p. 13.
25   A J Small, diary, 12 July 1903, MSS 3267/1, item 3, ML.

the European staff that worked in the Indo-Fijian mission, including Hannah Dudley and the Reverends Harold Nolan and John Wear Burton — the latter two having arrived in 1901 and 1902 respectively — and so his perspectives broadened and diversified as his engagement with the Indo-Fijian community and responsibility for administering to it within the mission grew.[26]

Small addressed the Wesleyan general conference in Brisbane, Australia, in May 1901 about the state of Fiji's changing society, and the result of this meeting contributed to the decision made later that year to create a separate Indian branch. Missionaries tended to explain the separation as a necessary adaption to practicalities, such as language difference. While some Fijian and Indo-Fijian people could speak Fijian and Indo-Fijian dialects, missionaries argued that the Christian message was best delivered in the convert's own mother tongue on the principle that the message and religious experience would be diluted or misconstrued if it were not.[27] The mission had, as with Williams and Dudley, endeavoured to employ Indian catechists and European missionaries who were familiar with Indo-Fijian languages and cultures. Dudley's six years in India with the Zenana movement had equipped her with a reasonable knowledge of Hindustani.[28] However, they struggled to find more people with such sound language skills at the time of segregation. The mission board's ideal was to have a European missionary who would act as superintendent to the Indian branch, with a few Indian catechists and ministers to support the work, an arrangement that would maintain the ethnicised categories that John Kelly has written about, that demarcated social and spatial distance, as well as European authority.[29]

The decision to split the mission was also based on demographic trends. Though historian Harold Wood has recorded that some 60 Indian converts attended a church service at Dudley's church in December 1901, in 1902 there were only seven people from the Indo-Fijian community who were actually

---

26 A J Small, diary, 13 Feb 1902, 5 July 1902, 15 October 1902, MSS 3267/1, Items 2,3, ML; A H Wood, *Overseas Missions of the Australian Methodist Church: Fiji-Indian and Rotuma*, vol. 3, Aldersgate Press, Melbourne, 1978, pp. 15, 19. Small's efforts to rein in Dudley's activities led to tensions, noted by J Garrett, *Footsteps in the Sea: Christianity in Oceania to World War Two*, Suva, University of the South Pacific in conjunction with the World Council of Churches, 1992, pp. 158–59.

27 L Sanneh, *Translating the Message: The Missionary Impact on Culture*, Maryknoll, NY, Orbis Books, 2009, p. 111; 'The Story of the Haunted Line: Totoram Sanadhya Recalls the Labour Lines in Fiji', translated by B V Lal and B Shineberg, in B V Lal, *Crossing the Kala Pani: A Documentary History of Indian Indenture in Fiji*, Canberra, Division of Pacific and Asian History, Research School of Pacific and Asian Studies, The Australian National University, Suva, Fiji, Fiji Museum, 1998, p. 102.

28 M Sidal, *Hannah Dudley: Hamari Maa: Honoured Mother, Educator, and Missioner to the Indentured Indians in Fiji, 1864–1931*, Suva, Fiji, Pacific Theological College Press, 1997, pp. 5, 18–19; J W Burton, *The Weaver's Shuttle: Memories and Reflections of an Octogenarian*, n.d., MLMSS 2899, add on 990, ML, p. 52.

29 The estimated cost of migration (£100), settlement in Fiji (£230) and then stipends per annum (£170). Mission District Minutes, Minutes of the Annual Synod of the Fiji District, Bau, 10 Oct 1901, MOM 175 CY2671, 1901–1903, ML, pp. 17–18; J Kelly, 'Threats to Difference in Colonial Fiji', *Cultural Anthropology*, vol. 10, no. 1, 1995, p. 64.

members of the Methodist mission.[30] Yet, missionaries believed that the separate branch was necessary despite the small membership. At the same Wesleyan general conference meeting, Small informed his Australian colleagues of Fiji's demographics according to the 1901 census, and voiced his concern about the rapid growth of the Indian community. Demographics also preoccupied colonial administrators during this period. Small pointed to the increasing Indo-Fijian birth rate, sitting at 6.18 per cent, and the death rate of 1.04 per cent for adults and 12.34 per cent for children.[31] The Fijian population, in the same period, had decreased to 94,397. With the Indo-Fijian population now totalling 14.2 per cent of the colony's peoples, and Fijian numbers dropping, observers believed that Indo-Fijians might one day outnumber Fijians and become the majority in Fiji.[32]

In the background to these discussions were bigger questions, relating to land and the economy, for the mission and its members. The formation of Fiji's land policies under British colonial rule were intrinsic to later policies which reflected a concern for indigenous rights. In 1876, Fiji's first governor, Arthur Gordon, called on the Council of Chiefs to detail the customary systems of land ownership, which would then be used for the administration of land registration. It took several years for the council to arrive at some sort of clear decision as to how land had been organised prior to European encroachment.[33] The Indo-Fijian community was setting down roots: despite the 1875 ordinance that forbade the alienation of Fijian lands, some lands had been bought by Europeans; Indian farmers were renting some of these plots and settling in the colony when they finished their indenture.[34] Eventually, just prior to the arrival of Indian labourers to the colony, legislation was established whereby land ownership was attributed to a *mataqali*, which would be registered by colonial administrator David Wilkinson. Each *mataqali* claim had to be approved by the *tikina* and the provincial council. The final approval was left to the governor of the colony. Land ownership thus ran according to lines of ancestral links and were inherited by families and individuals.[35] With the signing of land legislation in this manner, land ownership became an ethnically politicised commodity.

---

30   A H Wood, *Overseas Missions of the Australian Methodist Church: Fiji-Indian and Rotuma,* vol. 3, Aldersgate Press, Melbourne, 1978, pp. 15, 23.

31   'A Visitor from Fiji: The Rev J S [sic] Small: Progress of Mission Work: Coolie Labour and the Sugar Industry', *The Brisbane Courier*, Brisbane, 27 May 1901, p. 9.

32   Fiji Bureau of Statistics – Key Statistics: June 2012, Population, 1.2A Census Population of Fiji by Ethnicity, www.statsfiji.gov.fj/Key%20Stats/Population/1.2%20pop%20by%20ethnicity.pdf, accessed 22 March 2013; 'A Visitor from Fiji: The Rev J S [sic] Small: Progress of Mission Work: Coolie Labour and the Sugar Industry', *The Brisbane Courier*, Brisbane, 27 May 1901, p. 9.

33   P France, *The Charter of the Land: Custom and Colonization in Fiji*, Melbourne, Oxford University Press, 1969, pp. 110–11.

34   M Moynagh, 'Land Tenure in Fiji's Sugar Cane Districts Since the 1920s', *Journal of Pacific History*, vol. 13, no. 1, 1978, p. 53.

35   P France, *The Charter of the Land: Custom and Colonization in Fiji*, Melbourne, Oxford University Press, 1969, p. 113.

The ethnicised nature of Fijian land legislation was to complicate the potential sense of belonging for any other ethnic group that subsequently entered Fiji. It did not necessarily occlude access to land for non-indigenous peoples: by 1901, Small estimated that Indo-Fijian farmers had acquired 768 acres along the Rewa River for sugar cane farming. In the Navua district, 1,565 acres were under cultivation. Perhaps seeing the potential for Indo-Fijians to acquire considerable land and some wealth, Small told the Wesleyan general conference that it was essential that the mission expand their activities to cater to the 'increasing heathen coolie population of Fiji'.[36] The mission's leadership conceded that the Indian presence in Fiji was not temporary or transient, but one with great potential for longevity.[37]

In 1901, the mission tried to entice more catechists or missionaries from India into the Pacific. Despite support from the Methodist leader in India, Bishop James M Thoburn, their efforts were unsuccessful. The board relied instead on fresh ministers from Australia and New Zealand who were unfamiliar with Indian cultures or languages.[38] One of these was John Wear Burton. Despite having no prior experience in India, he was selected to work exclusively in the Indo-Fijian community.[39] He gathered up his belongings and got on board the boat, full of enthusiasm and trepidation at the thought of leaving New Zealand for the adventure that lay ahead. But Burton received a warning from the outspoken ship's captain during his passage in 1902: 'The Indians have their own religion and want none of yours.'[40]

Burton was undeterred, and after only a short time in Fiji felt assured enough to declare himself the leader of the mission's Indo-Fijian work.[41] He studied Urdu with a man named Daniel Nizam-ul-din. Nizam-ul-din had been working on a plantation as a *sirdar* (the title commonly given to Indian foremen on sugar

36 'Wesleyan General Conference: Sitting in Brisbane', *The Chronicle*, Adelaide, South Australia, 25 May 1901, p. 15.

37 It was unclear whether these farmers were renting the land or had bought it from those who had bought the land despite the 1875 colonial ordinance. 'Wesleyan General Conference: Sitting in Brisbane', *The Chronicle*, Adelaide, South Australia, 25 May 1901, p. 15; A H Wood, *Overseas Missions of the Australian Methodist Church: Fiji-Indian and Rotuma*, vol. 3, Aldersgate Press, Melbourne, 1978, p. 9. Between May 1905 and April 1908, 104,142 acres of Fijian land were sold despite the 1875 ordinance. M Moynagh, 'Land Tenure in Fiji's Sugar Cane Districts Since the 1920s', *Journal of Pacific History*, vol. 13, no. 1, 1978, p. 53.

38 Mission District Minutes, Minutes of the Annual Synod of the Fiji District, Bau, 10 October 1901, MOM 175 CY2671, 1901–1903, pp. 17–18.

39 Burton was originally from Lazenby, England, and had been living in New Zealand when he decided to join the mission. J W Burton, *The Weaver's Shuttle: Memories and Reflections of an Octogenarian*, unpublished manuscript, n.d., p. 5.

40 Ibid., p. 51.

41 A Thornley, 'The Methodist Mission and Fiji's Indians: 1879–1920', *The New Zealand Journal of History*, vol. 8, no. 1, 1974, p. 141; A Thornley, 'The Methodist Mission and the Indians in Fiji, 1900 to 1920', Masters thesis, University of Auckland, 1973, p. 18.

plantations).[42] They had met when Nizam-ul-din was serving time in prison, and Burton transferred Nizam-ul-din's indenture to his own name for £16, engaging in the indenture system in the process of trying to secure his own language tutor. He also enlisted Nizam-ul-din's help to recruit more converts to Methodism.[43] This complex relationship with Nizam-ul-din was in some ways mutually beneficial; while Burton was technically his employer, the balance of power passed between student and teacher as Nizam-ul-din instructed Burton in language. The process of exchange through language learning demonstrated Burton's vulnerability and empowered Nizam-ul-din. He became a bridge between Burton and the community not only as a type of recruiter but by enabling Burton to better converse with potential Indo-Fijian converts.

While Totaram Sanadhya, a leader of Sanatani Hinduism, viewed Nizam-ul-din and Burton as a team, in private, Burton adopted mannerisms typical of the colonial elite.[44] He did not offer Nizam-ul-din a seat at the table while he sat to learn his lessons. He also marked his prestige by building a large house for his own family, and a much smaller house for Nizam-ul-din. He was acutely aware of this and seemed somewhat ashamed in later recollections.[45] He knew that these actions had perpetuated a sense of hierarchy based not on ministerial experience or class, but on ethnic difference. Burton's efforts to develop his cultural and linguistic knowledge also elevated his own status within the mission, as cultural and linguistic knowledge were highly valued.

---

42   U Sharma and H Irvine, 'The Commodification of Labour: Accounting for Indentured Workers in Fijian Sugar Plantations, 1879–1920', www.apira2013.org/proceedings/pdfs/K028.pdf, accessed 6 March 2014, p. 6; A H Wood, *Overseas Missions of the Australian Methodist Church: Fiji*, vol. 2, Melbourne, Aldersgate Press, 1978, p. 21. Nizam-ul-din is mentioned by Totaram Sanadhya, who had worked as an indentured labourer in Fiji before returning home to India in 1914. Sanadhya referred to Nizam-ul-din as Badri Prasad Nizamuddin, the name he used before he converted to Christianity, after which time he took the name 'Daniel'. 'The Genesis of Hinduism Under Indenture', in B V Lal, *Crossing the Kala Pani: A Documentary History of Indian Indenture in Fiji*, Canberra, Division of Pacific and Asian History, Research School of Pacific and Asian Studies, The Australian National University, Suva, Fiji, Fiji Museum, 1998, pp. 117–18; J Garrett noted the relationship between Totaram and Burton, see J Garrett, *Footsteps in the Sea: Christianity in Oceania to World War Two*, Suva, University of the South Pacific in conjunction with the World Council of Churches, 1992, p. 160; B V Lal and B Shineberg, 'The Story of the Haunted Line: Totaram Sanadhya Recalls the Labour Lines in Fiji', *Journal of Pacific History*, vol. 26, no. 1, 1991, p. 107.

43   J W Burton, *The Weaver's Shuttle: Memories and Reflections of an Octogenarian*, unpublished manuscript, n.d., pp. 32, 53, 55; indenture could be transferred through the Agent General of the colony. 'Fiji Indian indenture ordinance no 1 of 1891', B V Lal, *Crossing the Kala Pani: A Documentary History of Indian Indenture in Fiji*, Canberra, Division of Pacific and Asian History, Research School of Pacific and Asian Studies, The Australian National University, Suva, Fiji, Fiji Museum, 1998, p. 61. Garrett commented that Burton's Hindustani was 'adequate rather than elegant', *Footsteps in the Sea: Christianity in Oceania to World War Two*, Suva, University of the South Pacific in conjunction with the World Council of Churches, 1992, p. 160.

44   B V Lal, *Broken Waves: A History of the Fiji Islands in the Twentieth Century*, Honolulu, University of Hawai'i Press, 1992, p. 40.

45   J W Burton, *The Weaver's Shuttle: Memories and Reflections of an Octogenarian*, unpublished manuscript, n.d., pp. 56–58.

Small and Burton worked closely together during this first decade of the twentieth century to establish the infrastructure for the Indian branch. In 1902, they travelled together along the shoddy road to Baker's Hill in Nausori, to the east of Suva, to select a site for the Indo-Fijian mission house that would act as a headquarters for its administration.[46] This was where Davuilevu, the facility for Fijian ministerial training, was located. Small and Burton walked around the existing site, plotting where additional buildings might be placed, and decided to position the Indo-Fijian activities across the creek from the existing Fijian compound. In 1909, Burton and Small named the block that they had dedicated for the Indo-Fijian mission 'Dilkusha', after a colony in Lucknow, India. The name means 'my heart is happy' in Hindi.[47] Through the processes of design and naming, there were sites of inclusion and exclusion constructed on the basis of race within this Methodist space.

The placement of buildings at Baker's hill reflected the growing confidence missionaries had in creating a racialised administration. This was also evident when the missionaries met at the 1903 synod and discussed the future of a Fijian church and how it might be organised. The minutes stated:

> the special conditions of the life and work in Fiji make it impossible to govern our native Church upon the same principles that are applicable to races which have advanced so much further in civilisation.[48]

It was unclear as to whether the Fijian community was being compared with churches in Europe or India, but this comment revealed that missionaries continued to see societies through a lens coloured by evolutionist theory: the Darwinian idea that cultures were at various hierarchical stages of civilisation, from 'primitive' to more modern. At this time, there was little distinction made between race and culture, with cultures generally perceived to be a reflection of a racial group's relationship to modernity. The 1903 district synod minutes demonstrate how deeply ingrained evolutionist theories had been amongst missionaries. While missionaries such as Lorimer Fison had challenged the evolutionary theories emerging from Europe throughout the 1860s and 1870s, by the turn of the twentieth century, missionaries were less questioning

---

46 A J Small, diary, 8 November 1902, MSS 3267/1, item 1, ML; A Thornley, 'The Methodist Mission and the Indians in Fiji, 1900 to 1920', Masters thesis, University of Auckland, 1973, p. 19.

47 Mission Board minutes 1910, MOM 204 CY3306, ML, p. 60; District meeting minutes, 1909, 14 October 1909, MOM 178 CY2706, ML, p. 5.

48 As cited in A H Wood, *Overseas Missions of the Australian Methodist Church: Fiji*, vol. 2, Melbourne, Aldersgate Press, 1978, p. 279; the colonial administration had the same approach. See A Ravuvu, *The Façade of Democracy: Fijian Struggles for Political Control, 1830–1987*, Suva, Fiji, Reader Publishing House, 1991, p. 45.

of the basic premise behind evolutionist theories. Missionaries were slow to reframe evolutionist ideas, and this in turn slowed the mission's efforts towards establishing a native church in Fiji.[49]

Ideas about racial essentialism continued to inform discussions in 1907 when missionaries worked at redrafting the mission's constitution, which needed to be changed in order to reflect the establishment of the Indo-Fijian branch in 1901. The process elicited responses from missionaries and locally trained ministers that demonstrated their commitment to developing a self-supporting, self-governing and self-propagating mission. A commission was sent by the board in Sydney to check on the mission's progress towards the 'three selves' church ideal.[50] When discussing the degrees to which the two branches of the mission's work would be separate, the commission concluded that Indo-Fijian and Fijian 'habits of life and modes of thought are dissimilar; and the languages spoken have no relation to one another'.[51] Again, missionaries drew on the rudimentary language of cultural difference to argue for the necessity of racial segregation. Missionaries, though implementing this segregated system according to race, referred more frequently to culture as the primary difference between peoples. All of these discussions coincided with Im Thurn's attempts to bring the young Fijian chief born on Bau Island, Ratu Sukuna, into the colonial administration. Im Thurn was concerned that a western-styled education would upset Sukuna's standing in the Fijian community, and he watched attentively for any signs of this.[52]

With the structure of the mission established in documents and deeds, efforts turned towards the work of evangelisation. Burton sought financial support from Australians with a sense of urgency, depicting Indo-Fijians as a threat to the Christian Fijian in public meetings.[53] He argued that if missionaries did not make a special effort to convert the Indo-Fijian community, 'the crescent of Mohamet' would 'displace the cross of Christ in the Pacific'.[54] The mission board continued to seek recruits who were familiar with Indian cultural practices in

---

49   For details on how Methodist missionaries in Fiji were influenced by anthropology in the late nineteenth century, and her suggestion that they were more convinced of these theories by the early 1900s, see H Gardner, *Gathering for God: George Brown in Oceania*, Otago, Otago University Press, 2006, pp. 107–9; H Gardner, 'Defending Friends: Robert Codrington, George Sarawia, and Edward Wogale', in K Fullagar (ed.), *Atlantic World in the Antipodes: Effects and Transformations since the Eighteenth Century*, Newcastle Upon Tyne, England, Cambridge Scholars Publishing, 2012, p. 154.
50   Fiji constitution meeting, 25 February 1907, MOM Ch OM 2, 1880–1898, number 3, 1906–1909, ML, pp. 57–58.
51   Commission to Fiji 1907, MOM Ch O M 2, 1880-1898/3, 1906–1909, 1907, ML, p. 45.
52   D Scarr, *Ratu Sukuna: Soldier, Statesman, Man of Two Worlds*, London, Macmillan Education for the Ratu Sir Lala Sukuna biography committee, 1980, p. 20.
53   M Sidal, *Hannah Dudley: Hamari Maa: Honoured Mother, Educator, and Missioner to the Indentured Indians in Fiji, 1864–1931*, Suva, Fiji, Pacific Theological College Press, 1997, pp. 29–30; M Tomlinson, 'Sacred Soil in Kadavu, Fiji', *Oceania*, vol. 72, no. 4, 2002, p. 240.
54   'Orientalisation of the Pacific', *Clarence and Richmond Examiner*, Grafton NSW, 9 March 1907, p. 15.

the hope that they would draw more Indo-Fijians into the mission, targeting students from the renowned Bareilly College in Uttar Pradesh.[55] Burton and the Reverend Charles Lelean travelled to India to find new workers in 1908.[56] They did not find any catechists or ministers who could come to Fiji immediately, but the voyage was more personally rewarding for Charles Lelean, who married Constance Howell while he was there. Howell, like Dudley, had worked with other female evangelists in the interdenominational Zenana mission movement in India, and her experience and knowledge of Indian cultures, as well as medicine, would undoubtedly benefit Charles Lelean in the decades ahead.[57] However, this meant that Europeans remained the face of Methodism to Indo-Fijians, and despite the growing tendency amongst Europeans to consider and respect the cultural protocols of Hinduism and Islam, this only served to maintain the sense of European dominance. The mission was widely perceived to be an extension of Britain's colonial rule.

The mission board in Australia was interested in building links between Fiji and India, and decided to establish a station in India 'from which this human tide is flowing upon its mission fields in the Pacific, so that this wave of coloured population may be touched, at its very starting point, with Christian forces'.[58] In March 1908, the board described the differences that existed between Indian and Pacific peoples:

> ... mission work in India must necessarily be of another type to that which has hitherto been carried on under its direction in the South Seas. In India we are face to face with a vast population, with a highly complex civilisation, and, with

---

55   Mission Board meeting, 1 August 1906, MOM Ch OM 2, 1880–1898/3, 1906–1909, ML, p. 78; Mission Board meeting, 3 October 1906, MOM Ch OM 2, 1880–1898/3, 1906–1909, ML, p. 16; Mission Board meeting, 4 January 1907, MOM Ch OM 2, 1880–1898/3, 1906–1909, ML, p. 50; J Garrett, *Footsteps in the Sea: Christianity in Oceania to World War Two*, Suva, University of the South Pacific in conjunction with the World Council of Churches, 1992, p. 163.

56   *Overseas Missions of the Australian Methodist Church: Fiji-Indian and Rotuma*, vol. 3, Aldersgate Press, Melbourne, 1978, p. 24; Mission Board meeting, 5 February 1908, MOM Ch OM 2, 1880–1898/3, 1906–1909, ML, p. 109; Mission Board minutes, 3 June 1908, MOM Ch OM 2, 1880–1898/3, 1906–1909, ML, pp. 141–42; Mission Board Minutes, 6 November 1908, MOM Ch OM 2, 1880–1898/3, 1906–1909, ML, p. 196; J W Burton to B Danks, 30 August 1905, CY3465, MOM 238, ML; 'Church Notes', *The Advertiser*, Adelaide, South Australia, 28 November 1908, p. 14; 11 April 07, MOM Ch OM 2, 1880–1898/3, 1906–1909, ML, p. 62; A H Wood, *Overseas Missions of the Australian Methodist Church: Fiji*, vol. 2, Melbourne, Aldersgate Press, 1978, p. 24; Mission Board meeting, 17 March 08, MOM Ch OM 2, 1880–1898/3, 1906–1909, ML, p. 118.

57   'Zenana Bible and Medical Mission', *Reporter*, Box Hill, Victoria, 30 September 1910; Mission Board minutes, 5 March 1909, MOM Ch OM 2, 1880–1898/3, 1906–1909, ML, p. 278; Mission Board Minutes, 2 June 1909, MOM Ch OM 2, 1880–1898/3, 1906–1909, ML, p. 288. For information on Zenana, see D L Roberts, *American Women in Mission: A Social History of their Thought and Practice*, Mercer University Press, 2005, p. 168; R Howe, 'The Australian Christian Movement and Women's Activism in the Asia-Pacific Region, 1890–1920s', *Australian Feminist Studies*, vol. 16, no. 36, 2001, p. 312; R A Semple, *Missionary Women: Gender, Professionalism and the Victorian Idea of Christian Mission*, Suffolk, The Boydell Press, 2003, p. 33.

58   Mission Board meeting, 17 March 08, MOM Ch OM 2, 1880–1898, no. 3, 1906–1909, ML, p. 119.

all the problems which such a type of civilisation creates. Nowhere else in the world is society so highly organised, so sharply stratified by differences of race and speech and social condition.[59]

The mission board depicted Indian society as more hierarchical than some Pacific societies, pursuing the argument that Indian civilisation was more complex and more sophisticated than those found in the Pacific, and feeding the idea of racial and cultural hierarchy. The mission board's minutes declared that India 'in the future will influence yet more directly, the mission fields under [the mission board's] care in the Pacific'.[60] While Britain continued to acquire labourers from India, who were referred to as 'the most docile and industrious of all the coloured races',[61] the minutes suggested that 'they threaten to turn Fiji into a mere fragment of India set in the Pacific'.[62]

Recording only 22 Indo-Fijian Methodist members in 1906, the Indo-Fijian branch was a considerable cost to the board, as its membership could not sponsor its own programs.[63] The Indo-Fijian branch relied almost entirely on the board's grants and supplementary financial contributions from supporters in Australia. The possibility of implementing a system of self-support — one of the elements of the 'three selves' church idea — was untenable. The board's secretary, the Reverend J G Wheen, commented in 1909 that the two branches were at two different stages of development as a result of the decision to separate. Reverend William E Bennett assured the mission's General Secretary Benjamin Danks in 1909: 'Cut off the Indian Mission from Fiji making it a charge on General Funds and we will undertake to be self-supporting.'[64] Bennett implied that self-support could only be achieved if the mission branches separated, and it was better to have one branch of the mission set on a clear course towards self-governance and financial self-support than to have the whole mission project derailed. From a financial perspective, this made sense to the mission's leadership. J G Wheen declared that the Fijian work would 'in the near future' be self-supporting, but the mission society would have to continue funding the Indo-Fijian work.[65] The mission board in Australia and the district synod in Fiji agreed that drawing money from the collections taken from the Fijian churches through

---

59   Ibid., p. 118; A Ravuvu, *The Façade of Democracy: Fijian Struggles for Political Control, 1830–1987,* Suva, Fiji, Reader Publishing House, 1991, p. 56.
60   Mission Board meeting, 17 March 1908, MOM Ch OM 2, 1880–1898, no. 3, 1906–1909, ML, p. 119.
61   Ibid.
62   Ibid.
63   A H Wood, *Overseas Missions of the Australian Methodist Church: Fiji-Indian and Rotuma,* vol. 3, Aldersgate Press, Melbourne, 1978, p. 23.
64   W E Bennett to B Danks, 2 February 1909, MOM106 Fiji In-Letters 1908–1910 (1–7).
65   Report, Wheen's visit to Fiji, 1 December 1909, MOM Ch OM 2, 1880–1898, no. 3 1906–1909, ML, pp. 358–59.

the *vakamisioneri* system — an arrangement developed to suit the communal, chiefly system that remained in Fijian villages — to fund the Indo-Fijian branch would only jeopardise the Fijian mission's transition to self-support.

Burton's ideas about 'native churches' and the 'three selves' church concept had been influential in the mission field. He left Fiji in 1909, but his influence over mission activities only grew. He accepted a position on the mission board in Australia. This placed him at the heart of the Methodist mission enterprise in the Pacific, which suited his ambitious nature. From his desk in Melbourne and then in Sydney, he continued to write and talk through his ideas about racial difference. He believed that the distinctions between Fijian and Indo-Fijian cultures were permanent; he was convinced that they sat at two different points on the spectrum of social progress and could not easily coexist. Burton framed his predictions for Fiji's future using theories of extinction and evolutionism, which informed his beliefs in the superiority of one race over another.[66] He was sure that Fiji would one day be predominantly Indo-Fijian.

After arriving in Melbourne in the midst of a dry, hot summer, Burton delivered a speech at Wesley Church where he informed his audience that there were 40,000 Indo-Fijians in Fiji, their number always increasing while 'the Fijians were dying out. In time, therefore, there would be a heathen Fiji once more, unless these people [Indo-Fijians] were won for Christ.'[67] From the podium he declared:

> The once-savage races indigenous to these lands are silently and swiftly passing away. The remnant that may be left can play only a very secondary and subordinate part in the great drama which the *Zeit-geist* is about to stage. Other races, more alert and vigorous, will surely people these shores and till these fields.[68]

---

66 A H Wood, *Overseas Missions of the Australian Methodist Church: Fiji-Indian and Rotuma*, vol. 3, Aldersgate Press, Melbourne, 1978, p. 22; L L Snyder, 'The Idea of Racialism: Its Meaning and History', in E Cashmore and J Jennings (eds), *Racisms: Essential Readings*, Thousand Oaks, California, London, 2001, p. 92; D Scarr, *Ratu Sukuna: Soldier, Statesman, Man of Two Worlds*, London, Macmillan Education for the Ratu Sir Lala Sukuna biography committee, 1980, p. 43.
67 'Methodism and Indian Missions', *The Spectator*, 5 March 1909, p. 381; see also 'The Annual Conference 1909 Ministerial Session', Victoria/Tasmanian Conference, *The Spectator*, 5 March 1909, p. 373.
68 J W Burton, *Our Work in Fiji*, Indian Mission House, Davuilevu, 1909, in B V Lal, *Crossing the Kala Pani: A Documentary History of Indian Indenture in Fiji*, Canberra, Division of Pacific and Asian History, Research School of Pacific and Asian Studies, The Australian National University, Suva, Fiji, Fiji Museum, 1998, p. 122.

Burton's argument was based on racial theories that he used to comprehend the high death rates amongst Fijians.[69] Missionary planning was therefore deeply informed by demographics and the depopulation debates mixed with 'popular ruminations', 'anthropological and psychological theories'.[70] Burton argued that Indo-Fijian labourers were not:

> the scum of India … They have brains! They are keen logicians, much harder to win than the simple minded Fijians. The Fijian looked up to the Englishman as a superior being. The Hindu looks down on him. Why, in his eyes, it is simply preposterous for this young nation of ours, with its juvenile philosophy, to offer to teach religion or philosophy to the ancient races of India, who have been specialists in these things for thousands of years before England was thought of![71]

Burton's predictions for Fijian society, in line with the thinking of many in Fiji's colonial service,[72] informed his ideas about mission strategy, which he published in international theology journals. It was around the time of this address that Burton's first article on mission policy and organisation appeared in the *Hibbert Journal*, titled 'Missions and Modernism: Christian Missions as Affected by Liberal Theology'.[73] In this article, Burton displayed his ideas about race that were underpinned by theological and demographic debates.[74] He claimed:

> from the Modernist's point of view of a Kingdom of God upon earth, some races are more worth saving than others. It is far more important, for instance, that Japan should be Christian in life and spirit than the whole of the South Seas should be converted. The inhabitants of these islands have evidently no function to perform in the great evolution of humanity, but he would be a bold man who would dare to outline the limits of Japan's or China's function … Some souls mean far more to the future than others, and this should not be lost sight of in the Missionary effort of the Church …[75]

Burton translated his ideas about racial hierarchies into global mission strategy, using 'racial virility' — population increases or decreases — as a predicator for evangelisation. Burton suggested a targeted approach to evangelisation,

---

69 S Jervis, 'Methodist Missionary Working in Fiji', cited in 'Notes from the Churches', *Chronicle*, South Australia, 30 August 1919, p. 50.

70 K Ram and M Jolly, *Maternities and Modernities: Colonial and Postcolonial Experiences in Asia and the Pacific*, Cambridge, Cambridge University Press, 1998, p. 183.

71 'Rev J W Burton in Wesley Church', *The Spectator*, 12 March 1909, p. 423.

72 D Scarr, *Ratu Sukuna: Soldier, Statesman, Man of Two Worlds*, London, Macmillan education for the Ratu Sir Lala Sukuna biography committee, 1980, p. 43.

73 J W Burton, 'Missions and Modernism: Christian Missions as Affected by Liberal Theology', *The Hibbert Journal*, vol. 7, 1908–1909.

74 J Fabian, *Time and the Other: How Anthropology Makes its Object*, New York, Columbia University Press, 1983, p. 2; B Douglas and C Ballard (eds), *Foreign Bodies: Oceania and the Science of Race, 1750–1940*, Canberra, ANU E Press, 2008, p. 46.

75 J W Burton, 'Missions and Modernism: Christian Missions as Affected by Liberal Theology', *The Hibbert Journal*, vol. 7, 1908–1909, p. 410.

encouraging missions to concentrate their efforts on converting only the races that would develop the world. He argued that the mission had to be selective about the fields they chose to work in:

> Common sense would seem to say that we ought first to attempt the living and progressive peoples who hold in their hand the keys of the future. But it may be asked in astonishment, 'Are you going to allow the natives of Africa and the South Seas to perish?' The reply might be well made 'Are *you* going to allow the millions in India and China to pass away without the hope of the Gospel?'[76]

Burton was addressing some of the ideas recently put forward by American mission leader John R Mott. Mott had inspired Burton and led him to missionary work. In 1909, Mott published *The Evangelisation of the World in this Generation*, in which he argued that missionaries had the duty of delivering the Christian message to all non-Christians throughout the world within the space of one generation, and of ensuring that the 'three selves' church policy was adopted in all lands.[77] Mott and the missionaries from across the globe that he interviewed on this question focused on whether it would be possible to introduce peoples to Christianity and convert them. Mott and Burton both believed that cultures might obstruct their desired outcomes, but agreed that Christianity could penetrate cultures and bring 'savage' or 'primitive' peoples into Christianity.[78] However, while Burton concurred fundamentally with the aim of converting all peoples from across the world, he argued that it was not necessarily worth devoting mission resources to all peoples, assuming that indigenous peoples of the South Seas and Africa had one foot in the grave. Both Mott and Burton had published their ideas on the eve of the International Missionary Council conference held in Edinburgh in 1910, where missionaries continued to discuss mission strategy.[79] Though Burton and his Methodist colleagues from the Fijian mission field did not attend this inaugural conference, the ideas generated by the International Missionary Council were evidently already influencing the Fijian mission's responses to the conditions in the colony.

In the years after he left Fiji, Burton continued to argue that the Indo-Fijian mission should be at the centre of the mission's activities, despite limited evangelical success in the field. The number of Indo-Fijian Methodists remained small, and there was widespread persistent resistance to Christianity and old reactions to apostasy — Hindus who converted to Christianity were often shunned and excluded from family and community. Hilda Steadman, the wife of missionary W Rex Steadman who worked in the Indo-Fijian branch, recorded

76   Ibid., p. 411.
77   J R Mott, *The Evangelization of the World in this Generation*, New York, Student Volunteer Movement for Foreign Missions, 1905, p. 16.
78   Ibid., pp. 33, 132–59.
79   B Stanley, *The World Missionary Conference, Edinburgh 1910*, Grand Rapids, Eerdmans, 2009.

that some of the girls who attended the Indo-Fijian school at Navua in 1912 were 'never allowed to return to their homes or see their mothers again', a reason in itself for despondency.[80]

Regardless, Burton felt that his argument was supported by the census figures, and through 1913 there was increasing media interest in the idea that the world was witnessing the extinction of the Fijian people.[81] In 1912, Henry Worrall, who had worked in the Rewa circuit amongst both Indo-Fijian and Fijian peoples, wrote a pamphlet named 'A Racial Riddle', printed in 1912. In it, Worrall described the Fijians as people of the past.[82] He used the biblical story of Jacob and Esau to describe the relationship between Indo-Fijians and Fijians. Jacob and Esau were twins in the Book of Genesis. Before they were born, God had said to their mother, Rebekah: 'You have two nations in your womb, and two peoples from within you will be separated', one to be stronger than the other, and the older to serve the younger. The Indo-Fijians were likened to Jacob, who was plain but strong. Worrall used Esau as a metaphor for the Fijians. On Esau's deathbed, Jacob had bought his birthright.[83] Worrall not only saw one race as stronger than the other, but considered them innately separate, with the Indians poised to purchase the birthright of the indigenous population of Fiji as they passed away. Burton, appointed as Conference Secretary of Methodist Foreign Missions, described the Fijians as 'futureless' in 1915.[84] Despite Burton's protestations that they should do otherwise, and other missionaries in Fiji agreeing that they were witness to the decimation of Fijians, the mission's attentions remained primarily focused on the Fijian branch. The story of Jacob and Esau would resonate with missionaries working in Fiji for years to come.

It is integral to view these discussions within the context of conversations that were occurring at the time in the corridors and courtrooms of Fiji's colonial administration, which seeped out into the press and circulated through the islands. Fiji's land legislation was being debated in earnest, particularly in April 1912, when the administration announced that all land grants would be restricted to leasehold.[85] There had been what the press called 'land disturbances'

---

80   Hilda Mary Steadman – papers, 1913–1975, PMB 1074; J Garrett, *Footsteps in the Sea: Christianity in Oceania to World War Two*, Suva, University of the South Pacific in conjunction with the World Council of Churches, 1992, p. 394.

81   'New South Wales: Hindoos in Fiji: A Missionary's Story', *Morning Post*, Cairns, 6 March 1907, p. 5; 'Race disappearance: The Case of the Fijians', *Northern Star*, Lismore, NSW, 17 January 1913, p. 3; 'Doomed Islanders: Decay of the Race: Ravages of Consumption', *The Sydney Morning Herald*, 24 May 1913, p. 19; 'Race Disappearance: A Vanishing Population: The Fijians Dying Out: And the Reason Why', *The Daily News*, Perth, Western Australia, 1 February 1913, p. 12.

82   H Worrall, 'A Racial Riddle: The Clash of Alien Races in the Pacific', *Life*, 1 August 1912, p. 141.

83   I referred to both the New International Version (NIV) and King James Version of the Bible. Genesis 25: 19–34.

84   'Welcome to Rev J W Burton', *The Spectator*, 1 May 1914, p. 719; 'The Call of the Pacific', *The Spectator*, 20 February 1914, p. 307; 'Foreign Mission Demonstration', *The Spectator*, 2 April 1915, p. 287–88.

85   'Fiji Land Grants', *The West Australian*, 24 April 1912, p. 12.

around Suva in the wake of this announcement. There was agitation from Fijians about the colonial legislation being designed to govern their land acquisition and holdings.[86] The 1915 decision to push through a motion in the Legislative Assembly that would open land up for European settlement only contributed to the growing sense of Fijian disempowerment.[87]

Segregation manifested not through one swift decision, but through a series of changes made in response to local factors and international ecumenical debates. Thus there was a clear transition from the mission's initial haphazard response to the presence of Indian indentured labourers in the colony to a more coherent strategy at the turn of the twentieth century. The main practical challenges highlighted in this chapter included language and cultural differences, and the mission board addressed these through the strategic recruitment of missionaries who had experience in India. Failing that, missionaries elected to be tutored in Indian languages and cultures. The other main practical reason for segregation was financial, linked to the mission policy of establishing a self-supporting church. The mission could not rely on its tiny Indo-Fijian membership to financially support its own activities. They also did not deem it appropriate to take funds from the Fijian membership for use in the Indian community. By keeping the mission branches separate, the Fijian mission could continue to support its own programs, and could be held up as an exemplar of a successful mission, well on the way to becoming financially independent. The Indo-Fijian branch, on the other hand, relied almost entirely on the Australasian Mission Board and private investors to fund its existence.

While those tangible issues were addressed, the segregation was also informed by the way that missionaries understood racial and cultural difference, which was generally in terms of evolutionism, essentialism, and a strong belief in extinction. The influence of evolutionist thought was evident in the writings and speeches of the rising leader John Wear Burton, who argued that the future of the mission in Fiji was Indo-Fijian. His claim was problematic for mission leaders who believed that there was almost no potential for the Indo-Fijian mission to become self-supporting, self-governing or self-propagating, and who had put endless efforts into the Fijian branch. There were no serious plans made for the devolution of the Indo-Fijian mission, but self-support remained a possibility for the Fijian community. Yet, missionaries also tended to agree that they were witnessing a significant change in Fiji which they believed would lead to these islands becoming an extension of India in the Pacific. Complex practical and theoretical realities of difference shaped the institution's strategy and organisation. Cultural difference and racial theories created the boundaries

---

86   'Fiji Land Disturbances', *The Advertiser*, Adelaide, 19 July 1912, p. 9.
87   D Scarr, *Ratu Sukuna: Soldier, Statesman, Man of Two Worlds*, London, Macmillan education for the Ratu Sir Lala Sukuna biography committee, 1980, p. 42.

and provided structure in a changing colonial society. Europeans maintained control of the mission through these times of change, their rationale informed by popularised and scholarly concepts of culture. These issues were equally evident in debates particular to the Fijian branch during this period, which will be the focus of the following chapter.

CHAPTER TWO

A National Church Built in 'Primitive' Culture: Communalism, Chiefs and Coins

Establishing a structure for the mission that separated it into ethnically defined spheres on 1 October 1901 had important implications for the Fijian branch of the church. As noted in the previous chapter, the decision was made on the chiefly island of Bau, where the mission's chairman, the Reverend Arthur J Small, was stationed. Holding the synod in this place highlighted the pre-eminence of Fijians in the institution. As noted earlier, the church had been separated on the premise that the two cultural groups in the colony were too different to be housed in the same mission. The separation allowed the 'three selves' church policy — a broad concept pushed through global mission networks — to be adopted in a homogenised shaping of Fijian identity: the Fijian branch was constructed in the 'Fijian way'. This was not dissimilar to the system established by the colonial administration, which had implemented distinct governance systems for the Fijian and Indo-Fijian communities. Both the mission and the administration translated the systems of Empire to hyper-local conditions, yet they were not always complementary. The colonial administration's policies were aimed at protectionism and sometimes stalled transformative processes that missionaries believed would help shape the 'native church'. Through the early decades of the twentieth century, missionaries also confronted the conceptual and practical challenges of progress, expecting that social change for the Fijian community would follow a linear trajectory through the stages of development towards 'modernity'.[1] This chapter highlights ways in which missionaries,

---

1   N Thomas, 'Sanitation and Seeing: The Creation of State Power in Early Colonial Fiji', *Comparative Studies in Society and History*, vol. 32, no. 1, 1990, p. 156.

informed by anthropological writings, responded to what they considered to be classic leaders of 'primitive' society — chiefs, communalism and subsistence economy — while constructing a distinctively Fijian 'native church'.[2]

Chiefs were central to the colonial administration's system of indirect rule and had for an even longer time been important to efforts at evangelisation. From Small's first day in the mission field in 1879, he had been stationed in Fiji's eastern islands, home to the highest-ranking chiefs. Here, Small was made aware of the complexities of chiefly hierarchies and the ways in which they continued to shape daily interactions between people. He met with missionary Lorimer Fison soon after his arrival in Fiji, and Fison introduced Small and his wife to the chiefs and people of Bau. Small's daughter, Winifred McHugh, later writing down her father's recollections, recorded that Ratu Tevita Uluilakeba II was away at the time of Small's arrival at Bau, but, in fact, by then Ratu Tevita, who was intended to be the Tui Nayau (paramount chief of the Lau islands) had already passed away.[3] That Small had noted Ratu Tevita's absence to his daughter indicated an awareness of the importance of this chief on Bau, despite the distorted way it has been recorded in McHugh's notes.[4] Small continued to notice interactions between chiefs and commoners through his career. In 1902, Small — an avid cricketer — was introducing some young Fijian men to the game, remarking that 'they were very enthusiastic, until the young chiefs had to bowl to the ordinary men, then they walked off the field and said it was not Fijian custom for chiefs to do that sort of thing'.[5] Historian David Wetherell described cricket as a game that levelled social hierarchies and boundaries in Papua New Guinea, but in the east of Fiji, deference to customary leaders remained intact.[6] Cricket provided a space where chiefly power might have been subverted, but the chiefs regained control of the situation by removing themselves from the game. Though a sporting incident might be considered trivial, the tensions that played out through the game of cricket demonstrated that while the contexts of engagement between chiefs and others were changing, the role of chief — a leadership model that had been solidified and made somewhat static through the systems of indirect rule — was challenged by new forms of leadership.[7]

---

2   Kuper has traced the development of the term 'primitive' throughout the nineteenth and twentieth centuries, see A Kuper, *The Reinvention of Primitive Society: Transformation of a Myth*, New York, Routledge, 2005, p. 5.

3   D Scarr, *A History of the Pacific Islands: Passages Through Tropical Time*, New York, Routledge, 2001, p. 136.

4   Memories of Winifred McHugh, PMB 156, p. 5.

5   Ibid., p. 10.

6   D Wetherell, *Charles Abel and the Kwato Mission of Papua New Guinea 1891–1975*, Melbourne, Melbourne University Press, 1996, p. 151.

7   N Thomas, 'Sanitation and Seeing: The Creation of State Power in Early Colonial Fiji', *Comparative Studies in Society and History*, vol. 32, no. 1, 1990, p. 149; A D Ravuvu, *The Fijian Ethos*, Suva, Institute of Pacific Studies, University of the South Pacific, 1987, pp. 18–19.

Small's ability to witness the maintenance of chiefly authority first-hand shaped his opinions, but missionaries in the field were also influenced by the debates occurring amongst anthropologists in Europe and America. His mentor, Fison, was also an avid anthropologist, corresponding with the leaders of the discipline and discussing his ideas with colleagues. Missionaries believed that chiefs were a mark of a less-modern society, an idea that Fison discussed with anthropologist E B Tylor during the early 1880s. Fison had engaged with anthropology while working in the Fijian mission field, particularly since reading American anthropologist Lewis Henry Morgan's kinship schedule in 1869.[8] From that time onwards, Fison entered readily into anthropological debates about race and culture. He was particularly interested in the work of E B Tylor, who in his seminal work *Primitive Culture*, published in 1871, had described cultures as being at various stages of evolution, and defined them according to certain characteristics as either 'savage', 'barbaric' or 'civilised'.[9] He utilised Fison and his knowledge of the Fijian chiefly and communal systems.[10] Fison, writing to Tylor in 1879 as he started to mentor A J Small, was sceptical of evolutionist theories emerging in Europe, particularly those put forward by John Lubbock, but in letters to Tylor he did try provide classifications of cultures relative to his experience in Fiji.[11] In 1879 he suggested that the relationship between chiefs and commoners demonstrated that Fijian society was 'savage'.[12] These were ideas that were taken up within the colonial administration, especially by Governor Arthur Gordon, who positioned himself as an expert in Fijian customs and engaged with ideas about social evolution, and whether social development was uni-linear or otherwise.[13]

---

8   P McConvell and H Gardner, 'The Descent of Morgan in Australia: Kinship Representation from the Australian Colonies', *Structure and Dynamics: eJournal of Anthropological and Related Sciences*, vol. 6, no. 1, 2013, p. 5.

9   G Stocking, *Race, Culture and Evolution: Essays in the History of Anthropology*, London, Collier-Macmillan Limited, 1968, pp. 80–81.

10   E B Tylor, *Primitive Culture: Researches into the Development of Mythology, Philosophy, Religion, Art, and Custom*, vol. 2, London, John Murray, 1871, p. 406; H Gardner, *Gathering for God: George Brown in Oceania*, Dunedin, Otago University Press, 2006, pp. 15, 108.

11   H Gardner, 'Defending Friends: Robert Codrington, George Sarawia, and Edward Wogale', in K Fullagar (ed.), *Atlantic World in the Antipodes: Effects and Transformations since the Eighteenth Century*, Newcastle-Upon-Tyne, England, Cambridge Scholars Publishing, 2012, p. 154.

12   L Fison to E B Tylor, 17 August 1879, transcribed and available online at Pitt Rivers Museum, web.prm. ox.ac.uk/sma/index.php/primary-documents/primary-documents-index/411-fison-1-tylor-papers-prm.html, accessed 19 March 2014.

13   I Heath, 'Toward a Reassessment of Gordon in Fiji', *Journal of Pacific History*, vol. 9, no. 1, 1974, p. 84; P France, *The Charter of the Land: Custom and Colonization in Fiji*, Melbourne, Oxford University Press, 1969, p. 125.

Yet, despite the perceived 'savage' nature of chiefly rule, missionaries generally conceded that they needed to incorporate chiefs into the mission's systems of governance.[14] Chiefly support helped to legitimise the mission's position in the community in the eyes of non-chiefly Fijians and colonists. The colonial administration had ensured a measured continuation of chiefly predominance through establishing the Great Council of Chiefs. In the mission, deference to chiefs, the practice of *vakaturaga* protocols, was shown through personal daily interactions rather than the establishment of a committee of chiefs. They were included in the regular events of the mission, and whether consciously or not, became part of what characterised the church as Fijian, or at least what marked the difference between Fijian and Indo-Fijian work.[15] The relationships between chiefs and the mission staff became important when negotiating matters between villages and the colonial administration. For instance, Small had amicable relationships with the colony's governors as well as the chiefs, and governors often relied on his comprehension of Fijian language and history. On one occasion, Small acted as intermediary when the colonial administration were trying to find the best possible location for new water tanks on Bau. Small helped to ensure that they would not be placed on a burial site.[16] Chiefs were so much a part of Fiji's culture that the Methodist missionaries worked alongside them and integrated *vakaturaga* practice into their everyday procedures.

The mission's long-term aspirations to establish a financially self-sufficient church conflicted with the colonial administration's protectionist policies that sought to minimise wherever possible the transformative influence of colonialism.[17] The colonial administration's 1890 Labour Ordinance and Masters and Servants Ordinance excluded Fijian workers from the market economy in a bid to guard indigenous culture.[18] Fijians still operated in what anthropologists of the time, particularly those belonging to E B Tylor's school of thought, would then have classified as a 'primitive' economic system.[19] The mission's duty was

14 N Thomas, 'Sanitation and Seeing: The Creation of State Power in Early Colonial Fiji', *Comparative Studies in Society and History*, vol. 32, no. 1, 1990, p. 164; M Mamdani, 'Historicising Power and Responses to Power: Indirect Rule and its Reform', *Social Reform*, vol. 66, no. 3, 1999, p. 865.

15 R Norton, 'Ethno-nationalism and the Constitutive Power of Cultural Politics: A Comparative Study of Sri Lanka and Fiji', *Journal of Asian and African Studies*, vol. 28, no. 3–4, 1993, p. 188; R Norton, 'Chiefs for the Nation: Containing Ethnonationalism and Bridging the Ethnic Divide in Fiji', *Pacific Studies*, vol. 22, no. 1, 1999, p. 22.

16 By the time Governor O'Brien became governor in Fiji in 1901, Small had been in the colony for 18 years and was an invaluable resource. Memories of Winifred McHugh, PMB 156, p. 46.

17 L Veracini, '"Emphatically not a white man's colony": Settler Colonialism and the Construction of Colonial Fiji', *Journal of Pacific History*, vol. 43, no. 2, 2008, p. 196.

18 N Thomas, 'The Inversion of Tradition', *American Ethnologist*, vol. 19, no. 2, 1992, p. 221; A Bain, 'A Protective Labour Policy? An Alternative Interpretation of Early Colonial Labour Policy', *The Journal of Pacific History*, vol. 23, no. 2, 1988, pp. 119–36; B Knapman, 'Indigenous Involvement in the Cash Economy of Lau, Fiji, 1840–1946', *Journal of Pacific History*, vol. 11, no. 3, 1976, pp. 186–87.

19 E B Tylor, *Primitive Culture: Researches into the Development of Mythology, Philosophy, Religion, Art, and Custom*, vol. 2, London, John Murray, 1871, pp. 6–7.

to ensure that its communities moved towards financial self-support, and was able to continue without the need for overseas financial aid, but the cost of running the Fijian branch was calculated in 1901 as £4,762 3s 11d — an almost impossible target for the Fijian Methodist membership to generate. Despite some involvement in the colony's industries, most remained village-bound subsistence farmers.[20] This was slowly changing, with Fijians increasingly involved in the barter or cash economy that had developed in the early 1900s, and others had been drawn either willingly or unwillingly into the cotton and sugar industries. Others worked independently of their villages on their own plots of land.[21] In places where this had occurred, the mission often received greater contributions.[22] However, the mission's income was constrained by the colonial administration's labour policies.

While the colonial administration had endeavoured to keep Fijian society in a 'primitive' state, the goals of self-support required shifts away from the communal system. By carefully weaving Fijian traditions into the mission's identity and programs, missionaries hoped that the old and the new would be bridged, and that Fijian society would progress.[23] Chiefly rule was acceptable, but the mission required that its members be allowed to earn wages in order to ensure regular financial contributions were made to the mission's coffers, and so this issue of money became central to discussions. The concept of self-support challenged the notion that a church could be built in Fiji without alteration to customary social structures, as the institution relied on western systems of finance. A tithe collection system created throughout the nineteenth century, called *vakamisioneri*, had made circuit incomes dependent on the whim of chiefs as much as Fijian involvement in the cash economy.[24] Collections were taken at an annual rally.[25] Small recalled sitting at a table with a Fijian minister (then referred to as 'Native Minister') while a *meke* (dance) was performed 'and as the performers marched past they would give their offering for the year.'[26] Chiefs supervised the *vakamisioneri* collection, and their support was essential to successful fundraising. Historian Bruce Knapman, discussing the system as it

---

20   The Indian branch costs totalled Indian branch £614 15s 9d. See Mission District Minutes, MOM 175 CY2671, 1901–1903, ML; B Indigenous Involvement in the Cash Economy of Lau, Fiji, 1840–1946', *Journal of Pacific History*, vol. 11, no. 3, 1976, p. 173.

21   S H Sohmer, 'Idealism and Pragmatism in Colonial Fiji: Sir Arthur Gordon's Native Rule Policy and the Introduction of Indian Contract Labour', *Hawaiian Journal of History*, vol. 18, 1984, pp. 141–42.

22   B Knapman, 'Indigenous Involvement in the Cash Economy of Lau, Fiji, 1840–1946', *Journal of Pacific History*, vol. 11, no. 3, 1976, p. 170.

23   N Thomas, 'Sanitation and Seeing: The Creation of State Power in Early Colonial Fiji', *Comparative Studies in Society and History*, vol. 32, no. 1, 1990, p. 167.

24   B Knapman, 'Indigenous Involvement in the Cash Economy of Lau, Fiji, 1840–1946', *Journal of Pacific History*, vol. 11, no. 3, 1976, p. 173.

25   Ibid., p. 172.

26   Memories of Winifred McHugh, PMB 156, p. 10; similar account given by Small to W Sutherland, 4 June 1900, F/1/1900, NAF.

was between 1873 and 1905, has argued that *vakamisioneri* placed pressure on Fijian villagers, who might dedicate up to one third of their wage to the church, sometimes contributing an amount that exceeded the set tax rate in the Lau island group, in Fiji's eastern province. However, the mission persisted, driven not only by the need to fund its activities but by a determination to demonstrate that the mission had potential to become financially self-supporting.[27] Thornley argued that, theoretically, *vakamisioneri* was designed to indicate the extent to which the community was moving towards autonomy and fulfilment of self-support, and was not, therefore, an oppressive system.[28] *Vakamisioneri* drew together the tension between the ideals of creating a church that reflected a national character, and the perceived need to modify traditional Fijian society if these aims were to be achieved.[29] It was no surprise that the Reverend William Slade, working in the Fijian branch, argued in 1901 that the income was inconsistent, and that making the mission autonomous from Australia when its revenue was so unpredictable would be pure 'folly'.[30]

Missionaries also struggled to institute indigenous self-governance at the turn of the twentieth century. The mission failed to attract high-ranking chiefs into its ministry, with many instead opting to work in the colonial administration.[31] Many chiefs took part in the Council of Chiefs and were employed as *rokos* (district governors) and *bulis* (local administrators), for example.[32] This disappointed missionaries who seemed unsure about the capacity of non-chiefly people to lead the Fijian mission members.[33] This was not a view shared by Fijian men who were working as lay representatives and vied for a greater say in mission affairs. Money was central to missionaries' justifications for excluding Fijians from financial decision-making, arguing that they had no experience in managing their own finances, let alone those of a large organisation. The 1901 District Synod minutes illustrate conflicting positions adopted by the missionaries on this question:

27   B Knapman, 'Indigenous Involvement in the Cash Economy of Lau, Fiji, 1840–1946', *Journal of Pacific History*, vol. 11, no. 3, 1976, p. 180; B Knapman, 'The "vakamisioneri" in Lau, Fiji: A Reply', *Journal of Pacific History*, vol. 13, no. 2, 1978, pp. 113–14.

28   A Thornley, 'The "vakamisioneri" in Lau, Fiji: Some Comments', *Journal of Pacific History*, vol. 12, no. 2, 1977, p. 108; B Knapman, 'The "vakamisioneri" in Lau, Fiji: A Reply', *Journal of Pacific History*, vol. 13, no. 2, 1978, p. 113.

29   B Knapman, 'Indigenous Involvement in the Cash Economy of Lau, Fiji, 1840–1946', *Journal of Pacific History*, vol. 11, no. 3, 1976, p. 182.

30   Slade to B Danks, 27 February 1901, F/1/1901, NAF.

31   A Thornley, 'Custom, Change and Conflict: Fijian Wesleyan Ministers, 1835–1945', in R J May and H Nelson (eds), *Melanesia: Beyond Diversity*, Canberra, Research School of Pacific Studies, The Australian National University, 1982, p. 126.

32   A Ali, 'Fijian Chiefs and Constitutional Change, 1874–1937', *Journal de la Societe des Oceanistes*, vol. 33, no. 54–55, 1977, p. 55.

33   N Thomas, 'Sanitation and Seeing: The Creation of State Power in Early Colonial Fiji', *Comparative Studies in Society and History*, vol. 32, no. 1, 1990, pp. 149–70.

The Synod regards with very grave apprehension the immediate introduction into its councils of a number of native Lay Representatives who have no knowledge of finance, not to speak of the very intricate finance of a large Mission District. The Synod is not opposed to the principle of Lay Representation, but it feels very strongly that Fiji cannot, and ought not to be dealt with as are more advanced and intelligent communities, and that at the present time our Circuit Stewards are so unfitted for the responsibilities of Synodical representation, that their immediate introduction will cause very serious difficulties in the Financial and General affairs of the District.[34]

The Reverend Howard Nolan summarised his concerns, writing: 'It is altogether too Utopian to suppose that the Fijian in one generation is fit to sit side by side with equal vote on financial questions as ourselves.'[35] Despite village involvement in local sugar, copra and sandalwood industries, few missionaries believed that western economic practices would be fully adopted in Fiji when customary obligations — such as *solevu* — were still so prevalent, and were particularly sceptical about involving laymen who were considered of a lower class than ordained Fijians (*talatala*).[36] Yet the ideal of self-support required that they start educating Fijians in financial management, and it was also the opinion of the colony's governor, Henry Moore Jackson, that Fijians enter more firmly into the colony's commercial operations.[37]

European missionaries allowed *talatala* into the financial session of synod for the first time in 1902, while retaining almost complete control of the institution's funds.[38] Laymen were also included, but were carefully chosen. Small commented that Tomasi Naceba, Joeli Kete and Matiasi Vave would be able to learn the intricacies of the financial systems, though 'at times it was amusing to note the look of surprise on their innocent faces as they saw pile after pile of money disappear down the throat of the mission'.[39] Small saw the inclusion of Naceba, Kete and Vave in the meetings as an important step towards preparing the Fijian ministry for self-governance, recounting:

> … after sitting with the considering cap on … another of their number rose to say that tho' they could not see a way out of the difficulty they quite believed that we could see it alright, so they left the question with us.[40]

---

34 Mission District Minutes, Minutes of the Annual Synod of the Fiji District, Bau, 10 October 1901, MOM 175 CY2671, 1901–1903, screen 14, ML.

35 H H Nolan to B Danks 12 January 1901, MOM 628, ML.

36 B Knapman, 'Indigenous Involvement in the Cash Economy of Lau, Fiji, 1840–1946', *Journal of Pacific History*, vol. 11, no. 3, 1976, p. 167.

37 B V Lal, *Broken Waves: A History of the Fiji Islands in the Twentieth Century*, Honolulu, University of Hawai'i Press, 1992, p. 26.

38 Commission to Fiji, MOM Ch O M 2, 1880–1898/3, 1906–1909, 1907, ML, p. 13.

39 A J Small to G Brown, 4 November 1902, F/1/1902, NAF.

40 Ibid.

Small seemed confident about opening the financial synod to Fijian laymen, but sought the counsel of two of Fiji's pre-eminent missionaries on the matter. These were Frederick Langham and George Brown, who had since left the mission field but retained strong opinions on the matter of increasing Fijian responsibility. Brown favoured the idea of allowing lay representation in synod, as long as it did not diminish the authority of European missionaries. The presence of lay representatives at synod, he felt, could be managed because missionaries could sway the vote of *talatala*.[41] Langham, on the other hand, considered the prospect of any increase of Fijian power in the financial synod to be 'suicidal'.[42] Though there were variations in their perspectives, the elder statesmen of the mission agreed: Fijian power in the synod should be limited, and European control was required.

Small continued to correspond with Langham on the topic of Fijian self-governance. Two years later, in 1903, Langham suggested that enhancing the status of *talatala* would lead to social tensions and clashes with chiefs, and in turn reduce financial support for the mission. He wrote that native ministers:

> cannot resist the attraction of gold coin, against the English missionaries. It will wake the chiefs and people <u>envious of the NMs</u> [native ministers] — who will try and get larger and better houses — glass doors and windows etc. I pointed out to them that if they got these, the chiefs who hadn't got them would be envious of them and would lessen their gift to them. The Natives are good Christians, but they are not good financiers![43]

Unconvinced by Langham's argument, Small contested that 'it is absolute necessity for the safety of the district that some power of self-governance should be given to the Fijian people who contribute to the funds sent year by year'.[44] Small was committed to self-support as a means of assuaging the discontent about missionaries' efforts to institute European hegemony that he sensed was growing amongst *talatala* and their congregations. He felt that steps had to be made to promote Fijian authority, despite facing opposition from other European missionaries.[45] He established trials for financial self-support in what he considered to be the three most affluent circuits — Lau, Macuata and Bua.[46] Small responded to demands for Fijian autonomy by advancing

---

41 G Brown to A J Small 4 December 1901, F/1/1901, NAF; Heighway to A J Small, 5 February 1904, F/1/1904, NAF; J W Burton, *The Weaver's Shuttle: Memories and Reflections of an Octogenarian*, unpublished manuscript, n.d, p. 69.

42 A J Small to G Brown, 18 December 1901, F/1/1901, NAF.

43 Langham to Nolan, cited in Nolan to A J Small, 28 November 1903, F/1/1903, NAF; Anxieties on tensions between chiefs and Indigenous ministers also evident in Heighway to A J Small, 5 February 1904, F/1/1904, NAF.

44 A J Small to G Brown, 10 February 1903, F/1/1903, NAF.

45 Correspondence of CO Lelean 1905–1918, FF/6, M/25, ML; W Bennett to CO Lelean, 18 March 1905, FF/7, M/25, ML; W Bennett to CO Lelean, 6 May 1905, FF/8, M/25, ML.

46 Small to Danks 22 June 1900, MOM 625; B Danks, diary, 1900, 1913–14 [Visit to Fiji], MOM 627.

it in areas he considered to be stable, which happened to be in areas known to be strict in adherence to chiefly rule. There was thus a tension over the instillation of a hegemonic dominant culture within the mission — there was a constant process of negotiation, of accommodating the hegemonic cultures that had prevailed in Fiji prior to colonial rule, but also efforts to secure European power and authority. This was done by constructing particular discourses around indigenous engagement with capitalism. To return to the argument put forward by Jean and John Comaroff, hegemony was established through habitual activity, and European missionaries constructed the habit of dismissing indigenous peoples as unable to successfully engage in a capitalist system. These were habits that Small attempted to break, but against some stiff opposition.[47]

Some European missionaries were concerned about affording greater leadership responsibility to indigenous mission workers when there were so few chiefs amongst them; others saw the absence of chiefs as essential to ensuring a democratic leadership in synod.[48] The Reverend Charles Oswald Lelean, a missionary from Victoria who had arrived in Fiji in 1902 and was stationed at Nailaga in north-west Viti Levu,[49] commented:

> I think a Synod of big chiefs, NMs [native ministers] and missionaries means that what the chiefs set their minds on they will get, for their NMs will vote with them and where do we come in who have come here to rule and if we don't we will be ruled.[50]

Lelean's words show the performativity of colonial culture — discussions about rule and European dominance, and its necessity. He was clear about the intentions of the mission, clearly buying into the discourses of colonial governance and authority. His words suggest that while his intentions were clear, there needed to be a constant checking of systems to ensure that European power was not disrupted; it was never entirely guaranteed. Colonialist discourses were also laced with considerations for class and church. Small, who was perhaps influenced by his time in the New South Wales Methodist community, where the church tended to reflect more of the hierarchical Anglican tradition than it did in Victoria, responded:

---

47 Comaroff and Comaroff, *Of Revelation and Revolution: Christianity, Colonialism and Consciousness in South Africa*, vol. 1, Chicago, University of Chicago Press, 1991, p. 25.

48 Heighway to A J Small, 5 February 1904, F/1/1904, NAF; A Thornley, 'Fijians in the Methodist Ministry: The First Hundred Years, 1848–1945', in A Thornley and T Vulaono (eds), *Mai kea ki vei? Stories of Methodism in Fiji and Rotuma*, proceedings of the Fiji Methodist history conference, Davuilevu, 10–13 October 1995, Fiji Methodist Church Press, 1996, p. 37.

49 A H Wood, *Overseas Missions of the Australian Methodist Church: Fiji*, vol. 2, Melbourne, Aldersgate Press, 1978, p. 389.

50 C O Lelean to A J Small, 10 April 1904, F/1/1904, NAF.

> I do not much fear the double native vote[. A]s for 'ruling', we shall rule by our superior knowledge and ability ... there will be little fear that we shall get many high chiefs elected to Synod we shall get the middle-class chiefs who are the best kind ...[51]

Small projected his experiences of class and church in Britain and New South Wales on to the chiefly system, which informed his vision of the mission's organisational structure. He had sought 'middle class chiefs' to lead the mission, or 'minor chiefs' as historian Colin Newbury has described them. Small's articulated desires to attract middle-class chiefs to the ministry reflected a conscious effort to relate the chiefly leadership system to their own perceptions of class, and use this to inform the formation of a strong indigenous leadership.[52]

As mentioned in the previous chapter, the Australasian Mission Board sent a commission to Fiji in 1907 to investigate the state of the mission's progress towards self-support. Missionaries raised the same concerns, expressed earlier in the decade, about Fijian self-support and governance.[53] Reservations were again expressed, for example, about the inclusion of Fijians in the financial synod, despite Fijians remaining in a tutorage position. Missionaries were concerned that this had signified the 'balance of power being entrusted to native representatives'.[54] They still held 'doubts as to the capacity of the Fijians to understand and administer financial matters, especially on a large scale'.[55] Concerns remained about trying to establish a native church in an economically 'primitive' society, where chiefs led communal labour programs. Discussions occurring within the mission were part of a much larger debate occurring in the colony about the position of chiefs, and whether the existing system, established by Governor Arthur Gordon and Governor John Bates Thurston, was a mode through which chiefs could exploit those for whom they were responsible.[56]

The commission reports give us valuable insight into the response of *talatala* to the structural design that embedded European authority. The commissioners interviewed *talatala*, who took the opportunity to speak out against the missionaries' paternalism and the unequal wage scheme the mission had instituted. *Talatala* wages were considerably lower than those awarded to their European counterparts.[57] In 1907, a fully qualified *talatala*, having completed probation, was paid at graduated rates between £8 8s and £18 per annum,

---

51   A J Small to C O Lelean, 25 April 1904, F/1/1904, NAF.
52   C Newbury, '*Bose Vakaturaga: Great Council of Chiefs, 1875–2000*', Pacific Studies, vol. 29, nos. 1 and 2, 2006, pp. 82–127.
53   Fiji constitution meeting, 25 February 1907, MOM 2, 1880–1898, no. 3, 1906-1909, ML, pp. 57–58.
54   Commission to Fiji 1907, CY3465, MOM 238, ML, p. 16.
55   Ibid.
56   B V Lal, *Broken Waves: A History of the Fiji Islands in the Twentieth Century*, Honolulu, University of Hawai'i Press, 1992, p. 19.
57   Ibid., p. 8.

the former for those just starting, and the latter rate for those who had worked 16 years or more. The mission paid for ministers' government taxes, and 25 shillings per quarter was given to each minister from moneys raised by the Methodist membership. They were given 'gifts of food and a residence'.[58] By way of contrast, around this time, European missionaries were paid a rate of £200 per annum.[59] The Reverend Daniel Lotu requested that there be only two rates of pay for *talatala* — one for probationers, and a rate of £18 per annum for fully qualified ministers.[60] *Talatala* wages remained low due to the expectation that *talatala* would receive support — food, clothing and housing — from the communities where they were stationed. The mission relied on the communal system of reciprocity and the expectation that Fijians would continue to live a 'Fijian' lifestyle. The European wage, on the other hand, supported a 'European' lifestyle: European missionaries lived in European-style houses usually owned by the mission, consumed imported foods from Australia and New Zealand, and often sent their children to overseas boarding schools, as well as receiving gifts from local communities. The different wage rates were considered to be an extension of missionary efforts to accommodate cultural difference, but it entrenched a racialised system of pay as well as a class system translated into the Fijian context.[61]

The commissioners did not interrogate the structural inequities that were made visible through their reporting. Their report merely reminded missionaries of their obligation to move towards self-support, and did not reproach them for the lack of progress that had been made towards that goal. The commission's delegates endorsed the continued authority of European missionaries, stating that European circuit superintendents still held the balance of power.[62] *Talatala* were, the commission concluded, 'efficient, and are held by the people in very great respect, but they require supervision'.[63] The report declared that the mission was confronted with 'the world-wide problem as to the wisest methods of governing a native race',[64] and decided not to force a faster transition to Fijian self-governance, determining that adequate steps were being taken to ensure self-support.[65] The commission's findings reflected the paradox of mission

---

58   Ibid.
59   Ibid.
60   Other indigenous ministers present included Felix Kalou, Jonah Uluinaceba, Kemuel Ulukavoro, Arminius Bale, Caleb Naba, Paelus Muavesi, Samuel Chikaitoga, Peter Tuidela, Daniel Lotu, Alick Raloka, Timothy Salaca, Matthias Vave, Joel Cama, Enoch Buadromo (the scribe), Commission to Fiji 1907, CY3465, MOM 238, ML, pp. 10–11.
61   NB: Indian catechists were earning between £3 and £4 per month depending on their level of educational achievement. District meeting minutes, 1908, PMB 1138, p. 27.
62   Commission to Fiji 1907, CY3465, MOM 238, pp. 2, 4.
63   Ibid., p. 8.
64   Ibid., p. 17.
65   Ibid., p. 18.

strategy informed by ideas that placed Europeans at the top of a racial hierarchy, while simultaneously encouraging the 'three selves' policy that was supposed to diminish European control.

The communal system presented a challenge to the colonial administration as well as the mission. Small recorded a meeting he had with the colony's governor, Everard Im Thurn, on this topic in 1909.[66] The governor was intent on dismantling the communal system.[67] As Deryck Scarr put it, Im Thurn wanted to 'inculcate individualism while curtailing chiefly power'.[68] Small suggested to the governor that it be done 'slowly ... let a man earn his liberty ... and let him hold it conditionally'.[69] Both men revealed their uncertainty about how to govern the communal society and the resultant collaboration and consultation between missionaries and colonial administrators. These two men of the British Empire drew on humanitarian discourse and terms tightly bound to democratic ideals, believing that liberty would be afforded to the Fijian if the chiefly system were slowly dismantled, or that it would be 'earned'. They may not have truly hoped for social upheaval, but they were both clearly frustrated by the system as it was and the limitations that they believed it placed on indigenous people.

Others were more confident than Small in their assessment of what was required to govern indigenous peoples, and a lot of discussion centred on indigenous lands and how to utilise it. Most missionaries and colonial administrators agreed that the 'commoner' class of Fiji was best equipped for life as agriculturalists — they were not seen as future members of the colony's intellectual or spiritual elite.[70] Im Thurn was working on the presumption that indigenous Fijians were passing away and would not need their lands for much longer, and on this premise instituted a system that more easily allowed for their alienation.[71] John W Burton heard all of this and, still working in the Indo-Fijian mission, swayed 'between concepts of universal human potential' while believing in 'images of racial limitations and characters, "lower races" with vices and a backward national spirit'.[72] In 1909, Burton suggested matter-of-factly: 'None would look upon the Fijian as an intellectual type. Charming and naïve as he may be in his manners, he belongs to the category of the "lower races".'[73] He suggested that

66   A J Small, diary, 10 November 1909, ML MSS 3267/1, item 5.
67   Ibid.
68   D Scarr, *Ratu Sukuna: Soldier, Statesman, Man of Two Worlds*, London, Macmillan Education for the Ratu Sir Lala Sukuna biography committee, 1980, p. 22.
69   Ibid.
70   C White, 'Affirmative Action and Education in Fiji: Legitimation, Contestation and Colonial Discourse', *Harvard Educational Review*, vol. 71, no. 2, 2001, p. 246.
71   D Scarr, *Ratu Sukuna: Soldier, Statesman, Man of Two Worlds*, London, Macmillan Education for the Ratu Sir Lala Sukuna biography committee, 1980, p. 22.
72   J Kelly, *The Politics of Virtue: Hinduism, Sexuality and Counter-Colonial Discourse in Fiji*, Chicago, University of Chicago Press, 1991, p. 83.
73   Burton, cited in ibid., pp. 82–83.

the 'brain work' in Fiji would be the domain of the European community: 'but the native has land — land that he should be encouraged to use; he has labour stored away in his splendid physique — labour that he must call forth or die'.[74] Burton's perceptions of linear trajectories of human progress induced him to advocate industrial missions in the Pacific.[75] In his text *Fiji of To-day*, published in 1910 while he was superintendent of the mission's industrial institute, Burton postulated that it was 'far better' for the Fijian to 'master the prose of land manuring and swamp draining than the poetry of Milton'.[76] Land and labour were interconnected in discussions about the governance of indigenous peoples, and this intertwining of the two would form the foundations of mission policies in following decades. Encouraging labour was a way of ensuring that indigenous peoples retained their land while safeguarding their own survival — not just a way of filling the mission's coffers.

Both Burton and Small considered their promotion of indigenous engagement in agriculture to be progressive. Small read African American Booker T Washington's *Working with the Hands* in 1907 and was evidently influenced by Washington's other publication *Up from Slavery*, which seems to have informed his ideas about social progress in Fiji. Washington had been a slave and created the Tuskegee Institute to encourage others with the same background into more autonomous agricultural work.[77] Burton also seems to have been influenced by Washington's work and argued that in addition to their new faith, Fijians 'needed industrial and technical education in order that they might survive in the new conditions of the strange world that was closing in upon them'.[78] Thus, in 1914, Burton recommended industrial training for Fijians as a means of promoting 'purpose and accuracy' in their outlook in life:

---

74   Ibid.

75   1909 District Synod meeting, 4 November 1909, MOM Ch OM 2. 1880–1898, no. 3, 1906–1909, ML, pp. 356–57; J Fabian, *Time and the Other: How Anthropology Makes its Object*, New York, Columbia University Press, 1983, p. 17.

76   J W Burton, *Fiji of To-day*, London, 1910, p. 242; A Thornley, 'Fijian Methodism: 1874–1945: The Emergence of a National Church', PhD thesis, The Australian National University, 1979, p. 241; District meeting minutes, 1910, PMB 1138, p. 99.

77   A Thornley, 'Fijian Methodism: 1874–1945: The Emergence of a National Church', PhD thesis, The Australian National University, 1979, p. 241; A J Small, diary, 1907, ML MSS 3267/1 items 4. B T Washington, *Up from Slavery: An Autobiography*, London, Oxford University Press, 1945; B T Washington, *Working with the Hands: Being a Sequel to 'Up from Slavery', Covering the Author's Experiences in Industrial Training at Tuskegee*, New York, Doubleday Page and Company, 1904. Booker T Washington was an African-American man, a former slave who had gone on to develop the Tuskeegee Institute in Alabama where former slaves learnt agricultural techniques. See B T Washington, *The Story of My Life and Work*, New York, Cosimo, 2007; M R West, *The Education of Booker T Washington: American Democracy and the Idea of Race Relations*, New York, Columbia University Press, 2006, p. 218.

78   J W Burton, *The Weaver's Shuttle: Memories and Reflections of an Octogenarian*, unpublished manuscript, n.d., p. 70; J W Burton, *Fiji of To-day*, London, 1910, pp. 243–44.

> Like some sections of Western nations having all they want, the natives ask why should we work? And it is difficult to get them to understand why consecutive work is essential to their physical and spiritual welfare. This has given rise to the great problem of the alien population, and produced the crowded Indian coolies in Fiji, Chinese in Samoa, and Japanese in New Caledonia.[79]

Burton drew on the debates of the day relating to indigenous health and wellbeing to support his argument for increasing industrial missions in the Pacific, reflecting his concern about indigenous depopulation. He was simultaneously engaging with debates about mission practice espoused by delegates at the Edinburgh International Missionary Council conference. Several mission societies submitted reports to the conferences' commission on industrial education that resembled Burton's argument.[80] Though believing that Fijians were doomed, Burton felt that industrial work would help to prolong their existence.[81] He also intended to instil some conformity to western styles of commerce, which he argued would in turn aid evangelisation: 'The gold of commerce is stained with the red blood of brown people. If we could Christianise our commerce, there would be more hope of Christianising both native and alien.'[82] Indeed, as the Comaroffs have argued, Christianity and commerce were seen as the antidote to 'primitive' communal systems, and would have a civilising effect.[83]

In 1917, Burton continued to air his doubts over the intellectual capacity of Fijian peoples, and linked this to his doubts of the legitimacy of their conversion to Christianity. He had perhaps started to doubt the ability of missions to evangelise the world within one generation, as Mott had suggested.[84] Similar to thinkers of the Victorian era as described by George Stocking, Burton was pessimistic about the potential for indigenous peoples to progress through the stages of development and 'acquire' civilisation.[85] 'It would be folly to expect deep rooting of faith among the child races', he told the audience at the 'Laymen's Missionary Lecture' at Wesley Church in Melbourne, 'who not only receive the seed from our hands, but who are dependent upon us for the very

---

79 'The call of the Pacific', *The Spectator*, 20 February 1914, p. 307.
80 *Report of Commission III: Education in Relation to the Christianisation of National Life, with supplement: presentation and discussion of the report in the Conference on 17th June 1910 together with the discussion on Christian literature*, Edinburgh and London, Oliphant, Anderson and Ferrier, 1910, p. 267.
81 'Foreign Mission Demonstration', *The Spectator*, 2 April 1915, p. 287–88.
82 'The Call of the Pacific', *The Spectator*, 20 February 1914, p. 307.
83 J Comaroff and J Comaroff, *Of Revelation and Revolution: The Dialectics of Modernity on a South African Frontier*, vol. 2, Chicago, University of Chicago Press, 1997, p. 120.
84 J R Mott, *The Evangelization of the World in this Generation*, New York, Student Volunteer Movement for Foreign Missions, 1905.
85 G Stocking, *Race, Culture and Evolution: Essays in the History of Anthropology*, London, Collier-Macmillan Limited, 1968, p. 123.

intellectual soil in which it must grow'.[86] However, while Burton was pessimistic about Fijian potential for progress up the evolutionary ladder, he did not see indigenous peoples as static in their imagined place on the scale of civilisation. He believed that people were constantly moving and progressing through stages of change, as evidenced when he quoted his favourite poet, Robert Browning:

> man is hurled
> From change to change unceasingly,
> His soul's wings never furled.[87]

Burton constantly reflected on the process of social change over the following decades. Browning's depiction of it as an almost violent event resonated with him. Change, he suggested, was not something that could or ought be resisted, as it was inevitable, but it was not necessarily easily engaged with. Burton spoke of progress as a series of temporal phases that included Christianity. He suggested that 'western civilisation has opened the door of the non-Christian world. Christianity must enter and take possession else the last state of that world will be worse than the first'.[88]

This chapter has touched on the ideas of several missionaries about the purpose and method of constructing the Fijian Methodist mission, with particular focus on the ideas held by key leaders Arthur J Small and John W Burton. These two men worked to implement the self-supporting church strategy, despite being absent from the 1910 Edinburgh International Missionary Conference at which these ideas were discussed.[89] Anthropological theories about primitive cultures helped to shape both Burton and Small's responses to the ideal of the 'three selves' church policy. The self-support strategy in Fiji brought tensions between concepts of the 'past' and 'present', tradition and modernity to the fore. In particular, debates about self-support centred on the role of chiefs. The decision to train ministers from the non-chiefly 'class' challenged customary leadership, but consultation with chiefs continued as a means of gaining legitimacy, ensuring financial self-support and ensuring that the colony's 'national character' was reflected in the mission.[90] Chiefly power could not be easily undermined while the colonial administration continued to employ chiefs. Small and Everard Im Thurn expected that chiefly power would eventually diminish, but that change would be slow. Missionaries saw

---

86   J W Burton, 'Laymen's Missionary Lecture: Inaugural lecture delivered at Wesley Church, Melbourne, May 22nd 1917, before the members of the General Conference of the Methodist Church of Australasia', Layman's missionary movement of Victoria, (Methodist Branch), Melbourne, Spectator Publishing, 1917, p. 43.
87   Ibid., p. 9.
88   Ibid., p. 30.
89   C Weir, 'The Work of Mission: Race, Labour and Christian Humanitarianism in the South-west Pacific, 1870–1930', PhD thesis, The Australian National University, 2003, p. 277.
90   A D Ravuvu, *The Fijian Ethos*, Suva, Institute of Pacific Studies, University of the South Pacific, 1987, p. 324.

themselves as overseers and instigators of very slow social transformation, believers in evolutionism, and attached this understanding of society to the 'three selves' church policy. Change, through 'progress' towards civilisation, was considered necessary for church devolution to occur.

The mission was also defined by the colonial administration's approach to indigenous labour. Burton's and Small's attitudes and arguments, and those of their colleagues, support historian Brian Stanley's assertion that 'neither the missionary societies nor their individual agents set out with the intention of challenging the structures of colonial society'.[91] In the Fijian context, where the colonial administration was resistant to implementing change to customary practices, the missionaries were the more typical imperialists; to them, their institution's progress necessitated change, and by 1917, as Burton continued to work with the mission board, he was defining the role that missionaries would take in facilitating social change in the Pacific. The approach that they took, including the creation of ethnically divided administrative structures, had important impacts.

In this chapter we have already identified signs of resistance to European authority and its assertion through the mission's structure. Debates around wages illustrated this most clearly. Fijian ministers, *talatala*, were conscious of European hegemony and took opportunities where possible to call for wages to be levelled out and critique colonial authority. There were signs that the formidable front held by the European missionaries acted to forge a unified response from *talatala* in synod. The processes of categorisation and organisation devised by missionaries at the turn of the twentieth century helped to solidify existing identities in this Pacific centre.

---

91 B Stanley, *The Bible and the Flag: Protestant missions and British Imperialism in the Nineteenth and Twentieth Centuries*, Leicester, England, Apollos, 1990, p. 90.

CHAPTER THREE

Theories of Culture: Responding to Emergent Nationalisms

This chapter explores missionaries' conceptions of 'culture' and 'race' that were influenced by both their experience in the mission field and by international debates.[1] The 1920s saw the General Secretary for Methodist Overseas Missions of Australasia, John W Burton, engaging heavily in international discussions about mission policies. This chapter outlines his efforts to enact those policies through the mission's institutions. The International Missionary Council called on missionaries everywhere to support the establishment of a 'native' church, yet missionaries were convinced that European control was required, and were therefore reluctant to push too strongly for indigenous self-governance. Burton used the policies discussed at the International Missionary Council as guiding principles for all the mission sites in the region, which roused different responses depending on the local context. In Fiji, his adaptation of these principles both stirred and quelled tensions as the Indo-Fijian community increasingly articulated anti-colonial feeling. Some missionaries tried to alleviate racial sentiment but others intensified it, exacerbating competition over land and often advocating for Fijian rights in the face of the increasing Indo-Fijian population. This chapter examines the development of ideas grounded in the 'three selves' church policy that related to indigenous autonomy and access to land throughout the 1920s, as missionaries and colonial administrators used essentialist ideas of Fijian and Indo-Fijian 'culture' to determine colonial Fiji's racial hierarchy.

---

1   M Kaplan and J Kelly, 'On Discourse and Power: Cults and Orientals', *American Ethnologist*, vol. 26, no. 4, 2000, p. 852.

To fully understand the changes in the Fijian mission, it is crucial to understand the broader networks the Methodist Overseas Missions operated within. The Methodist mission aided Australia's colonial administration of Papua New Guinea through provision of infrastructure, and the administration, under Sir Hubert Murray in the 1920s, relied heavily on government anthropologists. This meant that there was considerable overlap between discussions about governance and those within the anthropological discipline. By the 1920s, anthropologist Bronislow Malinowski's criticisms of missions — that missionaries (particularly in Papua New Guinea, where he had conducted his fieldwork in 1914) were forcing change on indigenous communities — had encouraged some missionaries to question their thinking and gradually gravitate towards the lessons of 'functional anthropology'. Functional anthropology encouraged people to think of society not in terms of 'aims', such as the aim to move from a primitive to a more civilised state, but rather in terms of function: each cultural practice was considered to serve a purpose.[2] Mission leaders involved in Fiji were engaging with ideas about 'culture' and filtering anthropological discourse into mission debates.[3] These concepts of difference helped missionaries address the practicalities of ministering to the colony's various communities. As historian David Wetherell discussed in his study on Charles Abel, an Anglican missionary in Papua New Guinea, the shift to functional anthropology promoted acceptance of the difference between indigenous and European culture; it encouraged missionaries to discard evolutionist conceptualisations of society, and adopt methods that they hoped would create a 'tranquil colonialism' where their authority would not be disputed. Anthropologists were starting to explore the potential for cultures to continue in the 'modern' colonial world, rather than be altered to suit European expectations.[4]

Contrary to some anthropologists' criticisms, there was evidence that missions had tried to maintain traditional customs in Fiji. Evidence of this can be found in the movement established around 1920 at Davuilevu called the *Viti Cauravau*, the Young Fijian Society, which sought to promote Fijian culture and values to

---

2   D Wetherell, *Charles Abel and the Kwato Mission of Papua New Guinea 1891–1975*, Melbourne, Melbourne University Press, 1996, p. xvi; T H Eriksen, *Small Places, Large Issues: An Introduction to Social and Cultural Anthropology*, third edition, New York, Pluto Press, 2010, p. 91. Peter Pels has noted that anthropologists had been criticising mission policies as early as the 1870s, with F Max Mueller. P Pels, 'Anthropology and Mission: Towards a Historical Analysis of Professional Identity', in R Bonsen, H Marks and J Miedema (eds), *The Ambiguity of Rapprochement: Reflections of Anthropologists on their Controversial Relationship with Missionaries*, Vondalstaat, Focaal, 1990, p. 82. He notes also that W H R Rivers made similar comments in 1920, p. 84. See Malinowski's comments on p. 85.
3   H Gardner, 'The Culture Concept and the Theological Colleges', unpublished conference paper, Pacific History Association conference, Wellington, 2012.
4   D Wetherell, *Charles Abel and the Kwato Mission of Papua New Guinea 1891–1975*, Melbourne, Melbourne University Press, 1996, p. xvi.

the extent that they protested against Fijian women marrying non-Fijian men.[5] The *Viti Cauravau* was an embryonic ethno-nationalist movement. That it had emerged from one of the central sites of Methodism in Fiji is perhaps not surprising considering the approach the Methodists had taken in shaping the mission around tradition, despite the limitations its foreign leaders placed on emerging indigenous leaders.[6]

The mission board consciously also strived to foster separate cultural and ethnicised branches within the Indo-Fijian branch, through continuing to deliberately recruit workers with knowledge of Indian cultures and languages. Among those who had travelled to Fiji after working in India was the Reverend Leslie Muir Thompson, who spent two years in northern India studying language before relocating to the mission station at Navua, Fiji, in 1916, where he remained until 1931.[7] Similarly, Frank L Nunn traversed the two colonies, working in India from 1909 to 1913 and then again from 1920 to 1926, and in Fiji from 1914 to 1920 and from 1928 to 1937.[8] European missionaries hoped that their cultural and linguistic comprehension of Indian society would set them apart from European settlers as anti-colonial sentiment rose in the Indo-Fijian community. The greatest attribute sought was language proficiency. Language was seen as a distinctive element of a national character, and became an essential pillar in the identity of a 'national' or 'native' church. As Indo-Fijians were considered 'natives', despite not being 'indigenous' to the colony, there was a sustained focus on this construction of a distinctive Indian 'native' identity.

Since his first trip to India in 1908, John W Burton had not only aided the recruitment of missionaries from India to Fiji, but had ensured that lasting networks were built between the two British colonies. He travelled to India in 1926, visiting numerous sites. At the end of his trip, he met with Charles Freer Andrews, an English Anglican missionary who became the globally recognised Indian nationalist leader, Gandhi's emissary.[9] Burton had already caught Andrews' attention when he published *Fiji of To-Day* in 1910. Andrews read this book before travelling to Fiji in 1917 to report on the condition of

---

5   D Scarr, *Ratu Sukuna: Soldier, Statesman, Man of Two Worlds*, London, Macmillan Education for the Ratu Sir Lala Sukuna biography committee, 1980, p. 108.

6   Ibid., p. 109.

7   'Church News', *Advertiser*, Melbourne, 13 May 1916, p. 2; T M O'Connor, 'Thompson, Leslie Muir (1885–1975)', *Australian Dictionary of Biography*, National Center of Biography, The Australian National University, adb.anu.edu.au/biography/thompson-leslie-muir-11850/text21211, accessed 6 February 2013; J Garrett, *Footsteps in the Sea: Christianity in Oceania to World War Two*, Suva, University of the South Pacific in conjunction with the World Council of Churches, 1992, p. 166.

8   A H Wood, *Overseas Missions of the Australian Methodist Church: Fiji-Indian and Rotuma*, vol. 3, Aldersgate Press, Melbourne, 1978, p. 77.

9   Indian Visit 1926, 3 November 1926, MLMSS 2899 Add On 990; C F Andrews, *India and the Pacific*, London, George Allen and Unwin Ltd, 1937, pp. 18, 23.

indentured Indian labourers.[10] Both Burton and Andrews, moving between Fiji and India to call for the end of the indenture system, had engaged with popular notions about the inevitability of Fijian extinction in the face of the more 'industrial' Indo-Fijian race.[11]

Despite the efforts of Burton and some other missionaries to advocate for the rights of Indo-Fijian workers, the majority of the Indians who remained in Fiji after indenture saw missionaries as part of the colonial machine.[12] When indenture ended, no one seemed particularly sure about how much of the Indian community would remain in the colony.[13] From 1915 onwards, missionaries in the agricultural areas of Viti Levu and Vanua Levu, in particular, watched as Indian families settled on 10-acre blocks leased from the Colonial Sugar Refining Company.[14] This consolidated the expectations held by many observers that Fiji would be increasingly populated by Indo-Fijian peoples.

With the cessation of indenture, there was trepidation about empowering Indo-Fijians with the same rights as Europeans, such as voting privileges.[15] Indo-Fijian labourers staged widespread riots against oppressive labour conditions throughout January and February 1920.[16] Charles Freer Andrews, during his trips to Fiji in 1916 and 1917, had discussed Gandhi's work and ideas with both Indo-Fijians and Fijians,[17] adding weight to the argument of historian Ken Gillion that, by 1920, Gandhi's ideas about home rule were already stirring opinion in the Indo-Fijian community.[18] The Reverend Richard Piper, stationed at the mission's Indo-Fijian branch in Lautoka, believed that these riots had

---

10 C Weir, 'An Accidental Biographer? On Encountering, Yet Again, the Ideas and Actions of J W Burton', in B V Lal and V Luker (eds), *Telling Pacific Lives: Prisms of Process*, Canberra, ANU E Press, 2008, p. 216.

11   C F Andrews, *India and the Pacific*, London, George Allen and Unwin Ltd, 1937, p. 63; C Weir, 'An Accidental Biographer? On Encountering, Yet Again, the Ideas and Actions of J W Burton', in B V Lal and V Luker (eds), *Telling Pacific Lives: Prisms of Process*, Canberra, ANU E Press, 2008, p. 216; A Pande, 'Indians and the Struggle for Power in Fiji', *Diaspora Studies*, vol. 3, no. 1, 2010, p. 59; J Garrett, *Footsteps in the Sea: Christianity in Oceania to World War Two*, Suva, University of the South Pacific in conjunction with the World Council of Churches, 1992, p. 161.

12 'Indians in Fiji: Indenture system: Address by Visiting Missioner', *The West Australian*, 17 April 1917, p. 4.

13   K L Gillion, *The Fiji-Indians: Challenge to European Dominance, 1920–1946*, Canberra, Australian National University Press, 1977, p. vii.

14 M Moynagh, 'Land Tenure in Fiji's Sugar Cane Districts Since the 1920s', *Journal of Pacific History*, vol. 13, no. 1, 1978, p. 54. The mission also benefited from assistance from CSR. For example, in 1904, the church at Lautoka was placed on land 'given as a grant' by the CSR, which also contributed to a church built at Davuilevu. Fiji District Synod Minutes 1904–1905 in A Thornley ,'The Methodist mission and the Indians in Fiji, 1900 to 1920', Masters thesis, p. 19.

15   K L Gillion, *The Fiji-Indians: Challenge to European Dominance, 1920–1946*, Canberra, Australian National University Press, 1977, p. vii.

16 'Indian Strike Riots in Fiji: Report by the Governor', *The Mercury*, Tasmania, 20 February 1920, p. 5; K L Gillion, *The Fiji-Indians: Challenge to European Dominance, 1920–1946*, Canberra, Australian National University Press, 1977, pp. 26–7.

17   C F Andrews, *India and the Pacific*, London, George Allen and Unwin Ltd, 1937, p. 68

18   K L Gillion, *The Fiji-Indians: Challenge to European Dominance, 1920–1946*, Canberra, Australian National University Press, 1977, pp. 19–20.

a racial undercurrent, which was exacerbated by the colonial administration opting to use Fijians as strike breakers. Anti-colonial sentiment similarly drove Indo-Fijian opposition to European missionaries preaching the gospel.[19] There was a correlation between the frustrations aired in the strikes against European employers, and those that were starting to simmer amongst Indo-Fijian catechists who laboured under the superintendence of European missionaries. Catechists believed that they were being denied promotion on the basis of their race. In both spheres of life — work and mission — European efforts to assert their own cultural hegemony had spawned unequal labour conditions.

European missionaries used their international networks to develop responses to anti-colonial sentiment. By 1921, Burton was a member of the Methodist mission board in Sydney. That year, he was one of 60 mission leaders who attended the International Missionary Conference at Lake Mohonk, New York, which was led by his mentor John R Mott, American leader of the Student Christian Movement.[20] As at previous International Missionary Council conferences, there was talk of incorporating national customs and cultures in missions, but many mission leaders simultaneously sought to promote indigenous progress to an end point of 'Christian civilisation'.[21] There was a tension between the perceived need not only to convert communities to Christianity but also to 'modernity', while trying to dispel accusations of imperialist attitudes. The Mohonk conference was pinned on Mott's optimistic message about evangelising all of the world's people and the need to establish 'native churches' throughout the world.

At this time, members of the International Missionary Council suggested that a mission's first line of defence against anti-colonial nationalist movements should be a demonstrated celebration of culture. They argued that an 'Indian church', an 'African church', and a 'Japanese church' — indigenous, self-supporting churches — should be built, and reflect the national character.[22] Acculturating Christianity appeared to missionaries to be in some respects more straightforward than elevating indigenous ministers to positions of authority, as racialist beliefs persisted and diminished belief in indigenous capability. This is certainly what appeared to be happening in Fiji.[23] Acknowledging the importance of culture became particularly important when the mission was competing against the highly

---

19   'India in Fiji', *The Spectator*, 9 June 1920, p. 422; K L Gillion, *The Fiji-Indians: Challenge to European Dominance, 1920–1946*, Canberra, Australian National University Press, 1977, p. 73.

20   J W Burton, *The Weaver's Shuttle: Memories and Reflections of an Octogenarian*, unpublished manuscript, n.d., pp. 32, 100; W R Hogg, *Ecumenical Foundations: A History of the International Missionary Council and its Nineteenth Century Background*, New York, Harper and Brothers, 1952, pp. 150, 202.

21   F Lenwood, 'The International Missionary Council at Lake Mohonk, October 1921,' *International Review of Missions*, vol. 11, 1922, p. 37; G R Doss, 'John R Mott, 1865–1955: Mission Leader Extraordinaire', *Journal of Applied Christian Leadership*, vol. 4, no. 1, 2010, p. 79.

22   K Saunders, 'The Passing of Paternalism in Missions', *Journal of Religion*, vol. 2, no. 5, 1922, p. 468.

23   F Lenwood, 'The International Missionary Council at Lake Mohonk, October 1921,' *International Review of Missions*, vol. 11, 1922, p. 41.

active Indo-Fijian nationalist group, the Arya Samaj, which was grounded in Hindu faith. Linking culture to emergent nationalisms, missionaries considered incorporating certain elements of Hinduism in the Indo-Fijian mission branch.[24] Nationalism and culture were bound in this mission project of the 'three selves' church, but in these discussions were being disengaged from racialist thinking.

The International Missionary Council's ideas were lofty, and the reality on the ground was markedly more complex. By 1921, the Indo-Fijian branch of Fiji's Methodist mission had only 70 members and conversion remained an important focus of mission work.[25] Frustrated with the slow progress, Richard Piper wrote in support of acculturation in 1922. He described the tendency of 'European' Christianity to lead to the disintegration of 'the ancient faiths and social systems of India'.[26] Piper believed efforts to incorporate Indian culture into Methodism had been lacklustre, attributable to the lack of contact between European mission staff and the wider community. European missionaries remained aloof, he claimed, too mindful of maintaining a distinction between themselves and the Indo-Fijian community. This had limited the linguistic attainments of mission staff, which Piper said was 'much lower than would be tolerated in India'. For example, missionaries used rough Hindustani rather than Urdu, the language associated with India's educated elite.[27] Missionaries working in India had described their work as being defined by language rather than geographical boundaries. Edgar W Thompson, himself a Methodist missionary in India, wrote in 1912 that it was 'useless to attempt an approach to a Muslim through the medium of Tamil or Telugu', saying that mission workers should use Urdu (Hindustani) and be familiar with Islam.[28] Piper may have failed to realise that there was a new language evolving in Fiji — Fiji Hindi — which blended Bhojpuri and Avadhi.[29] However, aware of a growing race-consciousness in the colony, Piper's primary concern was that the divide between European missionaries and the Indo-Fijian community could be deepened if their approach was interpreted as racist.

---

24   Arya Samaj was a strong anti-colonial force in Fiji and South Africa during the early twentieth century. See also J Kelly, *The Politics of Virtue: Hinduism, Sexuality and Counter-Colonial Discourse in Fiji*, Chicago, University of Chicago Press, 1991, pp. 202–3; N Green, 'Islam for the Indentured Indian: A Muslim Missionary in Colonial South Africa', *Bulletin of the School of Oriental and African Studies*, vol. 71, 2008, p. 530; P N Vedalankar and M Somera, *Arya Samaj and Indians Abroad*, Durban, South Africa, Sarvadeshik Arya Pratinidhi Sabha, 1975, p. 122.

25   J Garrett, *Where Nets Were Cast: Christianity in Oceania since World War Two*, Suva, Institute of Pacific Studies, University of the South Pacific in association with the World Council of Churches, 1997, p. 243.

26   'India in Fiji', *The Spectator*, 9 June 1920, p. 422.

27   R Piper, 'Indian mission: problems in Fiji: a report, compiled and printed by R Piper, December 1922, Lautoka', MOM 238 CY3465, screen 490; A Dalby, *Dictionary of Languages: The Definitive Reference to More Than 400 Languages*, London, Bloomsbury, 1999, p. 663.

28   E W Thompson, *The Call of India: A Study in Conditions, Methods and Opportunities of Missionary Work Among Hindus*, London, The Wesleyan Methodist Missionary Society, Bishopsgate, 1912, pp. 159–60.

29   B V Lal, 'Bahut Julum: Reflections on the use of Fiji Hindi', *Fiji Studies: A Journal of Contemporary Fiji*, vol. 3, no. 1, 2005, p. 153.

Piper was concerned that efforts towards the 'three selves' church policy appeared tokenistic in the Indo-Fijian branch, and warned that unfulfilled promises of self-governance would 'lead to the same old troubles that have marred the usefulness of our work'.[30] One of the problems that he identified was a jealousy between the mission's branches: the mission's workers could cooperate on matters that were of mutual interest, but he believed that the Fiji district synod was overbearing, had become 'big and unwieldy' and was 'breaking down under its own weight'.[31] The chairman was expected to preside over all three sessions of the district synod, but business was conducted separately for each racial group over several days. There was little energy to hear about matters relating to the Indo-Fijian mission, which was discussed at the end. With the Indo-Fijian work relegated to the back end of proceedings in every synod, those working within the Indo-Fijian community felt dejected. It would be better, Piper argued, to separate the proceedings, so that the mission's leaders were able to listen to concerns with fresh ears.[32] Piper also suggested that to address the growing resentment about the pre-eminent position given to Fijians in the mission, the Indo-Fijian branch needed its own representative, rather than a member of staff designated to European or Fijian work. This formed part of his case for increasing separation, and suggested that autonomy could be achieved with a 'divorce' from the district synod — Piper believed that Methodism in Fiji was already 'a house divided against itself'.[33]

The 1923 constitution amendments achieved some of what Piper hoped for with the establishment of the united European session at synod.[34] The institution segregated through a system that ensured European authority remained intact. The united European session included all of the European ministers and probationers who were involved in the Fijian and Indo-Fijian branches. The mission's constitution held that 'all questions relating to the character or work of the European missionaries shall be considered in the absence of the native ministers', the exclusion of Fijian and Indo-Fijian mission staff removing any chance that they might have any say in European staff appointments.[35] While the European session was an exclusive arena, the Fijian session included all European ministers and probationers, and one Fijian minister to represent each circuit.[36] A separate financial session included members of the pastoral

---

30 R Piper, 'Indian Mission: Problems in Fiji: A Report', MOM 238 CY3465, screen 490, ML.
31 Ibid.
32 Ibid.
33 Ibid.
34 M Pickering-Bhagwan, 'A Historical Examination of the Indian Synod's Amalgamation into the Conference of the Methodist Church of Fiji and Rotuma', thejournalofaspiritualwonderer.blogspot.com.au/2013/05/a-historical-examination-of-indian.html; 1923 Constitution, Constitution of Methodist districts in Samoa, Fiji, Tonga and New Britain, 1936, MOM 317, ML, p. 5.
35 Ibid., p. 4.
36 Ibid.

session, with one lay representative from each Fijian circuit nominated by the European superintendent. The Indo-Fijian session included Europeans and any Indo-Fijian ministers and probationers working in the Indo-Fijian branch, as there were so few of the latter.[37]

Despite their exclusion from some areas of governance, Fijian paramountcy seemed impenetrable. Fijians were working as ministers and were involved at almost every other level as probationers, catechists, circuit stewards, sectional stewards and in the local teaching community. They also worked as local preachers and class leaders, and attended quarterly meetings with European missionaries. Circuit stewards were charged with communicating the business of mission to local chiefs and villages. This process of dissemination was embedded within the constitution and showed the importance placed on communal involvement in mission affairs.[38] The mission's staff was required to report to chiefs, bringing together the 'ancient' and 'modern' forms of leadership in Fiji, and delivering ideas from the International Missionary Council debates on cultural accommodation to the local village level.

Church structures became a focal point for discussions about acculturation in the early 1920s. The architectural design and the process of building churches was expected to reflect the national character. The Reverend Richard McDonald, who succeeded A J Small as chairman of the mission the following year, believed the incorporation of Fijian cultural traditions into the church was a reflection of 'true' religious life, and also a sign that the church had become self-propagating. McDonald explained the need to respect Fijian custom in providing houses for Fijian ministers, saying that this was:

> native custom through and through and the natives claim this as a right. Their *tavi* as they call it is to supply planting land and residence for the Minister of God appointed to them. This they regard as a sacred obligation and we must be very careful how we interfere in the matter.[39]

McDonald had noted that Fijian ministers benefited from the communalist ideal of reciprocity. Churches reflected the efforts to demarcate cultural identities, through incorporating structural designs and decorations that were seen as typically 'Fijian' or 'Indian'. There were efforts to reify communalism through the way in which whole communities were involved in the construction of Fijian churches, including the buildings themselves. The Reverend Robert Green, stationed in the Lau group during the following decade, was convinced of the importance of incorporating cultural insignia in church buildings. He watched a new church being built, describing the concrete as representing

---

37 Ibid.
38 Ibid., p. 3.
39 R L McDonald to J W Burton, 26 January 1923, F/1/1923, NAF, pp. 1–2.

European culture, the 'curved and rounded ends and roof' as being Tongan, and the 'artistry and beauty of workmanship' as being essentially Fijian.[40] A suitably modified mixture of cultures were therefore captured and celebrated within the mission in a variety of visible ways in order to demonstrate the successful adoption of Christianity and its being intertwined with a 'national character' or culture.

Burton and McDonald did not always see eye to eye, with Burton keen to push for social change and McDonald tending to promote the status quo. McDonald's favourable opinion about the support offered to Fijian ministers in the communal society was evidence of this. Burton, on the other hand, worried that the communal system hindered rather than aided progress towards self-support, and expressed the need to give Fijian ministers 'definite responsibility in an area that they can cover. That seems to me to be the only way to build up a real Native Church.'[41] McDonald was more concerned about the influence chiefs still had on the church — chiefs were rarely challenged by Fijian ministers, and could potentially control and limit the ministers' stipends. McDonald wrote to Burton:

> The majority of Native Ministers do NOT desire that they shall be left to the tender mercies of their chiefs in regard to their stipends. Central control is to them sure control. Their appointment is assured as is their stipend whether they are near home or in the land of strangers. And you must take the NATIVE MIND into consideration when attempting to put responsibility on him. You cannot give him responsibility if he does not want it and refuses to accept it.[42]

Missionaries saw themselves as the protective buffer between chiefs and ministers. If European missionaries were to retreat — as the 'three selves' church policy seemed to recommend — Fijian ministers would be subject to the whim of the chiefs. McDonald argued that Fijian ministers should not have to concede part of their pay to their chiefs. At the core of his argument was doubt in the ability of the Fijian people to make the transition from a 'primitive' to more 'modern' society, and a belief that European missionaries could intervene to prevent chiefs exploiting their subjects.

They had differing opinions, but both Burton and McDonald depicted Fijian culture as 'primitive', just as this anthropological characterisation of indigenous people was becoming outdated. In his preface to Bronislow Malinowski's *Pacific Argonauts*, published in 1922, Sir J G Frazer stated that the terms made popular

---

40   Circa 1934. R H Green, *My Story: A Record of the Life and Work of Robert H Green*, Melbourne, 1978, p. 182.
41   J W Burton to R L McDonald, 9 January 1923, F/1/1923, NAF, p. 2.
42   R L McDonald to J W Burton, 26 January 1923, F/1/1923, NAF, pp. 1–2.

by E B Tylor's work were becoming redundant.[43] Missionary discourses lagged a little behind developments in the discipline, although McDonald flagged his engagement with the fairly current work of W H R Rivers, for example, when he referred to the 'native mind', and his belief that it negated the fulfilment of the self-government principle espoused by the International Missionary Council.[44] McDonald suggested that the ministers were content working within the new system rather than reverting to a system of governance that might open the door to greater chiefly control of the institution and ministers' wages.

McDonald and Burton were at odds on the question of what characteristics marked a society's potential to transition from 'primitive' to 'civilised'. As Burton's beliefs provoked frustration, missionaries in the field simultaneously juggled Indo-Fijian needs and Fijian paramountcy. In 1925, responding to these concerns, another draft constitution was circulated that established two separate synods, rather than just organising distinct sessions of the one synod as per the 1923 constitution. A united European synod would continue to decide European ministerial appointments and make decisions relating to lay missionaries, mission sisters, and mission finances, without the input of non-European mission workers.[45]

Piper was again a key advocate for separate synods, citing a fear of Fijian dominance and resultant marginalisation of Indo-Fijian Methodists. He was supported by others working in the Indo-Fijian branch, such as G H Findlay, who agreed that Indo-Fijians and Fijians were too different to be organised through a shared administration.[46] Findlay later suggested that 'Europeans, Fijians and Indians formed an "eternal triangle" of races, which created a strong unsettled feeling, although manifestations of it were rare'.[47] Findlay saw separation as necessary for the mission's functionality, relaying his opinion to mission meetings in Australia.[48] Through this systematic categorisation and organisation of peoples, missionaries were integral to the 'othering' process, widening the sense of difference between Fijians and Indo-Fijians, all the while seeking a 'nativising', acculturating project.[49]

---

43   J G Frazer, 'Preface' in B K Malinowski, *Argonauts of the Western Pacific: An Account of Native Enterprise and Adventure in the Archipelagoes of Melanesian New Guinea*, Long Grove, Illinois, Waveland Press, 1984, p. x.

44   G W Stocking, *After Tylor: British Social Anthropology, 1888–1951*, London, Anthlone, 1996, p. 108.

45   1925 draft constitution; District Synod minutes, appendix 2, F/4/E, PMB 1138.

46   A H Wood, *Overseas Missions of the Australian Methodist Church: Fiji-Indian and Rotuma,* vol. 3, Aldersgate Press, Melbourne, 1978, pp. 65, 98; Findlay is mentioned in J Kelly, *Politics of Virtue*, p. 217; A Ravuvu, *The Façade of Democracy: Fijian Struggles for Political Control, 1830–1987*, Suva, Fiji, Reader Publishing House, 1991, p. 56.

47   'Liquor Laws and Mixed Races: Fijian System Aggravates Racial Feeling', *The Advertiser*, Adelaide, SA, 6 May 1932, p. 16.

48   Ibid.

49   M Kaplan and J Kelly, 'On Discourse and Power: Cults and Orientals', *American Ethnologist*, vol. 26, no. 4, 2000, p. 854.

John R Mott, acting as envoy for the International Missionary Council and expressing the Methodist ideal of unity in diversity, visited Melbourne for the National Missionary Conference in 1926. Mott outlined the church-planting project, challenging missionaries to articulate exactly what constituted an 'indigenous church'.[50] He envisaged a church that would 'not interfere with native ideals and good customs'.[51] He hoped that church buildings would incorporate local architectural styles, appropriate to the climate. He also hoped that indigenous converts would 'be given a larger freedom of expression in the way they worshipped God'.[52] Self-governance was important, but 'vitality was more important than autonomy'.[53]

Mott's ideology, created at a considerable distance from any mission field, offered a theoretical vision for the missionaries in the audience who believed that their role was to bridge the divide between ancient and modern societies. Mott was concerned about public opinion that suggested missions were not capable of meeting the challenges of rapidly changing societies.[54] In response, Burton called for a united, inter-denominational and national missionary training college to equip men and women who intended to apply for foreign mission service.[55] Students would study a history of missions, tropical medicine and hygiene, other religions, bookkeeping, and mechanics. He also argued for training in phonetics and the science of language, suggesting this was important because, without knowing the local language, 'it is impossible to enter into "The Shrine of a People's soul"'.[56] Mott recommended missionaries also be taught elementary social anthropology:

> Too often missionaries, with the best of intentions, but entirely ignorant of the social customs of the people, have done considerable damage to the delicate fabric of native social life. In some cases that damage has been irreparable, and it may not be long before some farther-seeing governments will place a ban upon those coming into intimate contact with native peoples unless they have had some preliminary training in anthropological science.[57]

50   Mott was leader of the student volunteer movement, and had established the World Student Christian Federation in 1895, G R Doss, 'John R Mott, 1865–1955: Mission Leader Extraordinaire', *Journal of Applied Christian Leadership*, vol. 4, no. 1, 2010, p. 76; 'Courageous Meeting: International Missionary Council', *The Brisbane Courier*, 10 April 1928, p. 11.
51   'Missionary Conference: Native Church Problems: Address by Dr J R Mott', *The Argus*, Melbourne, 13 April 1926, p. 13.
52   Ibid.
53   Ibid.
54   Memorandum on United Kingdom Training, J W Burton Memo on missionary training R Hicken, circa 1926, MOM 319, ML.
55   Ibid., p. 2.
56   Ibid., p. 3.
57   Ibid., p. 4.

The Australian National Missionary Council nominated Sydney as the site for the college, as this was:

> the port of departure for missionaries to the Pacific and to the Far East, and secondly, and more important, is the fact that the Sydney University alone provides courses in Anthropology, native linguistics and tropical medicine and hygiene.[58]

A special arrangement was made with the University of Sydney for the provision of discounted anthropology courses for missionary training.[59] Not only, then, did missions and colonial administrations work together to provide health and education to indigenous peoples throughout this period, but now they were receiving the same training in the same classrooms. Colonial and mission programs were increasingly aligning as staff were funnelled through courses at the University of Sydney.

Burton capitalised on Mott's support for missionary education while continuing discussions about the Fijian mission structure with McDonald. The ideal of self-governance was never far from their minds, with Burton pointing out:

> The trouble is that we have taken our circuit system of the Home Land and applied it without distinction on the field. The European Superintendent is rather the Chairman of a district, and we shall have to rethink this whole matter it seems to me before very long.[60]

Despite their differences of opinion, Burton and McDonald agreed that a centralised system of governance would best suit Fiji.[61] Superintendents, scattered throughout the islands, had considerable authority, even though Burton and McDonald believed that the greatest power should lie with the district's chairman, who was charged with defining the parameters of each mission branch. The chairman was charged also with defining the parameters of the Indo-Fijian and Fijian synods.[62] Believing that a centralised system suited Fijian hierarchical social structures, which since the 1860s had elevated Cakobau to the centre at Bau, McDonald's democratic roots made him wary of how missionaries might react if there were any move made to limit their autonomy.[63] Contemplating constitutional change once again, McDonald was concerned that advocating for an increase in his own powers would place him 'in a most invidious position if he has to decide between the desires of European

---

58   Ibid., p. 5.
59   Ibid.
60   J W Burton to R L McDonald, 22 April 1926, MOM 524, Fiji 1926, ML, p. 2.
61   Centralised systems of governance had been difficult to establish in Fiji due to the many tiers in the social order from *mataqali* to *tokatoka*. C Newbury, 'Chieftaincy in Transition', *Journal of Pacific History*, vol. 43, no. 2, 2008, pp. 168, 175–76.
62   R L McDonald to J W Burton, 23 June 1926, Fiji 1926, MOM 524, ML.
63   Ibid.

members of synod and the claims of the Indian and Native members according to the terms of the constitution'.[64] McDonald wanted to absolve himself of stirring the racial tension brewing in the colony, and maintain European authority, and thus advised Burton to adopt a 'hastening slowly' approach towards change. Concerned about tipping the existing social balance, McDonald believed that alterations to existing systems of power should be slow but deliberate.[65]

While these debates occurred amongst European missionaries, they were starting to be held accountable for excluding Indo-Fijians from ministerial positions.[66] The first Indo-Fijian minister, Ishwari Prashad, was ordained in 1921, but he had been trained in India at Bareilly College.[67] Davuilevu, the theological college that had been established in Fiji in 1908, was not open to Indo-Fijian candidates.[68] Ramsey Deoki, an Indo-Fijian catechist, constantly challenged the lack of autonomy afforded to non-European Methodists in Fiji. Deoki was from a reasonably successful family of Methodist business owners from the Nausori area.[69] During an illness early in life, Deoki decided to join the ministry, but upon finding that he was barred from theological education at Davuilevu Theological College, was forced to do his ministerial training overseas. His father enrolled him at Melbourne High School at the age of 21.[70] He made an impression on Burton on one of his trips back to Fiji in 1924, when he sighted Deoki's 'shining face' as he delivered a Hindustani service in Suva.[71] Even as a young man, Deoki was clearly identifiable as a rising talent in the Indo-Fijian Methodist community — right at a time when the broader Indo-Fijian community was demanding greater representation in Fijian affairs.[72]

Just as the Indo-Fijian political leadership was rebuked during the mid-1920s, so too were Deoki and John Bairagi. Both catechists were recommended for ministerial training in 1926, but the European synod voted against their acceptance. European missionaries' rejection of their application for ministerial

---

64   Ibid.

65   R L McDonald to J W Burton, 15 May 1926, Fiji 1926, MOM 524, ML.

66   This is similar to the argument made by John Kelly regarding the colonial administration's efforts to support the continuation of indigenous power structures through the chiefs through indirect rule, but had not done the same with the Indo-Fijian community. J Kelly, 'Fear of Culture: British Regulation of Indian Marriage in Post-indenture Fiji', *Ethnohistory*, vol. 36, no. 4, 1989, p. 374.

67   A H Wood, *Overseas Missions of the Australian Methodist Church: Fiji-Indian and Rotuma*, vol. 3, Aldersgate Press, Melbourne, 1978, p. 67.

68   I K Susu, 'The Centennial Anniversary of the Davuilevu Theological College (1908–2008)', in *Light on the Hill: To Commemorate the 100 years of Davuilevu Methodist Theological College, 1908–2008*, Suva, Davuilevu Theological College, 2008, p. 18.

69   R J Miller, 'Victory in the Constant Struggle: The Life and Times of Reverend Ramsey R H H Deoki', Honours thesis, Queen's College Library, p. 4.

70   A H Wood, *Overseas Missions of the Australian Methodist Church: Fiji-Indian and Rotuma*, vol. 3, Aldersgate Press, Melbourne, 1978, p. 81.

71   J W Burton, diary, 10 August 1924, MLMSS 2899 Add On 990, ML.

72   D Scarr, *Ratu Sukuna: Soldier, Statesman, Man of Two Worlds*, London, Macmillan Education for the Ratu Sir Lala Sukuna biography committee, 1980, pp. 68–69.

training in Fiji revealed the pre-eminence of Fijian interests over those of Indo-Fijians. European members argued that they were 'acting in what they felt were the best interests of Fijian students for the ministry'.[73] The promising Indo-Fijian candidates were therefore forced to seek promotion overseas, or to remain catechists. This limited access to education exacerbated antagonism towards the mission's racialist organisational structure.[74] Begrudgingly, Deoki returned to Australia in 1927 to study for the ministry at the Methodist Home Missionaries Training College in Kew, Melbourne, and completed the course in 1929.[75] He received the same basic training as all missionaries coming via Victoria into the Pacific, yet was still not ordained upon his return.

Indo-Fijian catechists were admitted into the synod in 1926, but they were not given any considerable degree of influence. Burton and McDonald ensured European missionaries were able to maintain control over mission business. Burton reminded McDonald that:

> the Indian brethren will have no power to vote money, they can merely recommend and their recommendations will have to pass the gauntlet of the United European Session as well as the Annual Meeting of the board. I think that these safeguards will be ample, and I can see that there is a considerable advantage in letting these men see that there is only a limited amount of money that can be expended upon the Indian side of the work.[76]

Burton felt this concession was necessary to 'give much more power to our Indian Laymen on the mission field than they at present possessed',[77] but saw the Indo-Fijian session of the synod as merely a committee. It was interesting that, in the same year, Burton had visited India and spoken with Charles Freer Andrews. Burton had looked to India for inspiration on how to manage anti-European sentiment. He had promised to make 'very strict enquiries while I am in India as to what is the custom amongst the various societies there', suggesting that 'I do not think that there will be any who will say that we should give our Indian Christians in Fiji less opportunity of expression than Christians in India have'.[78]

73   Bairagi had been educated at Dilkusha, see A H Wood, *Overseas Missions of the Australian Methodist Church: Fiji-Indian and Rotuma*, vol. 3, Aldersgate Press, Melbourne, 1978, p. 78, and regarding their being disallowed from ministerial training, see p. 67; P Gaunder, *Education and Race Relations in Fiji, 1835–1998*, Lautoka, Fiji, Universal Printing Press, 1999, p. 88.
74   A L Stoler, 'Sexual Affronts and Racial Frontiers: European Identities and the Cultural Politics of Exclusion in Colonial Southeast Asia', in A Brah and A Coombes (eds), *Hybridity and its Discontents: Politics, Science, Culture*, London, Routledge, 2000, pp. 19–20. This had changed by the late 1930s. Both Indo-Fijian and Fijian ministers trained at Davuilevu. R H Green, *My Story: A Record of the Life and Work of Robert H Green*, Melbourne, 1978, p. 240.
75   'Mission Work Exemplified', *Frankston and Somerville Standard*, Victoria, 6 July 1929, p. 4; 'The Churches', *Albury Banner and Wodonga Express*, 20 December 1929, p. 14; 'Shipping', *Examiner*, Launceston, 1 January 1927, p. 1.
76   J W Burton to R L McDonald, 30 August 1926, MOM 524, Fiji 1926, ML.
77   J W Burton to R L McDonald, 7 September 1926, MOM 524, Fiji 1926, ML, p. 1.
78   Ibid., p. 2.

While in Ceylon (Sri Lanka), Burton attended the 1926 Ceylon Mission Synod, recording elements of the synod's discussions, including the local missionaries conceding that they felt it would take time to 'build up efficient staff' for self-government.[79] Following the discussions about the Fijian mission, he recognised the struggle to train ministers that European missionaries felt were sufficient for the task of self-governance; the same argument had been used to justify limiting self-governance in Fiji. With Deoki in the midst of ministerial training in Melbourne, Burton's argument would soon lose momentum.[80]

Racial evolutionary theories pervaded Burton's thoughts through this period. In 1927, he told a Darwin newspaper that the Pacific was:

> peopled with child races. One must remember that it is childhood with which Australia has to deal and our minds must be oriented accordingly. It is child-vices — black as they have been; child faces — though old and wrinkled; child minds — though cunning and treacherous; and child virtues — neither deep nor strong, which occupies our attention.[81]

Burton had by this time abandoned the idea that the Fijian people were a vanishing race, but still believed that they required European leadership and guidance. He saw Pacific Islanders as not only ethnically distinct, but as lagging behind Europeans in social development.[82]

Burton's paternalism did not extinguish his belief in the potential for 'native' churches, but he continued to limit progress towards Fijian and Indo-Fijian autonomy in both mission branches. In 1927, seeing no opportunities in Fiji, John Bairagi decided to leave his appointment in Fiji and go to India for further training. He offered to pay his own fare and intended to return to Fiji after completing his studies, arguing that training in India would further assist him in his work in the Indo-Fijian community.[83] These plans changed, and he resigned from the Fiji mission the following year. He explained his decision to McDonald:

> The hearts and minds of the Missionaries in question, who, by virtue of their ecclesiastical vocation give others the impression that they are the votaries of the Christian religion, are not permeated by the great love of Christ. This is shown in the unjust ways in which the Indians and other coloured races are treated by these Missionaries in their business and other every day dealings with them.[84]

---

79   J W Burton, 14 October 1926, diaries, MLMSS 2899 Add On 990, ML.
80   S Neill, *A History of Christian Missions*, London, Penguin, 1964, p. 522.
81   'Australia's Responsibility in the Pacific', *Northern Standard*, Darwin, 8 July 1927, p. 2.
82   C Weir, 'An Accidental Biographer? On Encountering, Yet Again, the Ideas and Actions of J W Burton', in B V Lal and V Luker (eds), *Telling Pacific Lives: Prisms of Process*, Canberra, ANU E Press, 2008, p. 218; B Stanley, *The Bible and the Flag: Protestant Missions and British Imperialism in the Nineteenth and Twentieth Centuries*, Leicester, England, Apollos, 1990, p. 172.
83   1927 Fiji District Synod minutes, Chairman's notes, CY 3038, shot 42, ML, p. 32.
84   J Bairagi to R L McDonald, 16 March 1928, F/1/1928, NAF.

Bairagi pointed to the inherent contradiction between the mission's goals of equity and inclusion, and the lived reality of European superiority.[85] Missionaries were accustomed to performing their European prestige and acted in a way that allowed them to associate with the colonial cohort.[86] Missionaries had practised a form of 'cultural work' — a way of acting out their racial superiority through practising selected cultural practices — to inscribe difference between them and their Indo-Fijian colleagues.[87] Burton's enthusiasm for the Indo-Fijian branch could not overcome the realities of Indo-Fijian marginalisation. Bairagi ended up staying on in Fiji, becoming a pastor for the Indian Christian Society, but evidently he was utterly disaffected with the Methodist mission because of the slights shown to him and Deoki.[88]

The mission continued to seek European missionaries with prior experience in India — and therefore prior knowledge of cultural practices and language — to lead the Indo-Fijian mission. The Reverend T C Carne was a missionary in India during the 1920s who had influence in Fiji well before he transferred to the Fiji district in 1948.[89] At the 1927 Methodist Laymen's Memorial Lecture in Melbourne, Carne presented a paper, entitled 'Christ of the Indian Mind', in which he spoke about harnessing nationalist sentiments through Christianity, suggesting that 'in Christ alone can national ideals be fulfilled'. Missions needed to link 'our universal message to what is good in the cultural heritage of India'.[90] He spoke of a 'national Christ' and 'a national Christianity',[91] but warned that there were dangers in isolating the church if there was too much emphasis on creating an Indian church rather than connecting it to the church universal.[92]

85   This is an inversion of the Comaroff's argument about encouraging the adoption of new habits to demonstrate conversion. J Comaroff and J Comaroff, *Of Revelation and Revolution: Christianity, Colonialism and Consciousness in South Africa*, vol. 1, Chicago, University of Chicago Press, 1991, p. 25; A L Stoler, 'Rethinking Colonial Categories', *Comparative Studies in Society and History*, vol. 31, no. 1, January 1989, p. 138.
86   S Sullivan, *Revealing Whiteness: The Unconscious Habits of Racial Privilege*, Bloomington, Illinois, Indiana University Press, 2006, p. 4.
87   E J Popke, 'Managing Colonial Alterity: Narratives of Race, Space and Labor in Durban, 1870–1920', *Journal of Historical Geography*, vol. 29, no. 2, 2003, p. 250; A L Stoler, 'Sexual Affronts and Racial Frontiers: European Identities and the Cultural Politics of Exclusion in Colonial Southeast Asia', in A Brah and A Coombes (eds), *Hybridity and its Discontents: Politics, Science, Culture*, London, Routledge, 2000, pp. 19–20.
88   R L McDonald to W R Steadman, 6 June 1931, F/1/1931, NAF.
89   A H Wood, *Overseas Missions of the Australian Methodist Church: Fiji-Indian and Rotuma*, vol. 3, Aldersgate Press, Melbourne, 1978, p. 83.
90   T C Carne, 'The Christ of the Indian mind', eighth Methodist Laymen's Memorial Lecture, Melbourne, 15 November 1927, Methodist Laymen's Missionary Movement, Victoria, digital.slv.vic.gov.au/view/action/singleViewer.do?dvs=1377806583753~29&locale=en_US&metadata_object_ratio=10&show_metadata=true&preferred_usage_type=VIEW_MAIN&frameId=1&usePid1=true&usePid2=true, p. 7.
91   Ibid., p. 8.
92   Ibid., p. 9. Ian Breward has recently suggested that Carne was vehemently against syncretism, but this did not deter some engagement with Indian cultures. I Breward, *Dr Harold Wood: A Notable Methodist*, Preston, Australia, Uniting Academic Press, 2013, p. 125.

Carne brought a lot of these ideas with him to Fiji.[93] His theoretical work, sensitive to culture and nationalism, was absorbed into mission policy and practice.

Carne was the sort of deep-thinking missionary Burton hoped his new training scheme would produce, though he never seemed to be quite so personally involved in debates about the acculturation of Christianity as Carne. In 1928, Burton spoke more confidently about the future potential for 'native' churches, but believed that self-support required indigenous communities to undergo cultural and social change. By then, the Methodist mission had invested in a property for its missionary training in Sydney. Instruction included lectures in anthropology by University of Sydney anthropologist A P Elkin, pushing missionaries beyond the bounds of theology and requiring their broader education in the humanities.[94] Burton's 'new' missionary would have higher academic qualifications, and be an amateur anthropologist. Anthropology, he agreed with Mott, could assist missionaries to negotiate cultural and societal change.[95]

That same year, the Reverend T N Deller similarly argued that in Fiji 'it was more a conversion to civilisation than a conversion to Christianity that had to be attempted'.[96] The International Missionary Council promoted agricultural education for converts, as well as industrialisation and mechanised forms of farming as part of this social transition. In 1928, international support for industrial missions affirmed the Fijian mission's efforts at Navuso Agricultural School, near Davuilevu. Navuso students worked a 33-hour week maintaining crops and livestock, growing sugar cane, rice, maize, bananas, on top of which they learnt to take 'care of stock' and studied 'botany, carpentry, drawing, farming, arithmetic, records, English, sanitation and hygiene, geography, and civics'.[97] These subjects provided a general education, but the main objective was to train young farmers. While other areas of the mission celebrated cultural difference, Navuso placed greater emphasis on a western-style education, encouraging the

---

93 J Garrett, *Where Nets Were Cast: Christianity in Oceania since World War Two*, Suva, Institute of Pacific Studies, University of the South Pacific in association with the World Council of Churches, 1997, p. 243.

94 'Missionary Societies: Conference in Melbourne', *Examiner*, Tasmania, 14 April 1928, p. 14.

95 P Pels, 'Anthropology and Mission: Towards a Historical Analysis of Professional Identity', in R Bonsen, H Marks and J Miedema (eds), *The Ambiguity of Rapprochement: Reflections of Anthropologists on their Controversial Relationship with Missionaries*, Vondalstaat, Focaal, 1990, p. 84.

96 Deller worked in Fiji 1921 to 1935. A H Wood, *Overseas Missions of the Australian Methodist Church: Fiji*, vol. 2, Melbourne, Aldersgate Press, 1978, p. 369; 'Returning to Fiji: Rev D N Deller Farewelled', *The Brisbane Courier*, 26 May 1927, p. 9.

97 *The Missionary Review*, 4 November 1928, pp. 7–8.

acquisition of markers of modernity.[98] The principal, Benjamin Meek, desired to 'create a Fijian yeomanry, which, by the intelligent and industrious use of idle lands for the production of commercial crops, will obtain the means to satisfy the growing needs of the community'.[99] Ultimately, Meek believed that Fijian farmers would acquire skills at Navuso that would lead to 'greater positions of trust and responsibility'.[100] Agrarian forms of labour provided a stepping-stone to the next station in the model of social progress, a means of advancement. While this required some alterations to Fijian relationships with the land, farmers continued to practise rituals of the past when planting and harvesting, combining cultivation, tradition and worship.[101] It was a process that did not bring an immediate eschewing of customary farming practices but rather served as a space in which to bring together old methods for land production with new techniques for land management.

Figure 2: 'Navuso', Benjamin Meek and students.

Source: Photo by R H Rickard and others for the Methodist Church of Australasia, Department of Overseas Missions, 'Series 01: Photographic prints of missionaries and Indigenous people in the Northern Territory, Papua New Guinea, Fiji, Samoa and India, ca 1885–1938', PXA 1137, 490-535, pic acc 7061, neg 46, Mitchell Library, State Library of New South Wales. Published with permission of Uniting Church of Australia.

---

98   Other schools established for indigenous students throughout British colonies functioned in a similar way. For example, see discussion on Lincoln University in South Africa in A D Kemp and R T Vinson, '"Poking holes in the sky": Professor James Thaele, American Negroes, and Modernity in 1920s Segregationist South Africa', *African Studies Review*, vol. 43, no. 1, special issue on the diaspora, 2000, p. 146; J Comaroff and J Comaroff, *Of Revelation and Revolution: Christianity, Colonialism and Consciousness in South Africa*, vol. 1, Chicago, University of Chicago Press, 1991, p. 15; D Hanlon, 'Converting Pasts and Presents: Reflections on Histories of Missionary Enterprise in the Pacific', in B V Lal and P Hempenstall (eds), *Pacific Lives, Pacific Places: Changing Boundaries in Pacific History*, Canberra, Coombs Academic Publishing, 2001, p. 147.

99   B Meek, 'Agricultural Education in Fiji', *The Missionary Review*, 5 March 1928, p. 14.

100 Ibid.

101 A R Tippett, *Oral Tradition and Ethno-history: The Transmission of Information and Social Values in Early Christian Fiji, 1835–1905*, Canberra, St Marks Library, 1980, p. 53.

Industrial missions elicited discussion about indigenous relationships to land and indigenous engagement in labour. Both were crucial tenets that needed to be addressed as part of the civilising project devised by missionaries. Both land and labour needed to be managed effectively in order to promote social and spiritual progress. Meek wrote an article for the Australian Methodist publication *The Spectator* in 1928, stating:

> The Fijian's birth right is his land, but he is in danger of losing it altogether because he has neglected to use it. Great fertile areas have been leased away, and the Fijian has been quite content to draw his rent and to live a life of comparative idleness.[102]

Meek blamed the land lease system adopted by the colonial administration for creating an 'idle' society, as many Fijian could exist on land rent moneys alone. Meek associated low virility with idleness, adopting some of the ideas Burton had espoused in the previous decade regarding the virility of Fijians.[103] 'Everywhere the progressive races of the world are pushing out from their old boundaries', he wrote, 'overflowing into the less densely occupied lands, seeking raw materials for their factories and food for their industrial population'.[104] In such a world, indigenous lands should not be left vacant and unutilised:

> Humanity is dependent on the soil for its food, clothing and other necessities of life, and with the increase of population comes the search for new fields of production. The result is, that where we find peoples occupying lands, but not developing them, the urge of civilisation and progress demands that such lands must be cultivated to meet world needs.[105]

Meek perpetuated some of Burton's earlier philosophies regarding the strength of various races and need to target selective groups for selective causes. Meek revealed his concern about what would occur if Fijians left land 'unproductive':

> If they cannot or will not produce, then history teaches that others will. Those who occupy and use land eventually become the owners of it. The industrious Indian, since the discontinuance of the indenture system, has leased lands, and is now digging out of the soil wealth that might have gone to the native owner, had he realised his opportunities. Unless the Fijian learns, before it is too late, to farm his lands, he will most surely in the future be the labourer on the land instead of its owner.[106]

---

102 B Meek, 'Agricultural Education in Fiji', *The Missionary Review*, 5 March 1928, p. 12.
103 C Toren, *Mind, Materiality and History: Explorations in Fijian Ethnography*, London, Routledge, 1999, p. 68. See p. 78 for notes on an interview where an indigenous Fijian man used similar rhetoric in the 1980s.
104 B Meek, 'Agricultural Education in Fiji', *The Missionary Review*, 5 March 1928, p. 12.
105 Ibid.
106 Ibid.

Meek believed that engaging in western forms of farming and turning the land to generate profit would ensure that the *vanua* (land) remained in Fijian hands. Concerns about land were prominent in public discourse about Navuso, and contributed to the increasingly exclusionist rhetoric about Indo-Fijians. The predominance of Fijian students at Navuso, combined with the principal's discourse about the need for Fijians to protect their land, revealed support for Fijian ascendancy that often went unspoken within the mission's daily correspondence. Education in western modes of agriculture was seen as essential to ensuring Fijian land rights in the colony as the Indo-Fijian community increased in size. It was a way of empowering Fijians in preparation for what was being flagged as an inevitable battle for land.[107]

These discourses reinforced ideas about Fijian identity and its connectedness to land: the *vanua*. Meek had specific ideas about the Fijian relationship with the *vanua*, believing that Navuso students would learn much from 'scientific study of the possibilities of the soil'.[108] Meek suggested that 'supernatural agencies have not to be placated, but common sense and thought used instead'. He was not entirely against customary Fijian farming techniques, but wrote:

> A stumbling block to true religion is in the superstition and tradition in the native mind about natural phenomena and eternal processes. The simple facts taught in Hygiene, Agriculture, Animal Husbandry, and Nature Study, make him aware that nothing is haphazard or subject to the caprice of evil spirits; but everything is the natural unfolding of laws laid down by a supreme beneficent Being.[109]

Meek's article resonated with similar discussions occurring in Australian anthropology. Two years after Meek published these comments, Elkin published his ideas on the connection between indigenous culture and the land. Indigenous connection to land formed the basis for modes of inclusion and exclusion in Fiji.[110] Meek's comments suggest a fluid movement of ideas between mission and anthropology in Australasia in the late 1920s.

Meek's vision of a 'Fijian yeomanry' was realised when Navuso graduates started to secure their own plots of land for agricultural production. In October 1929, Mr Young of the Colonial Sugar Refinery (CSR) wrote to the Reverend Leslie M Thompson, principal of Dilkusha school, to offer CSR's assistance in 'placing on farms any who complete their course [at Navuso], if they desire to start out for themselves'.[111] This provided additional incentive for Fijian men to

---

107 B V Lal, *A Time Bomb Lies Buried: Fiji's Road to Independence, 1960–1970*, Canberra, ANU E Press, 2008, p. 10.
108 B Meek, 'Agricultural Education in Fiji', *The Missionary Review*, 5 March 1928, p. 12.
109 Ibid.
110 J Lane, 'Anchorage in Aboriginal affairs: A P Elkin on Religious Continuity and Civic Obligation', PhD thesis, University of Sydney, 2008, p. 288.
111 Young to Thompson, 8 October 1929, F/1/1930, NAF.

finish the course. Ten Navuso graduates accepted this offer, acquiring blocks of land of seven or eight acres the following year at Baulevu, north of Nausori.[112] The mission and CSR thus collaborated in the training and deployment of Navuso students after their graduation, enabling Fijian and Indo-Fijian land acquisition. With low numbers of Indo-Fijian students at Navuso, however, the efforts of CSR and the school only sharpened the image of Fijian paramountcy evident in Meek's earlier comments.

At the same time, the structures of the mission reinforced the categories for and perceptions of Indo-Fijian identities. Missionaries advanced their explicit calls for a separate 'indigenous Indian church' for the Indo-Fijian Methodist community. G H Findlay wrote encouragingly to T C Carne about his hopes for an Indo-Fijian church. Findlay hoped that devolution would 'offer our Indian Christians a fuller opportunity of self-expression in Church life'.[113] Progress towards this goal was slow, leaving some Indo-Fijian mission members disillusioned. European missionaries voiced their desire to eventually establish an autonomous Indo-Fijian church conference, but in the next breath offered a multitude of reasons why it was not yet possible: it was not financially feasible; they had not 'won' enough converts; and they did not have adequate 'native' leaders. The concept of a self-supporting, self-governing and self-propagating Indo-Fijian church was still entirely academic.

It was perhaps not surprising that conversion rates in the Indo-Fijian community remained low at the end of the 1920s. Burton continued to push for European ascendancy in missions when he published a blueprint for native churches in his 1930 publication *The Pacific Islands Survey*. While he argued that European missionaries were not 'integral' to the 'native church', he said that Europeans were essential for training indigenous peoples in all matters theological, administrative and financial. The foreign missionary:

> should be there as a helper and advisor, rather than as a superintendent and an administrator. He should be regarded as on loan from the Home Church to be withdrawn whenever the Native Church is strong enough to do without him. If that were the acknowledged policy and objective of missions throughout the Pacific, there would be doubtless greater responsibility laid upon native shoulders which would grow stronger by having to bear it.[114]

---

112 To V Clark, 14 May 1930, F/1/1930, NAF.
113 G H Findlay to TC Carne, 8 November 1929, F/1/1929, NAF.
114 Burton used terms such as 'native' and 'indigenous' broadly to discuss the 'three selves' church concept. He was essentially referring to all 'non-Europeans'. J W Burton, *The Pacific Islands: A Missionary Survey*, London, World Dominion Press, 1930, p. 21.

In Burton's opinion, missions were still in the process of preparing indigenous peoples for self-governance. The missionaries would play an essential role in coordinating and driving the devolution of power. He favoured increased responsibility for *talatala*, but also suggested that ongoing European missionary presence was justified by the poor quality of indigenous ministerial training. He did not believe that the local ministry as it existed in 1930 was adequately qualified to stand equal to Australian and New Zealand-trained colleagues. This stance reflected his perspectives on class and race. Burton wrote:

> In the early days of missionary enterprise in the Pacific, ministers were ordained much too easily. Their education was scanty, and their knowledge of Christian truth was wholly inadequate. The test was character rather than attainment, and none would plead that the test of spiritual fitness should ever be lowered, but equipment is important, and steps, all too tardy, are now being taken to remedy this state of things.[115]

Burton projected that autonomy would elude indigenous ministers for some time yet. It certainly appeared to be the case for Fiji. Europeans had managed to maintain certain aspects of hegemony through the construction of the Fiji mission's 1926 constitution. European missionaries could still veto decisions made in synods, effectively diminishing the voting power of any non-Europeans present. The president general — based in Sydney — had ultimate control over mission affairs, despite fielding recommendations from the Fiji district synod and the mission board in Sydney.[116] Increasing Fijian and Indo-Fijian representation in the district synod therefore did not concurrently increase their power.

Burton used ideas similar to those of anthropologist George Pitt Rivers to describe what he saw in Fiji. Pitt Rivers' *The Clash of Culture and the Contact of Races*, published in 1927, outlined a Darwinian theory of one racial group contributing to the destruction of another.[117] Burton continued to write in terms of 'primitive' and 'advanced' societies, retaining an evolutionist paradigm as

---

115 J W Burton, *The Pacific Islands: A Missionary Survey*, London, World Dominion Press, 1930, p. 21; A Thornley, 'Custom, Change and Conflict: Fijian Wesleyan Ministers, 1835–1945', in R J May and H Nelson (eds), *Melanesia: Beyond Diversity*, Canberra, Research School of Pacific Studies, The Australian National University, 1982, p. 127.
116 Constitution of the Fiji District: Amendments, see pages 48 and 49 of 1929 General conference minutes; Constitution of Methodist districts in Samoa, Fiji, Tonga and New Britain, 1936, p. 2, General conference minutes, p. 145; Constitution of the Fiji district: Amendments, see pages 48 and 49 of 1929 General conference minutes and constitution of Methodist districts in Samoa, Fiji, Tonga and New Britain, 1936, Book of laws, p. 140, MOM 317, ML.
117 G H L Pitt Rivers, *The Clash of Culture and the Contact of Races*, New York, Negro Universities Press, 1927, p. 1.

his theoretical anchor.[118] He believed that the institution's Eurocentric structure inhibited the development of an indigenous church, but could not yet see a way to overcome it. In his 1930 publication, Burton wrote:

> Perhaps the most serious criticism of missions in the South Pacific is that they have institutionalised the Native Church after our more advanced European fashions instead of following the simpler and more natural ways of primitive life. This tendency to huge expenditure on elaborate plant still goes on, and while, from our European point of view, it means efficiency, yet, if it stultifies native initiative and native control, it is ineffective in the end.[119]

Richard McDonald had become chairman of the Methodist mission in Fiji in 1925, and from his vantage point in Suva felt that there were already several indicators that Fijian culture was reflected in the mission, or, to use Burton's words, that the mission had been fashioned 'following the simpler and more natural ways of primitive life'.[120] McDonald pointed to visual and material manifestations of Methodism in the landscape and the people, writing to benefactor Robert Smith in 1930: 'Without any urging from us he [Fijian Methodists] erects the House of God in his own town and pays for it and in most cases it is far and away the best house in the village.'[121] If European missionaries were withdrawn from Fiji, McDonald argued, 'it would have an effect on his advance and progress in the Christian way; but I am convinced that his spiritual experience is a real one, and his religion is the mainspring of his whole life'.[122] Finally he told Smith: 'He is a child in the faith and needs help and guidance, but he is developing at a great rate and the progress of the last decade gives us much hope.'[123]

118 J Fabian, *Time and the Other: How Anthropology Makes its Object*, New York, Columbia University Press, 1983, p. 17.
119 J W Burton, *The Pacific Islands: A Missionary Survey*, London, World Dominion Press, 1930, p. 20.
120 R L McDonald to R Smith, 4 July 1930, F/1/1930, NAF, p. 1.
121 Ibid.
122 Ibid.
123 Ibid.

Figure 3: Richard McDonald in front of Methodist Mission Office, Suva.

Source: Photo by R H Rickard and others for the Methodist Church of Australasia, Department of Overseas Missions, 'Series 01: Photographic prints of missionaries and Indigenous people in the Northern Territory, Papua New Guinea, Fiji, Samoa and India, ca 1885–1938', PXA 1137, 327535, pic acc 7061, neg 2, Mitchell Library, State Library of New South Wales. Published with permission of Uniting Church of Australia.

There were a variety of ways in which European missionaries addressed the question of self-support during the 1920s. The promise of greater autonomy was extended as an olive branch to appease anti-colonial sentiment. This became increasingly important as Indo-Fijians demonstrated their discontent with inequitable work conditions. This was as much an issue within the mission as it was on the streets of Fiji's towns. By the end of the decade the Methodists had already lost John Bairagi, one of its talented Indo-Fijian ministers, due to missionary attitudes. These mission structures, supposed to cater to culture, had concurrently given 'natives' something to rail against. When categories were clear, the 'natives' were better able to define the processes of exclusion, and to unify in their efforts against them.

Despite this quiet protest from the mission's non-European staff, European hegemony remained in place. European missionaries struggled to respond to anthropology's criticisms of the mission's use of race and culture to design mission strategy throughout the 1920s. Opinions varied about the place culture should take in the mission — whether change should be enforced, and how.

Most opinions depended on an essentialised view of the culture the missionaries were working within. Yet, the debates between mission leaders McDonald and Burton illustrated the various ways in which concepts of culture were enlisted to respond to the 'three selves' church policy. The self-supporting church concept continued to provide an avenue by which European missionaries could promise greater autonomy to Fijian and Indo-Fijian people. However, the theories about 'race' and 'culture' informing their approach to the 'three selves' church concept, and their experience in the field, made them reluctant to increase indigenous authority, particularly in the 'Indo-Fijian' branch.

CHAPTER FOUR

Indigenous Agrarian Commerce:
Yeoman Claims to Soil

The villages and farms in the north-west of Fiji's Viti Levu seemed sometimes to be a long way from the mission's leadership in Suva, and a lot could be done without the chairman's knowledge or approval. This region was part of the Ra circuit, an area renowned for its history of anti-colonial movements. Many of the indigenous Fijian nationalists in this part of Viti Levu had been, at one time or another, members of the Methodist mission. Though directed not to be involved in economic or political enterprises, Methodist missionaries were often drawn into these potentially volatile spheres of village debate and agitation. Responding to the politics, several missionaries contributed to the development or maintenance of a Fijian yeomanry through support for industrial training and agricultural endeavours. Leaders of this movement included the Reverends A Wesley Amos and Arthur Drew Lelean, nephew of the Reverend Charles Oswald Lelean who had been working in Fiji since the 1890s. These men sometimes operated outside the bounds of the mission and colonial administrations' regulations and legislations, and challenged the conceptualisations of the 'ancient' and the 'modern'.[1] Missionaries and other supporters — usually individuals from Australian-based businesses and banks — sometimes pushed beyond the bounds of the labour regulations designed by the colonial administration. Administrative distinctions between Fijians and Indo-Fijians had established unique challenges for Fijian farmers, who — contrary to the separatist agendas of some administrators — sometimes worked on sugar crops that neighboured Indo-Fijian farms. This went against the standard protocol enacted by the British administration which sought to

---

1   N Thomas, 'The Inversion of Tradition', *American Ethnologist*, vol. 19, no. 2, 1992, p. 223.

clearly delineate the two communities, as John Kelly has argued.[2] Colonial bids to construct boundaries between the two communities were therefore not finite; there were moments of fluidity and contact between the two, but certainly a developed sense of competition. This chapter examines the ways in which Methodist missionaries mediated and sometimes exacerbated tensions between the Fijian and Indo-Fijian communities around issues of land and labour during the 1920s and 1930s, and the ways in which they negotiated colonial legislation and cultural systems to pursue nationalist, or even ethno-nationalist, ideas. This chapter also highlights missionary efforts to transform indigenous peoples 'from the ground up'; induction in to systems of commerce and commodification that they hoped would shift Fijian society from communalism to a more civilised, if agrarian, capitalist social stage.[3]

Ensuring Fiji's Methodist mission could become financially self-supporting required a steady and significant income from the mission circuits. Missionaries were therefore concerned about Fijians' limited ability to engage in paid labour. Sometimes the only money coming into villages was from leasing *mataqali* land.[4] The colonial administration's 1912 Labour Ordinance required that Fijians perform communal labour obligations rather than gain employment in the colony's various industries, and was seen to protect indigenous workers from abuse and exploitation. It limited the mobility of Fijians beyond their villages.[5] Conscious of demands for greater flexibility, the ordinance did establish a *galala* (independent) farming system. This section of the ordinance was designed to allow men to leave their village and work for themselves, but only if they paid a tax.[6] This provision acted as a release valve, letting the steam out of the anti-colonial feeling resulting from the strictures placed on Fijian wealth acquisition. Brij V Lal has claimed that the *galala* system promoted individuality, undermined chiefs and disrupted the version of traditional Fijian society that the colonial administration under Governor Sir Arthur Gordon had tried to preserve.[7] In the 1920s, debate about Fijian labour followed two main streams within the mission,

2   J Kelly, 'Threats to Difference in Colonial Fiji', *Cultural Anthropology*, vol. 10, no. 1, 1995, pp. 64–65.
3   J Comaroff and J Comaroff, *Of Revelation and Revolution: The Dialectics of Modernity on a South African Frontier*, vol. 2, Chicago, University of Chicago Press, 1997, p. 120.
4   K J Brison, 'Imagining Modernity in Rural Fiji', *Ethnology*, vol. 42, no. 4, 2003, p. 338.
5   A Bain, 'A Protective Labour Policy? An Alternative Interpretation of Early Colonial Labour Policy', *Journal of Pacific History*, vol. 23, no. 2, 1988, p. 121; M Mamdani, *Define and Rule: The Native as Political Identity*, Cambridge, Massachusetts, Harvard University Press, 2012, p. 25.
6   T Macnaught, 'Chiefly Civil Servants? Ambiguity in District Administration in the Preservation of the Fijian Way of Life, 1896–1940', *Journal of Pacific History*, vol. 9, 1974, p. 15; G Ward, 'Internal Migration in Fiji', *Journal of the Polynesian Society*, vol. 70, no. 3, 1961, p. 262; Brookfield depicts *galala* farming as an anti-chiefly movement but the case study I present here demonstrates the pre-World War II *galala* communities still involved chiefs. See H C Brookfield, 'Fijian Farmers Each on his Own Land: The Triumph of Experience Over Hope', *Journal of Pacific History*, vol. 23, no. 1, 1988, pp. 15–35, 17; J Overton, 'A Fijian Peasantry: Galala and Villagers', *Oceania*, vol. 58, no. 3, 1988, p. 194
7   B V Lal, *Broken Waves: A History of the Fiji Islands in the Twentieth Century*, Honolulu, University of Hawai'i Press, 1992, pp. 70–71.

with commentators arguing either that Fijian 'salvation' depended on their moving into individualistic agricultural enterprise, or that traditional village life should be maintained due to concerns that agricultural work would lead to social fragmentation and the loss of culture. Missionaries were constantly considering how the 'ancient' and 'modern' social systems could coexist.[8]

Missionaries were highly alert to developing nationalisms that repudiated Fijian traditions. Throughout the early twentieth century, opposition to labour restrictions were channelled into support for Apolosi Ranawai, who was born into a chiefly *mataqali* (family), a son of a Wesleyan minister from Narewa village near Nadi.[9] He was known almost exclusively as 'Apolosi'. Apolosi established the Fiji Produce Company in 1913, which became the *Viti Kabani* (Fiji Company). The *Viti Kabani*'s main aim was to advocate for Fijian economic autonomy, liberating those Apolosi believed were bound 'hand and foot to European and Chinese traders' by the colony's labour regulations.[10] It sold Fijian produce directly to consumers, increasing the income of Fijian farmers.[11] Apolosi's advocacy for Fijian farmers and his involvement in 'occult' activities had important ramifications and influenced discussions around the 'three selves' church principle, especially financial self-support.[12] His business ideals aligned with the goals of industrial missions, which were established internationally throughout many mission fields to encourage indigenous peoples into agricultural and industrial education. Both Apolosi and the Methodist missionaries sought to inspire Fijian involvement in the colony's economy through industry, and promoted indigenous commerce and wealth acquisition.[13] Such an endeavour relied upon some movement towards individualism and an eschewing of communal obligations — what missionaries generally perceived as a move away from primitivity towards modernity.

Apolosi's movement did not symbolise a complete break from Fijian traditions. It was not entirely against chiefly claims of authority because of Apolosi's chiefly ancestry and the support he received from people such as Ro Tuisawau,

---

8   T Macnaught, 'Chiefly Civil Servants? Ambiguity in District Administration in the Preservation of the Fijian Way of Life, 1896–1940', *Journal of Pacific History*, vol. 9, 1974, p. 14.
9   M Kaplan, *Neither Cargo nor Cult*; R Nicole, *Disturbing History: Resistance in Early Colonial Fiji*, Honolulu, University of Hawai'i Press, 2011, p. 80.
10   T Macnaught, *The Fijian Colonial Experience: A Study of the Neotraditional Order Under British Colonial Rule Prior to World War II*, Canberra, Australian National University Press, Pacific Research Monograph Number 7, 1982, p. 77–8; R Nicole, *Disturbing History: Resistance in Early Colonial Fiji*, Honolulu, University of Hawai'i Press, 2011, p. 80.
11   N Thomas, 'The Inversion of Tradition', *American Ethnologist*, vol. 19, no. 2, 1992, p. 223.
12   When visiting villages for fieldwork in 2010, many people described the practices of Apolosi and his followers. People who believe Apolosi might return continue them today. K Close, fieldnotes, December 2010.
13   A D Couper, 'Protest Movements and Proto-cooperatives in the Pacific Islands', *Journal of the Polynesian Society*, vol. 77, no. 3, 1968, pp. 269–72; N Thomas, 'The Inversion of Tradition', *American Ethnologist*, vol. 19, no. 2, 1992, p. 223; J Heartfield, '"You are not a white woman!": Apolosi Nawai: The Fiji Produce Agency and the Trial of Stella Spencer in Fiji', *Journal of Pacific History*, vol. 38, no. 1, 2003, p. 69.

a 'dissident high chief of Rewa'.[14] However, the primacy given to Fijian economic advancement necessitated, as Nicholas Thomas suggested, 'an indigenous modernism that repudiated the custom-bound past, and various forms of obligation and constraint that epitomised it'.[15] In 1917, Apolosi told a crowd at Tavua that chiefs were the reason for the ignorance of the rest of Fijian society, and that chiefs effectively sold their men's labour for their own benefit.[16] Historian Timothy Macnaught has argued that Apolosi spoke a new language that united Fijians, bridging the provincial and village-level divisions that had previously disconnected people, as well as those detached through status and parochial affiliations. Apolosi crafted a new nationalistic discourse that highlighted the shared experience of Fijians under an exploitative colonial system to conjure a 'radical pan-ethnic Fijian consciousness'.[17] The *Viti Kabani* went beyond addressing inequity in the colonial economy, giving rise to a new nationalism that had implications for the Methodist mission.[18]

Though he enjoyed widespread support from villagers and some European missionaries, including Arthur Small, the colonial authorities loathed Apolosi.[19] Ratu Sir Lala Sukuna, the highest-ranking indigenous Fijian in the colonial administration in the early 1920s, had a different vision for Fiji to Apolosi, and the two became enemies. Regarding the propensity for Fijians to get ahead, Sukuna said:

> the native appears to have reached the height of prosperity commensurate with his degree of development. Any call for the modification of a social system, if it is to be of any lasting advantage, must come from within, from those whose lives are likely to be affected by it.[20]

---

14   D Scarr, *More Pacific Island Portraits*, Canberra, Australian National University Press, 1978, p. 179; R Nicole, *Disturbing History: Resistance in Early Colonial Fiji*, Honolulu, University of Hawai'i Press, 2011, p. 87; K Gravelle, *Fiji Times: A History of Fiji*, Fiji Times and Herald Ltd, 1979, pp. 180–81.

15   N Thomas, 'The Inversion of Tradition', *American Ethnologist*, vol. 19, no. 2, 1992, p. 223.

16   Cited in B V Lal, *Broken Waves: A History of the Fiji Islands in the Twentieth Century*, Honolulu, University of Hawai'i Press, 1992, p. 51.

17   T Macnaught, *The Fijian Colonial Experience: A Study of the Neotraditional Order Under British Colonial Rule Prior to World War II*, Canberra, Australian National University Press, Pacific Research Monograph Number 7, 1982, p. 79; R Nicole, *Disturbing History: Resistance in Early Colonial Fiji*, Honolulu, University of Hawai'i Press, 2011, p. 85; T Teaiwa, 'An Analysis of the Current Political Crisis in Fiji', in B V Lal and M Pretes (eds), *Coup: Reflections on the Political Crisis in Fiji*, Canberra, ANU E Press, 2008, p. 31; J Baledrokadroka, 'Fijian Ethno-nationalism', in J Fraenkel, S Firth and B V Lal (eds), *The 2006 Military Takeover in Fiji: A Coup to end all Coups*, Canberra, ANU E Press, 2009, p. 416; T Macnaught, *The Fijian Colonial Experience: A Study of the Neotraditional Order Under British Colonial Rule Prior to World War II*, Canberra, Australian National University Press, Pacific Research Monograph Number 7, 1982, p. 111; R Norton, 'A Preeminent Right to Political Rule: Indigenous Fijian Power and Multiethnic Nation Building', *The Round Table: The Commonwealth Journal of International Affairs*, vol. 101, no. 6, 2012, p. 522.

18   R Nicole, *Disturbing History: Resistance in Early Colonial Fiji*, Honolulu, University of Hawai'i Press, 2011, pp. 88–89.

19   Ibid., p. 89.

20   CSO 17/1906 as cited in D Scarr, *Ratu Sukuna: Soldier, Statesman, Man of Two Worlds*, London, Macmillan Education for the Ratu Sir Lala Sukuna biography committee, 1980, p. 47.

Sukuna's statement demonstrated the hold of evolutionist ideas over Europeans and educated Fijians.[21] Evolutionism was being construed in a variety of ways, morphing over time and being deployed in numerous contexts. The colonial administration had designed legislation that would support the chiefly and communal systems, on the pretext that disrupting chiefs and communalism would incite social chaos. As a high chief of Lau, Sukuna had a vested interest in maintaining a communal system that encouraged commoners to pay homage to chiefs. Apolosi's movement, which promoted the rights of commoners and their access to income, did not impress Sukuna in the slightest. While Sukuna suggested that lasting social change should come from within, he never supported Apolosi's grassroots efforts. Sukuna also had his own fraught relationship with the Methodist mission, whose leadership had at times been supremely patronising of the young chief.[22]

Sukuna condemned Apolosi's depiction of Indo-Fijians as a threat, suggesting that he exacerbated 'racial feelings' to acquire status.[23] Apolosi continued to emphasise Fijian interests, however, especially Fijian rights to land. Apolosi hoped all lands alienated since cession would be returned to Fijian ownership, and that his company would expand to acquire all Indo-Fijian and European-run businesses.[24] In 1917, soon after his release from prison after serving an 18-month sentence for embezzlement, Apolosi discouraged Fijians from leasing their land, advising villagers to ignore chiefs who had been courted by colonial authorities.[25] He urged a crowd gathered at a meeting held in Tavua to:

> stay in your own town, dig the soil — your own soil, make use of it. Take the profit of it yourself for this is the time for it, and the things we can do for our individual benefit in these days cannot be hidden from us. It is open to us to put money in the bank, to have cheque books, and over drafts of over 20 pounds.[26]

While his statement suggests otherwise, Fijians at this time were not able to open their own bank accounts without a European guarantor. Banks in Fiji during this period tended to practise what economist Adrian Tschoegi has called 'ethnic banking', catering to expatriates from their own countries that worked in Fiji,

---

21   C M White, 'Minority Status as a Contested Terrain: Defining the Parameters of Subordinate Status in Post-independent Fiji Discourse', *Social Identities: Journal for the Study of Race, Nation and Culture*, vol. 8, no. 1, 2002, pp. 19–20.

22   D Scarr, *Ratu Sukuna: Soldier, Statesman, Man of Two Worlds*, London, Macmillan Education for the Ratu Sir Lala Sukuna biography committee, 1980, pp. 30–31.

23   Macnaught, *The Fijian Colonial Experience: A Study of the Neotraditional Order Under British Colonial Rule Prior to World War II*, Canberra, Australian National University Press, Pacific Research Monograph Number 7, 1982, p. 89.

24   Ibid., p. 80; R Nicole, *Disturbing History: Resistance in Early Colonial Fiji*, Honolulu, University of Hawai'i Press, 2011, p. 87.

25   K Gravelle, *Fiji Times: A History of Fiji*, Fiji Times and Herald Ltd, 1979, p. 182; T Macnaught, *The Fijian Colonial Experience: A Study of the Neotraditional Order Under British Colonial Rule Prior to World War II*, Canberra, Australian National University Press, Pacific Research Monograph Number 7, 1982, p. 85.

26   Enclosure 4 in confidential despatch, 6 December 1917, in CO 83/139, as cited in B V Lal, *Broken Waves: A History of the Fiji Islands in the Twentieth Century*, Honolulu, University of Hawai'i Press, 1992, pp. 51–52.

rather than to all people within the colony irrespective of ethnicity or nationality.[27] The colonial administration's response to Apolosi's subversive message was harsh. Authorities monitored his activities and reported on the speech he had made in Tavua. He was declared an enemy of the colonial administration, and a warrant was issued, leading to his arrest and exile to the distant island of Rotuma until 1924.[28] Despite his absence from Ra, Apolosi influenced the Methodist membership and the approach of missionaries in the circuit for several decades.

Aware of Apolosi's ideas, European mission superintendents based at Nailaga actively supported Fijian industrial education. The Reverend Charles Oswald Lelean, stationed at Nailaga from 1902 to 1909, oversaw the Nasinu Experimental Farm in 1921.[29] His replacement was the Reverend Arthur Wesley Amos, who observed the *Viti Kabani* at its most active, while anxieties about Fijian land ownership were at fever pitch.[30] In Fiji from 1912 until 1924, Amos witnessed the development of a bifurcated land-use system with the lease of many 10-acre blocks of CSR land to Indo-Fijians at the end of their indenture.[31] When he was transferred from Nailaga to Lakeba in 1919, Amos tried to meet with Ratu Sukuna to discuss his concerns but was continuously snubbed and grew frustrated with the Fijian leader.[32] His ideas about the need for Fijian economic advancement were at odds with Sukuna's.[33] In that same year, Amos trialled a local system of financial self-support in the Lau islands, which, despite being unsuccessful, illustrated his willingness to move towards this goal.[34] As missionaries increasingly encouraged Fijians to abandon the strictures of their prescribed daily labour tasks, the mission circuits became sites of change and social adaptation — 'laboratories of modernity'. As Stoler and Cooper suggest, colonies provided spaces where different methods

27   A E Tschoegi, *Foreign Banks in the Pacific: Some History and Policy Issues*, d1c25a6gwz7q5e.cloudfront. net/papers/1096.pdf, accessed 25 January 2014, p. 8.

28   R Nicole, *Disturbing History: Resistance in Early Colonial Fiji*, Honolulu, University of Hawai'i Press, 2011, p. 70, 96; T Macnaught, *The Fijian Colonial Experience: A Study of the Neotraditional Order Under British Colonial Rule Prior to World War II*, Canberra, Australian National University Press, Pacific Research Monograph Number 7, 1982, p. 91.

29   A J Small to A W Amos, 6 December 1921, F/1/1921, NAF; A W Amos to A J Small, 15 December 1921, F/1/1921, NAF, pp. 1–2.

30   A W Amos was also involved with the National Missionary Council of Australia which was formed in 1926. He became Chairman of the Council in 1949. 'Personal', *The Argus*, Melbourne, 6 August 1949, p. 12.

31   'Task for Church After War: New Methodist President's Concern', *The Argus*, 1 March 1945, p. 2; M Moynagh, 'Land Tenure in Fiji's Sugar Cane Districts Since the 1920s', *Journal of Pacific History*, vol. 13, no. 1, 1978, p. 54.

32   A W Amos to A J Small, Fiji District Correspondence, 1919, 16 September 1919, cited in D Scarr, *Ratu Sukuna: Soldier, Statesman, Man of Two Worlds*, London, Macmillan Education for the Ratu Sir Lala Sukuna biography committee, 1980, pp. 40, 57. Sukuna used the mission's boat as if it were at his disposal, to Amos's frustration.

33   A Thornley, 'Fijian Methodism: 1874–1945: The Emergence of a National Church', PhD thesis, The Australian National University, 1979, p. 272.

34   'Commission re: Native Church: Information Collected for the Consideration of the Commission', Melbourne, The Methodist Society of Australasia, Spectator Publishing Company, 1923, p. 9.

for 'social engineering' and order could be tested on a small or large scale, and this was done at various mission sites depending on the degree of support from the mission's headquarters.[35]

All of this occurred amidst constant concern about demographics in Fiji. The 1921 census revealed that the Fijian population was now 84,475, and counted for 53 per cent of the population, while the Indo-Fijian community numbered 60,634 and constituted 38 per cent of the population. Indo-Fijians had been only 28 per cent of the population 10 years before.[36] Observers were anxious about the growing number of Indo-Fijians in the face of the high death rates and low birth rates in the Fijian community.[37] This only added to unease about the divisive nature of Apolosi's calls for Fijian rights. Wanting to avoid controversy, Amos started associating with a like mind who had a less dubious reputation, the Ratu Rawaidranu, chief of Navatu in Ra, who established the Navatu Company in 1921, at a time when Fijians were being excluded from the most effective modes of obtaining money through their being forced into low-paying employment.[38] The Navatu Company was similar to the *Viti Kabani* in that it demonstrated a blend of cultural 'continuity and change'.[39] A graduate of Fiji's medical school, Rawaidranu was astute and progressive. Rather than relying on money from leases, he sought a higher income for his community by encouraging them to earn a wage.[40] In earlier decades, he had organised men from his village to work on Taveuni's copra plantations, and to cut mangroves across Ra province to supply timber to the Fiji Sugar Company.[41] His Navatu Company farmed sugar cane, peanuts and watermelons, and had two cargo ships. At its inception, however, Rawaidranu was forced to think creatively about how he would establish the company, which would have been impossible had he not had the support of Europeans who he had befriended — including, in this instance, Amos. He needed their support in order to open a bank account with one of the foreign banks that had been established in the colony, and he sought their advice on business ventures. Establishing a business account was one complication; the payment of the company's employees — many of whom were

---

35   F Cooper and A L Stoler, 'Introduction', in F Cooper and A L Stoler (eds), *Tensions of Empire: Colonial Cultures in a Bourgeois World,* Berkeley, University of California Press, 1997, p. 5.

36   Fiji Bureau of Statistics – Key Statistics: June 2012, Population, 1.2A Census Population of Fiji by Ethnicity, www.statsfiji.gov.fj/Key%20Stats/Population/1.2%20pop%20by%20ethnicity.pdf, accessed 22 March 2013.

37   'Fiji', *Townsville Daily Bulletin,* 23 September 1926, p. 3.

38   D Scarr, *Ratu Sukuna: Soldier, Statesman, Man of Two Worlds,* London, Macmillan education for the Ratu Sir Lala Sukuna biography committee, 1980, p. 71.

39   Senivalati Toroki and Emosi Tabumasi, nephews of Nacanieli Rawaidranu, personal communication, June 2013; Thornley, 'Fijian Methodism: 1874–1945: The Emergence of a National Church', PhD thesis, The Australian National University, 1979, p. 277; C Forman, *The Island Churches of the South Pacific: Emergence in the Twentieth Century,* Michigan, Orbis Books, 1982, p. 133.

40   M Moynagh, 'Land Tenure in Fiji's Sugar Cane Districts Since the 1920s', *Journal of Pacific History,* vol. 13, no. 1, 1978, p. 55.

41   K Close, fieldwork notes, December 2010.

illiterate — provided another challenge. Rawaidranu opened an account with Morris Hedstrom supermarkets where workers could obtain basic necessities such as rice and sugar. He appealed to relatives and friends, such as his nephew Samisoni Lalaqila from Nadogaloa, to leave their villages and relocate to a plot of land at Toko near Tavua to start sugar cane crops. The company was established in the face of great opposition from Ratu Sukuna, and tax collectors regularly visited the village settlements and harassed the workers.[42]

Rawaidranu's venture had support at all levels of the mission, including from the Reverend John W Burton. In 1922, Burton advocated industrial training as a method for 'uplifting of races', and 'development of the territory through the natives themselves being trained for agricultural pursuits'.[43] Involving Fijian people in the market economy was seen as essential to ensuring 'permanent progress and prosperity in the Pacific'.[44] Burton claimed that 'the function of the white man would be to train the native, and to act as a commercial intermediary between the native producer and the markets of the world'.[45] Missionaries were not supposed to be involved in business or political ventures, but in Burton's opinion this did not limit their potential to be trainers.[46] Fijian peoples, according to his social evolutionist philosophy, would have to pass through the inevitable stages of human progress and be incorporated into the market economy, rather than cling to the 'old' communal system. Missionaries saw increased economic engagement as a means of ensuring financial self-support in Fijian communities, which would sustain the future 'native church'.

Questions about both land and labour elicited conjecture about the potential for Indo-Fijian dominance in the colony. Burton collected submissions for a commission into the progress of self-support in 1923, receiving responses from Methodist missionaries throughout the Pacific region.[47] In light of their comments, Burton wrote an article about Fijian labour for the *Sydney Morning Herald* in 1924:

> Will labour conditions be so difficult that there will be a further withdrawal of European capital, and the country sink back into a state where the inhabitants cultivate only so much land as will suffice their meagre needs? Or will Fiji, under a system of peasant proprietorship, of both Indian and Fijian, develop into a

---

42 Senivalati Toroki and Emosi Tabumasi, nephews of Nacanieli Rawaidranu, personal communication, June 2013.
43 'Missionary Enterprise: Stimulating the Work: Interview with J W Burton', *The Register*, Adelaide, South Australia, 9 October 1922, p. 8.
44 Ibid.
45 Ibid.
46 Stanley has noted that missionaries elsewhere had similar ideas. B Stanley, *The Bible and the Flag: Protestant Missions and British Imperialism in the Nineteenth and Twentieth Centuries*, Leicester, England, Apollos, 1990, pp. 71, 76.
47 'Commission re: Native Church: Information Collected for the Consideration of the Commission', Melbourne, The Methodist Society of Australasia, Spectator Publishing Company, 1923, p. 3.

wealthy and prosperous native state as some West African possessions have done? Will the European be gradually eliminated and his place taken by the Indian and Chinese? None may say.[48]

Burton seemed impervious to the political ramifications of statements such as these. The colonial administration and mission were aware that promoting agricultural education for the Indo-Fijian community so soon after indenture proved politically problematic; perpetuating the colonial system required keeping the Indo-Fijian community as a peasant class. An anonymous missionary, trying to raise funds for the Davuilevu industrial mission, had suggested that 'the Indian invariably improves mentally, morally and physically under indenture'.[49] The Reverend Richard Piper was unnerved by such statements, worried that if he and others working in the Indo-Fijian mission had not managed certain mission workers, the Methodist mission might have:

> owned a coolie line and its complement of indentured coolies just at the time when the agitation in India was getting to fever heat. The agreement to take up this coolie proposition and then borrow the money to pay for them was actually drawn up ready to sign and the Indian missionaries had not even been advised or consulted. Yet if the plan had come off our name would have stunk in India.[50]

He felt that it was not so hard to understand why there was 'trouble with the Indian mission'.[51] The European arrogance that Piper described exacerbated the growing rift between Indo-Fijians and Europeans within the Methodist community.

Those who, like Piper, were conscious of racial tensions, monitored anti-colonial sentiment as it brewed. In the wake of the Indo-Fijian strikes in 1920, Amos observed that 'there was a definite attempt on the part of the Sadhu to enlist the sympathy of the Fijians in a racial dispute and for a time there was a danger of a repetition of the Apolosian doctrine of black versus white'.[52] While Amos was relatively supportive of Apolosi's aims, he was clearly anxious about the potential for a merger between Indo-Fijian and Fijian anti-colonial groups, and this no doubt influenced his vision of mission self-support as an effort to quell any disgruntlement. In this environment, the alliance between Fijians and missionaries became crucial, as it was believed to stall alliances between Fijian and Indo-Fijian dissidents.

In 1923, only two years after Ratu Rawaidranu had established the Navatu Company, Indo-Fijian settlers pressured Fijian farmers who had established themselves on the Pfluger estate near Tavua for access to some of the land. Amos wrote to Chairman Small in 1923:

48   J W Burton, 'Fiji: Labour and the Future', *Sydney Morning Herald*, 27 September 1924, p. 11.
49   R Piper, 'Indian Mission: Problems in Fiji: A Report', screen 490, item 9, MOM 238, ML.
50   Ibid.
51   Ibid.
52   A W Amos to A J Small, 30 August 1921, F/1/1921, NAF, p. 2.

> My people are with me in trying to keep out the Indians from settling on 'Toko' (part of the Pfluger estate), side by side with our *Vuli* [school] town. It would make a useful piece of planting ground for our schools, which are pinched out on all sides by the [CSR] and growing Indian settlement.[53]

Amos managed daily tensions over land, and defended the mission's land that had been designated for the Methodist school in the face of rapidly expanding Indo-Fijian settlement. His reference to the Fijian Methodists as 'my people' suggested that this had enhanced solidarity between the missionary and the Fijian Methodists; there was a sense of 'us' and 'them'.

Amos continued to support Rawaidranu's work after he returned to Victoria in 1924 to become Secretary of the Wesleyan Overseas Mission Department. His backing proved essential to the farming scheme. Arthur D Lelean replaced Amos at Nailaga in 1923 after five years working on Fiji's eastern island of Taveuni, where he had learnt Fijian custom and protocols.[54] He knew chiefs were essential to ensuring support for the mission, as they dictated how the community's funds would be spent.[55] Lelean entered Ra circuit ready to meet the challenge produced by Apolosi's supporters, and collaborated with Rawaidranu, carrying on where Amos left off.

Burton visited Nailaga in 1924, and while there scrawled a quick note in his diary about a conversation he had with Arthur Lelean about Apolosi. Burton was wary of the local leader, describing Apolosi as a source of 'trouble' and a 'big problem of Fijians'.[56] Burton mentioned that Lelean and Rawaidranu had established Fijian farmers on 48 acres of land leased from CSR.[57] The farmers had secured a seven-year lease at a rent price of 3/- per acre, with no right of renewal unless CSR decided to renew again or they bought the land from the owners.[58] The costs were high, and the initiative relied on generous donations from the Victorian Methodist community.[59] Money raised through selling the crops went directly to their chief, with one crop harvested in 1927 earning approximately £200.[60] Arthur Lelean

---

53   A W Amos to A J Small, 16 January 1923, F/1/1923, NAF.

54   A D Lelean to A J Small, 25 April 1922, F/1/1922, NAF; A D Lelean to A J Small, 19 June 1922, F/1/1922, NAF; A D Lelean to A J Small, 8 September 1922, F/1/1922, NAF, p. 2.

55   A D Lelean to A J Small, 8 September 1922, NAF, F/1/1922, NAF, p. 2; A J Small to A D Lelean, 19 September 1922, F/1/1922, NAF. High copra prices in the early 1920s allowed for steady *vakamisioneri* contribution in the Lau islands: B Knapman, 'The "vakamisioneri" in Lau, Fiji: A Reply', *Journal of Pacific History*, vol. 13, no. 2, 1978, pp. 113–14.

56   J W Burton, diary, 16 August 1924, MSS 2899 add on 990, ML.

57   B Knapman, 'Capitalism's Economic Impact in Colonial Fiji, 1874–1939: Development or Underdevelopment?', *Journal of Pacific History*, vol. 20, no. 2, 1985, p. 73.

58   J W Burton, diary, 15 Aug 1924, MSS 3267/2, ML.

59   A W Amos to R L McDonald, 8 March 1931, F/1/1931, NAF, p. 3; R L McDonald to A D Lelean, 4 March 1931, F/1/1931, NAF; Re Cable a/c A D Lelean, A W Amos to R L McDonald, 10 March 1932, F/1/1932, NAF; R L McDonald to Amos 22 March 1932, F/1/1932, NAF.

60   'The Great Ba Circuit', *The Spectator*, 20 April 1927.

filtered circuit funds into the scheme.[61] He poured his personal income into other areas of the mission work. In 1928, buildings at Matavelo School (next to the Methodist compound at Nailaga) were condemned after an epidemic and needed to be demolished and replaced. The cost was £1,307 and Arthur Lelean paid the bill, expecting some remittance from the mission, which was not forthcoming. After a committee was set up to discuss the matter in 1928, Mr F J Cato, a Methodist from Melbourne who had made large financial contributions to the mission and Burton's mentor, committed £400 to the buildings' reconstruction and another £200 was raised by the Fijian branch.[62]

Figure 4: 'Ploughing bullocks — Nailaga'.

Source: Photo by R H Rickard and others for the Methodist Church of Australasia, Department of Overseas Missions, 'Series 01: Photographic prints of missionaries and Indigenous people in the Northern Territory, Papua New Guinea, Fiji, Samoa and India, ca 1885–1938', PXA 1137, 490-535, pic acc 7061, neg 9, Mitchell Library, State Library of New South Wales. Published with permission of Uniting Church of Australia.

---

61   For example see R L McDonald to A D Lelean, 3 April 1930, F/1/1930, NAF; A W Amos to R L McDonald, 10 March 1932, F/1/1932, NAF.

62   Records re Commission to Fiji, August 1928, frame 302; 'Ra Circuit Finances', mission board minutes, MOM CY 3310 1927–1930, ML; J W Burton, *The Weaver's Shuttle: Memories and Reflections of an Octogenarian*, unpublished manuscript, n.d., p. 110.

Missionaries were involved in negotiating access to land. On 29 September 1929, Ratu Rawaidranu, Ratu Sukuna, and CSR representatives signed an agreement recognising the sugar settlements as part of the *galala* system.[63] This method of lease was not exactly the ideal system of land acquisition for Fijians so far as Sukuna was concerned; he had come to believe that one of the reasons why the Fijians were 'contented and loyal' was because customary forms of land ownership had been incorporated into the systems of the Native Lands department.[64] Regardless of Sukuna's personal and political sentiments, his signature made it possible for the first four farmers to settle on leases at the Toko Estate at Tavua one month later.[65] This formalised the support from the colonial administration and CSR.[66] Missionaries oversaw the project, with a council established at that year's synod. The council would be based at Nailaga, would be convened by Arthur Lelean, and would include the superintendent of the Indo-Fijian branch from Ba and Lautoka, as well as the headmaster of the Lautoka farm school, Mr R Stebbins. Committee members hoped that a manager from CSR would act as an advisor to the committee, and that a qualified accountant would be installed as auditor. A constitution, administrative system and parameters for the council had to be considered, as the responsibilities of the council were initially unclear.[67] The council deliberated not only on matters regarding industrial education throughout the district, but also independent sugar settlements and the mission's industrial schools, and asked 'whether we are satisfied with the farm helping to pay for feeding and clothing boys — or whether we are going to try and make farmers out of the boys'.[68] They thus queried their role in enacting and promoting change in the community and in this instance overrode the separation of Fiji's colonial society, administering the Fijian and Indo-Fijian communities simultaneously in one forum. Again, however, it was Europeans making decisions for all — much like the European synod.[69]

The *galala* farming scheme attracted considerable opposition. Victor Clark, a CSR employee, commented that there was 'opposition and propaganda from Indians and some of the die-hard chiefs' to the Toko farmers' project.[70] There were attempts to subdue references to racial antagonism, but the

---

63   K Close, *Talanoa*, Yaladro, fieldnotes, 2010.

64   D Scarr, *Ratu Sukuna: Soldier, Statesman, Man of Two Worlds*, London, Macmillan education for the Ratu Sir Lala Sukuna biography committee, 1980, p. 76.

65   V Clark to R L McDonald, 7 May 1930, F/1/1930, NAF, pp. 1–2.

66   Ibid., p. 3; T Macnaught, *The Fijian Colonial Experience: A Study of the Neotraditional Order Under British Colonial Rule Prior to World War II*, Canberra, Australian National University Press, Pacific Research Monograph Number 7, 1982, p. 140.

67   Fiji District Synod, European Journal, 1929, Screen Shot 55, CY 3038, ML, p. 45.

68   W Stebbins to R L McDonald, 5 May 1930, F/1/1930, NAF.

69   M Kaplan and J Kelly, 'On Discourse and Power: Cults and Orientals', *American Ethnologist*, vol. 26, no. 4, 2000, p. 852.

70   V Clark to R L McDonald, 7 May 1930, F/1/1930, NAF, p. 2.

farming scheme brought underlying antipathy to the fore. Earlier that year, Richard Piper, working at the Nadi station of the Indo-Fijian branch, wrote to McDonald complaining about statements published in *The Methodist* magazine. The retiring president of the Methodist mission, the Reverend Frank Lade, who had no experience in Fiji, reported that there was a 'bitter feud' between Indo-Fijian and Fijian communities. Piper argued that no missionary in Fiji would 'subscribe' to these comments, despite his personally recording the racial tensions in the mission throughout the previous decade.[71]

Clark had also mentioned chiefly opposition to the scheme and may have had Sukuna in mind as he wrote this, because the colony's labour regulations created several hurdles for *galala* farmers. Fijian workers required exemptions from their *tikina* (districts), but Rawaidranu acted as their chief.[72] Clark, stationed at the Varoko *galala* settlement in 1930, appealed to McDonald to see if the colony's governor, Sir Murchison Fletcher, would allow the workers exemption from communal work obligations. After McDonald's consultation with Sir Murchison Fletcher,[73] the labour laws were altered so that the 700 farmers working outside their villages could apply for exemption from communal duties for £1 each per annum, but they required support from CSR or the mission to do so.[74] The *galala* scheme did not entirely extinguish chiefly obligations, but rather reshaped the ways in which chiefs worked with their communities. The system at Tavua required a shift in chiefly allegiances. With Ratu Rawaidranu as the leader, a number of new farming settlements were established where men could work and take their families with them.

Prepared to condone chiefly systems, missionaries struggled more with continuity in non-Methodist faiths in the farming communities, aware of Apolosi's affiliation with occult practices. Within the international missionary community, there were suggestions that accommodating culture would appease strong nationalist elements, but this accommodation would not be to the point where communities were continuing traditions deemed to be non-Christian.[75] Charles Lelean attended the International Missionary Council conference in Jerusalem in 1928

---

71   R Piper to R L McDonald, 14 March 1929, F/1/1929, NAF, pp. 1–2.

72   H C Brookfield, 'Fijian Farmers Each on his Own Land: The Triumph of Experience Over Hope', *Journal of Pacific History*, vol. 23, no. 1, 1988, p. 17; R Nayacakalou, *Leadership in Fiji*, University of the South Pacific in association with Oxford University Press, 1975, p. 1.

73   Sir Murchison Fletcher was governor from 1929 to 1936. B Knapman, 'Capitalism's Economic Impact in Colonial Fiji, 1874–1939: Development or Underdevelopment?', *Journal of Pacific History*, vol. 20, no. 2, 1985, p. 77.

74   R L McDonald to V Clark, 14 May 1930, F/1/1930, NAF, p. 1; See also B Knapman, 'Capitalism's Economic Impact in Colonial Fiji, 1874–1939: Development or Underdevelopment?', *Journal of Pacific History*, vol. 20, no. 2, 1985, p. 79; T Macnaught, *The Fijian Colonial Experience: A Study of the Neotraditional Order Under British Colonial Rule Prior to World War II*, Canberra, Australian National University Press, Pacific Research Monograph Number 7, 1982, p. 139.

75   B Mathews, *Roads to the City of God: World Outlook from Jerusalem*, London, Edinburgh House Press, 1928, p. 10.

with his wife Constance. One speaker suggested that an indigenous church would be marked by an 'interpretation of Christ and its expression in worship and service, in customs, and in art and architecture, incorporate the worthy characteristics of the people, while conserving at the same time the heritage of the Church in all lands and in all ages'.[76] European missionaries would continue to play a role in deciding what 'worthy characteristics' would be incorporated into indigenous churches, but this development opened new avenues for missionaries to understand the acculturation of Christianity. Yet, in the Fijian branch, missionaries were unsure about the difference between syncretism and what could be considered a Fijian version of genuine Christianity.[77] McDonald and Charles Lelean were concerned when rumours emerged that Arthur Lelean was encouraging syncretic movements.

Charles Lelean heard that Apolosi — now back from exile — had established a 'new cult called the "*Lotu ni Gauna*"' (the 'religion of the new age').[78] The *Lotu ni Gauna* had followers in Nadi, Sabeto, Nawaka and Nadrau. Charles Lelean considered this more of a rogue movement than any attempt at an indigenous version of Christianity, but used this case to argue against reducing the European missionary presence in the Ra circuit, citing the need to ensure that Christianity was properly adhered to.[79] He was a hardliner, whereas Arthur Lelean seemed to have been slightly more open-minded. When Apolosi was arrested on the beach at Vuda on 30 January 1930, Arthur Lelean saw an opportunity to welcome members of the *Lotu ni Gauna* back to Methodism.[80] Many of Apolosi's supporters had left the mission prior to his first arrest due to the high demands of the Methodist's annual *vakamisioneri* contributions,[81] which had led to a significant drop in mission revenue, leaving missionaries scrambling to compensate.[82] During Apolosi's first exile, his supporters who had tried to return to Methodism were met with opposition by the mission, due

---

76   Ibid., pp. 43, 60; *Evangelical Dictionary of World Missions*, as cited in D Lindenfield and M Richardson, (eds), *Beyond Conversion and Syncretism: Indigenous Encounters with Missionary Christianity, 1800–2000*, New York and Oxford, Berghahn Books, 2012. This was likely the form of syncretism that missionary Jesse Carey feared would occur if the theological institution in Fiji had been transferred to Fijians in the 1870s. See A Thornley, '"Through a glass darkly": Ownership of Fijian Methodism, 1850–80', in P Herda (ed.), *Vision and Reality in Pacific Religion*, Canberra, Pandanus Books, 2005, p. 139.

77   Deryck Scarr has suggested that Apolosi Nawai's movement was syncretic. D Scarr *Ratu Sukuna: Soldier, Statesman, Man of Two Worlds*, London, Macmillan education for the Ratu Sir Lala Sukuna biography committee, 1980, p. 46.

78   C O Lelean to J W Burton 3 February 1930, F/1/1930, NAF.

79   Ibid.

80   A D Lelean to R L McDonald, 31 March 1930, F/1/1931, NAF.

81   R Nicole, *Disturbing History: Resistance in Early Colonial Fiji*, Honolulu, University of Hawai'i Press, 2011, pp. 88–89, 90; A D Lelean to R McDonald, 31 March 1930, F/1/1931, NAF.

82   R Nicole, *Disturbing History: Resistance in Early Colonial Fiji*, Honolulu, University of Hawai'i Press, 2011, p. 93.

to their involvement in what were described as occult activities. Arthur Lelean did not want to repeat the same mistake, and allowed their return to Methodist services.

Though Arthur Lelean acknowledged the practice of traditional or occult ceremonies among Apolosi's followers, he was more eager to address the nationalist and anti-colonial aspects of Apolosi's movement. Lelean's support for Fijian land acquisition revealed the impact of allegiances between Methodist missionaries and the Fijian community. He wrote to McDonald in 1930:

> The only solid argument Apolosi could put up against the Mission was that the M.M. [Methodist Mission] did not consult the Fijians when the Indians were turned loose to take up residence in Fiji after indenture. I explained that that was done by fools in Australia but not by those interested in the *Kai Viti* [*iTaukei*] here.[83]

Arthur Lelean pointed directly to the tensions between Fijians and Indo-Fijians, and Apolosi's belief that Australians — most likely CSR, whose headquarters were located in Australia — were complicit in the process of the dispossession of Fijian land in favour of Indo-Fijian settlement. Arthur Lelean was caught in a quandary, pressured to take part in this process of land alienation. McDonald wrote to Lelean, warning that some Europeans expected Lelean to act as an 'agent in the disposal of lands round there to Indians'.[84] McDonald advised that it was not their job:

> … there are solicitors and others who can do it and who make their living at it. We will bring ourselves severe criticism if we act in such matters and we will be well advised to keep clear altogether. Give them all the help we can in other ways — but to act as their agent — I think we ought not to agree to it.[85]

Arthur Lelean's knowledge of the local community placed him in a position where he was unable to avoid involvement in politics or business, both of which were attached to land negotiations. While it seems that he shirked the demands of a private European investor who had wanted his help to buy land, there is evidence that Arthur Lelean played a personal role in ensuring Fijian access to land, organising land leases for the farming scheme and the mission. In 1930, he informed McDonald that he had paid the lease at Nailaga, including the front garden, at £2 9s[86] He wrote again to McDonald about this property in September and apologised for not making the final payment for Vunidilo, one

---

83   A D Lelean to R L McDonald, 31 March 1930, F/1/1931, NAF, p. 1.
84   Ibid.
85   R L McDonald to A D Lelean, 10 December 1930, F/1/1930, NAF.
86   A D Lelean to R L McDonald, 14 August 1930, F/1/1930, NAF.

of the mission's 'revenue raising properties', through the mission — he had instead paid for it himself.[87] Arthur Lelean blurred the distinctions between his personal finances, those of the mission, and those for the farming estates.

By 1931, Arthur Lelean and Rawaidranu had established 75 farmers at Toko and another 30 men at Varoka, with CSR providing 10-acre plots of land to each farmer, along with plants, seeds and supervision.[88] Lelean leased 48 acres of farmland from CSR for rice, maize and sugar cane crops. In all, with the assistance of CSR, the colonial administration and local chiefs, Amos boasted that Arthur Lelean had aided 600 Fijian families to enter the sugar industry, creating a 'new type of Fijian farmer'.[89] Competitions were held at the Varoka settlement to judge who could cultivate the best garden and keep the neatest house. After touring these settlements, Chairman McDonald 'felt convinced that, with training, the Fijian will prove a first rate agriculturalist and a real asset to his country'.[90] Missionaries involved in both the Navuso agricultural school and the schemes in Ra sought to create an 'industrial man', but rather than being 'detribalised', the so-called 'Fijian Methodist industrial man' still had an avenue into 'traditional' Fijian society through his continued deference to the chiefly system and familial ties. This had the additional benefit of creating a more 'productive and predictable' society for easier governance.[91] *The Spectator* celebrated the farming schemes:

> The men told Mr McDonald they would never return to the old conditions. However, they still recognised their obligation to their towns and the old people, but such a chance of making good as they now had [,] they would not miss for anything.[92]

The farming schemes married missionary ideals of modernity, individualism, and progress with customary social practices. McDonald saw the scheme as a 'natural development of the Fijian today and nothing and nobody will be able to stop it'.[93] Through work, McDonald felt that Fijian communities could contribute to and engage with their nation, becoming active and useful citizens.

---

87 Ibid.

88 A W Amos to R L McDonald, 10 November 1931, F/1/1931, NAF.

89 A W Amos to R L McDonald, 10 November 1931, F/1/1931, NAF; A W Amos, 'Fiji Revisited', continued from 20 November 1935, *The Spectator*, 27 November 1935, p. 975; R Eves, 'Colonialism, Corporeality and Character: Methodist Missions and the Refashioning of Bodies in the Pacific', *History and Anthropology*, vol. 10, no. 1, 1996, pp. 85–138.

90 'Across Viti Levu: Rebuilding Towns: Successful Fijian Farmers', *The Spectator*, 30 September 1931.

91 F Cooper, *Decolonisation and African Society: The Labor Question in French and British Africa*, Cambridge, Cambridge University Press, 1996, p. 2.

92 'Across Viti Levu: Rebuilding Towns: Successful Fijian Farmers', *The Spectator*, 30 September 1931.

93 R L McDonald to A D Lelean, 7 July 1931, F/1/1931, NAF.

The colonial administration was suspicious of Arthur Lelean due to the persistent rumours that he was associating with Apolosi. The mission sister at Nailaga, Miss Brokenshire, reported in 1932 that she had heard that Lelean was permitting *Lotu ni Gauna* ceremonies on mission premises.[94] Lelean had described the *Lotu ni Gauna* to McDonald:

> [Apolosi's] *lotu* [church] consists of Methodism plus prayers to Degei, Lutunasobosobo, Savusavu and Vosavakadua. A bowl of grog is used for prayers, and then thrown outside along with this '*Duka*' or sins. Baptism is by a bowl of grog down the neck, and promising to obey when the command is given ... but I'm not out to make fun of those who have been deceived — they have returned, and the hot bed at Vuda (where the king kissed Apolosi's toe nail) started off yesterday with *Vakamisioneri* contributions £21-10-0 as a start for this year.[95]

Arthur Lelean was prepared to accept those who had been involved in syncretic practices into the church. He now had evidence that his inclusive approach would secure more finances for the mission. In May 1931, McDonald continued to interrogate Lelean about his affiliation with Apolosi, and warned:

> that someone has indisputable documentary evidence that [Patemo] is first, second and third and all the time to Apolosi, and that Government and Mission are nowhere. That [Patemo] is using you to further Apolosi's end.[96]

Though it is exceptionally difficult to find information about who Patemo was, it is obvious that he was one of Apolosi's followers. Arthur Lelean denied the accusation that he was associated with Apolosi in this way, writing: 'Is ADL [Arthur Drew Lelean] for Apolosi? No! As a padre, his friend.'[97] McDonald persisted, inquiring again in July, after receiving reports that the colonial administration had:

> Intercepted correspondence between Patemo and Apolosi in which our henchman makes it clear — though perhaps the meaning of his words would not carry all the Government gives them — that he is awaiting 'the day' which is very near at hand for the emancipation of the Fijian. They only await the return of A. [Apolosi] and the move contemplated will take place! It is interpreted as being all this settlement scheme &c is part of a big plan to pave the way for Apolosi's reign; while perhaps the real interpretation is that the settlement scheme is the objective and end in view and that as is one, but only one, of the avenues, by which it will be reached. However Government officials have accepted the earlier interpretation. In ALA's report,[98] ADL [Arthur Drew Lelean] is a good fellow &c,

---

94 P Brokenshire – private and confidential notes on the Lotu ni Gauna, Davui/a/2, 1932, as cited in A Thornley, 'Fijian Methodism: 1874–1945: The Emergence of a National Church', PhD thesis, The Australian National University, 1979, p. 157.

95 A D Lelean to R L McDonald, 31 March 1930, F/1/1931, NAF, p. 2.

96 R L McDonald to A D Lelean, 20 May 1931, F/1/1931, NAF.

97 A D Lelean to R L McDonald, 28 May 1931, F/1/1931, NAF.

98 I have not been able to identify who this acronym refers to. I assume it was a government official.

> but he is a missionary, and of course has the point of view of the missionary and is duped by these unscrupulous *kai vitis* [Fijians]. It was indeed fortunate that ALA went round when he did, as he was able to see for himself and size the position up and take immediate action to counteract the movement! That is the gist of this attitude and Government accepts it.[99]

In response to this, Arthur Lelean suggested:

> Apolosi does not present any great difficulty, but his life is safer where he is now, and there is not any need to unite the Fijians again under communism, now that each individual is trying to make good under European supervision. The genuine desire of the Fijian to become an economic factor in the colony is based on a determination to survive and grow. This is shared alike by those who hate Apolosi, and those who pledged themselves to him some 16 years ago.[100]

It was perilous to associate with Apolosi, scorned as he was by the colonial administration. Rawaidranu did not voice support for Apolosi, wanting to ensure the ongoing support of the colonial administration.[101] Arthur Lelean became withdrawn. His relationship with McDonald was strained throughout 1931, and correspondence became increasingly infrequent.[102]

Members of the Methodist leadership continued to support the aims of the scheme, but the large investment that it required had placed significant strain on the mission and its reputation. Conscious of Lelean's precarious financial position and having personally sent significant contributions, Amos scanned Burton's 1930 publication *The Pacific Isles* in the hope that the farmers still had his support.[103] Burton's endorsement was crucial to securing the goals of the farmers, so he excitedly quoted Burton to McDonald, that the Fijian 'requires education in those particular arts that will enable him to cultivate his land and develop the resources of his country'.[104] However, the Reverend Norman Wright, working in the Indo-Fijian mission at Lautoka in January 1933 had heard that a Mr A B Herrold had:

> suffered considerable financial loss through ADL [Arthur Drew Lelean] inducing him to make land available for Fijians and after considerable delay not doing anything. He further said that this had been done in several cases so that the Public were discussing it freely.[105]

---

99   R L McDonald to A D Lelean, 4 July 1931, F/1/1931, NAF.
100 A D Lelean to R L McDonald, 28 May 1931, F/1/1931, NAF.
101 K Close, Yaladro, *Talanoa*, fieldwork notes, 2010.
102 A D Lelean to R L McDonald, 5 March 1931, F/1/1931, NAF.
103 A W Amos to R L McDonald, 10 November 1931, F/1/1931, NAF, p. 4; J W Burton, *The Pacific Islands: A Missionary Survey*, London, World Dominion Press, 1930, pp. 16, 19.
104 J W Burton, *The Pacific Islands: A Missionary Survey, London*, World Dominion Press, *1930*, p. 26, cited in A W Amos to R McDonald, 8 March 31, F/1/1931, NAF, pp. 3–4.
105 N Wright to R L McDonald, 3 Jan 1933, F/1/1933, NAF.

McDonald came to Lelean's defence, stating that 'unless something more definite is reported to me, the matter must just drop'.[106] It was clear that the European community was becoming agitated by Lelean's efforts. As historian Bruce Knapman described, Lelean was attempting to stem a 'large-scale white settler development founded on dispossession and forced rural proletarianization of Fijians'.[107] While on furlough in Donald, Victoria, in 1933, Lelean wrote:

> I've tried to set the ball rolling to get help for Fijian farmers and Navuso, but have met with opposition so far. If only the Fijians had had Indian mothers and fathers!!! The fool who stands up for the Fijian has a hornet's nest about his ears in no time.[108]

In June, a Mr Birmingham, from the Fiji-based company Morris Hedstrom, claimed that Lelean owed him money. He reassured McDonald that Morris Hedstrom was well protected and that he was a friend and well-wisher of Lelean, but admitted:

> [he] would welcome some regulation by your governing body precluding him from any of these foolish advances of his to Fijians. I am sure he personally is a heavy loser through these advances but I would not be surprised to hear even he does not know by how much![109]

In 1933, Indo-Fijians were demanding greater access to land. Even Sukuna, who was more open than Apolosi to the legitimacy of Indo-Fijian claims to belonging in Fiji, would not concede the best land. Sukuna stated that he believed tracts of land should be set aside for Indo-Fijian use, giving particular mention to those who had been 'dispossessed through the also legitimate desire of natives to take up economic cultivation'.[110] Amos put Lelean in contact with F Oswald Barnett, a Methodist renowned for his Melbourne campaign against the state of the slums in Collingwood and Fitzroy during the 1920s.[111] An accountant by trade, Barnett offered his services to coordinate a company that would oversee the business affairs for the farming schemes. He said that men from the Victorian Methodist Laymen's Movement had 'voluntarily proposed the establishing of a

---

106 R L McDonald to N Wright, 7 Feb 1933, F/1/1933, NAF.

107 B Knapman, 'Capitalism's Economic Impact in Colonial Fiji, 1874–1939: Development or Underdevelopment?', *Journal of Pacific History*, vol. 20, no. 2, 1985, p. 81.

108 A D Lelean to R L McDonald, 1 May 33, F/1/1933, NAF.

109 Birmingham to R L McDonald, 6 June 1933, F/1/1933, NAF.

110 Sukuna, Legislative Council debates, 26 October 1933, cited in D Scarr, *Ratu Sukuna: Soldier, Statesman, Man of Two Worlds*, London, Macmillan education for the Ratu Sir Lala Sukuna biography committee, 1980, p. 107.

111 E W Russell, Barnett, Frederick Oswald (1883–1972)', *Australian Dictionary of Biography*, National Centre of Biography, The Australian National University, adb.anu.edu.au/biography/barnett-frederick-oswald-5138/text8599, accessed 26 June 2013; T Birch, '"These children have been born in an abyss": Slum Photography in a Melbourne Suburb', *Australian Historical Studies*, vol. 123, 2004, p. 2.

small trading company for the purpose of financing student farmers and other Methodist folks'.[112] The Reverend E A Thompson wrote that the commercial company would operate with:

> the main purpose of placing the native Fijian upon the land and assisting him to cultivate and secure the advantages gained thereby … for this purpose we propose to advance him sufficient finance, mainly upon the security of his own character, at a reasonably low rate of interest, which will, of course, vary according to circumstance.[113]

An Australian board would manage the company with a knowledgeable businessman appointed to manage 'Fijian affairs'.[114] Thompson reiterated to Lelean: 'You will understand that this is a purely Commercial Company established and to be worked on a business footing, but managed by business men not mainly for cash profits, but the ultimate advancement of the ideal that you and they have at heart.'[115]

Arthur Lelean was never clearer in his desire to sustain Fijian land access than in his discussions with Barnett's business group. The minutes of a meeting held on 28 April 1933 at Barnett's office in Temple Court, Melbourne, clearly stated that the main purpose of the company was 'to aid the Fijian to acquire his own native land', and to 'place Fijians back upon the land as leases fall in':[116]

> [Lelean] had received a letter from Rev. J W Burton advising caution in attaching himself to any company, but Mr Lelean pointed out that he had no intention of dabbling in business, nor doing anything contrary to the will of the Mission Board. He was of the opinion, however, that anything that could be done to establish the Fijian on his own land should be done, so that the Fijian should regain his birth-right, and the Fijian Church could become self-supporting.[117]

He stated that 'at present the Indian was rapidly securing the land, as the Fijian was unable through lack of finance to pay for the improvements as the leases fell in, so that the Indians retained the land under a perpetual lease'.[118] Lelean also suggested that one of the difficulties was that the 'Fijian is a minor in the eyes of the law', and this was why a company was potentially useful.

112 A W Amos to R L McDonald, 20 June 1933, F/1/1933, NAF, p. 1.
113 E A Thompson to A D Lelean, 19 June 1933, F/1/1933, NAF, p. 1.
114 Ibid.
115 Ibid.
116 Those present at the meeting were W A Towler, E H Moad, H A Hedley, A E Allan, H H Murray, S C Brittingham, J F Wilkinson, F O Barnett, E A Thompson, W B McCutcheon, E L Gault and A D Lelean. Minutes, enclosed in letter 15 May 1933, F/1/1933, NAF.
117 Minutes, enclosed in letter, 15 May 1933, F/1/1933, NAF.
118 Ibid., p. 2; B V Lal, *Broken Waves: A History of the Fiji Islands in the Twentieth Century*, Honolulu, University of Hawai'i Press, 1992, p. 71.

Finances were a critical point of discussion. Arthur Lelean admitted that he had guaranteed 'advances made by the banks and other traders' and had acted as a guarantor for many so that land could be secured.[119] Amos was convinced that this scheme was worth a trial, though he felt that it should not be led by a missionary.[120] McDonald was so anxious about it that he wrote to Barnett warning him not to trust Arthur Lelean due to his being 'most irregular in financial matters'.[121] He wrote again to Amos in July and suggested that:

> there are cases where land of extinct *mataqalis* is available for lease, and this might be secured by advances from such a fund as is suggested. Again, where a lad is on his land, and is just getting his crop going, and is in danger of being sent to gaol because he has not been able to pay his tax, a temporary loan against his crop would be a real service.[122]

But McDonald remained adamant that Fijians should make their own arrangements with CSR or the government, rather than have the mission involved.[123] He pointed out that 'lands are held tribally, and your advance is not to one person but to the tribe, and they disagree amongst themselves with regard to repayment'.[124] In 1936, Amos believed that to eliminate this issue, radical change to the village system was required which it would perhaps have a negative impact on the church, despite Rawaidranu's ongoing commitment to Methodism.[125] The Reverend Cyrus Taiveitaua had written to Amos about Ratu Rawaidranu, saying that he was 'giving splendid leadership to his companions in church affairs',[126] having supported men who had gone to work with the Reverend Theodor Webb at the Methodist mission in North Australia. Amos also recorded:

> At the last annual meeting they found their yearly missionary offering only reached £33, and gave them much concern. When Nathaniel [Rawaidranu] heard it he came forward with the balance of £27! This is an extraordinarily fine gift for a Fijian, and is a sign that in the changing order of Fiji he is carrying over to the new system the faith of his fathers. This gift, let it be noted, is to help us Australians discharge our obligations to our own aborigines!! Truly these children of the sun are rising up to challenge the older people of the West![127]

119 Minutes, enclosed in letter 15 May 1933, F/1/1933, NAF.
120 A W Amos to R L McDonald, 20 June 1933, F/1/1933, NAF, p. 2.
121 R L McDonald to F O Barnett, 8 June 1933, F/1/1933, NAF; F O Barnett to R L McDonald, 29 May 1933, F/1/1933, NAF; F O Barnett to R McDonald, 23 June 1933, F/1/1933, NAF.
122 R L McDonald to A W Amos, 3 July 1933, F/1/1933, NAF, pp. 1–2.
123 Ibid., p. 2.
124 Ibid.
125 A W Amos, 'The New Fiji', *The Spectator*, 29 January 1936.
126 Ibid.
127 Ibid.

Amos believed that Rawaidranu's donation demonstrated that the mission's programs could become financially self-supporting, and self-propagating as the investment facilitated *talatala* spreading the Word of God to non-Christian peoples in other lands. Despite the difficulties, Rawaidranu was seen to embody the successful efforts to institute the 'three selves' church policy.

Charles Lelean was concerned about his nephew's health, as rumours continued to circulate about the difficulties experienced by the farmers and investors. Charles Lelean had also heard that the 'CSR has been let down badly over one of his tenant farmer schemes at Nadroga'.[128] District Commissioner John Goepel claimed that Arthur Lelean was coordinating the migration of Fijians from their customary land to new sites without the colonial administration's knowledge or involvement. Goepel also claimed that the conditions on the farms were appalling, which was not noted in mission records.[129] Despite Amos's undying support, Arthur Lelean left Fiji in 1936, returning to the Ballarat circuit in Victoria to attend to both his and his family's health. He was devastated. He confided in his best friend in the field, the Reverend Robert Green: 'I determined to return outside the Mission, after a year or so, to die later on with the Fijians.'[130]

While Charles Lelean had not always agreed with his nephew's activities, he evidently shared Arthur Lelean's belief in the need to reinstate Fijian land ownership. He publicly challenged the colonial administration's attempt to open land to Indo-Fijian and European use. In October 1936, Sukuna and the Council of Chiefs passed resolution 30, opening for settlement all lands that were not required by Fijians. The administration would acquire this land for lease on behalf of Fijian *mataqalis*.[131] Two years later, on 27 February 1938, Charles Lelean, in a sermon at Suva's Jubilee church, commented:

> … we had better look after our lands. This is the time for us to get together, to wake up and do something about them! Things concerning our lands must be decided on here and not in any other place. Let us look after our lands, lest, in the future, the government of India will control them.[132]

128 C O Lelean to R L McDonald, 5 March 1934, F/1/1934, NAF. See also C O Lelean to R L McDonald, 10 July 1934, F/1/1934, NAF; C O Lelean to R L McDonald, 28 July 34, F/1/1934, NAF, p. 2; C O Lelean to R L McDonald, 28 July 34, F/1/1934, NAF, p. 2.
129 J Goepel to the Colonial Secretary, 15 April 1935, CSO F20/2 as cited in T Macnaught, 'Chiefly Civil Servants? Ambiguity in District Administration in the Preservation of the Fijian Way of Life, 1896–1940', *Journal of Pacific History*, vol. 9, 1974, p. 14.
130 A D Lelean to R H Green 26 March 1936, M/61, MF, in A Thornley, 'Fijian Methodism: 1874–1945: The Emergence of a National Church', PhD thesis, The Australian National University, 1979, p. 34.
131 Council of Chiefs, CP 36/1936 as cited in M Moynagh, 'Land Tenure in Fiji's Sugar Cane Districts Since the 1920s', *Journal of Pacific History*, vol. 13, no. 1, 1978, p. 59.
132 Colonial Secretary to C O Lelean, 2 March 1938, MOM F/2/vol 2, CSO 143; C O Lelean to colonial secretary, 7 March 1938, MOM F/2/vol 2, CSO 143.

Later that year, in a conference held at the Lilac theatre in Suva, land was again raised as an important issue, this time by Hindu scholar and community leader Pandit Hriday Nath Kinzru, with plans made for a commission to explore opportunities for greater Indo-Fijian access to land.[133] The issue of land was becoming increasingly inflammatory. Charles Lelean's comments were more exclusivist and effectively anti-Indo-Fijian than anything Arthur Lelean had written. The farming scheme had been one way in which missionaries were involved in responding to Indo-Fijian settlement. Charles Lelean's comments signalled the preparedness of missionaries to promote the sense of difference and competition between the two communities over land. The Leleans had walked a fine line, evidently not always utterly against the Indo-Fijian community yet also championing Fijian rights. They articulated the mission's propensity to promote Fijian paramountcy.

Missionaries played a crucial role in facilitating land negotiations in the Pacific during the 1920s and 1930s. This position as broker left ministers, such as those involved in these farming schemes in north-west Viti Levu, to contend with a situation more complicated than a simplistic binary condition of colonisers against colonised. Nor was it simply a matter of determining the position of chiefs against commoners. Fiji's colonial society was a site of complex interactions and contests over land, money, power and prestige.[134] Ethnicity and status did play a role but this was never in a strictly binary relationship, although there were often allegiances between Europeans and Fijians. Indo-Fijian settlement elicited strong responses from missionaries, including a protectionist response that they perceived to be humanitarian. The farming movement did not promote Fijian engagement with Indo-Fijian workers, but rather developed in competition with them. Fijians formed a nationalist consciousness through Apolosi Ranawai's movement, based on the sense of competition they felt towards Indo-Fijian farmers over land as well as through their endeavours to establish a Fijian church working towards a sense of citizenship and 'Fijianness'. The *galala* farming schemes were based on chiefly, communal systems of social organisation and contributed to the construction of Fijian nationalism at the village level, paralleling the mission and administration's native protectionist policies.[135]

The *galala* farming scheme ignited tensions over land, with a pro-Fijian stance developing and being articulated more frequently by European missionaries. This was a similar attitude to that displayed by British administrators, as John

---

133   B V Lal, *A Vision for Change: A D Patel and the Politics of Fiji*, Canberra, ANU E Press, 2011, p. 46.

134   A L Stoler, *Carnal Knowledge and Imperial Power: Race and the Intimate in Colonial Rule*, Berkeley and Los Angeles, University of California Press, 2002, p. 8.

135   J Leerssen, 'Nationalism and the Cultivation of Culture', *Nations and Nationalism*, vol. 12, no. 4, 2006, p. 559.

Kelly has illustrated in his research. The administration and the missionaries were using the same lexica of alterity, and were working simultaneously, if not in collaboration, to promote the codification of land use based on perceptions of race.[136] Ratu Rawaidranu and Arthur Lelean had — through the way that they had organised and discussed the scheme — solidified a sense of difference, both cultural and racial, between Fijian and Indo-Fijian farmers in the north-west of Viti Levu. The concept of land as the birthright of the Fijians had been sustained in missionary discourse and enhanced the sense of Fijian paramountcy. While not indulging in anti-Indo-Fijian sentiment, A Wesley Amos, and Arthur and Charles Lelean, promoted the rights of indigenous Fijians, which was illustrated through their commentary about land — the *vanua*. The farming scheme at Toko exemplified the interest in the self-support concept at the local village level. It was no longer an internationally renowned humanitarian ideal, but a frame for Fijian efforts to gain control of their church. The international church concept of self-support had been converted to a grassroots movement.

---

136 E A Thompson to A D Lelean, 19 June 1933, F/1/1933, NAF, p. 1; J Kelly, 'Threats to Difference in Colonial Fiji', *Cultural Anthropology*, vol. 10, no. 1, 1995, p. 66.

CHAPTER FIVE

Leadership with Limitations: Constrained Leadership for Indo-Fijian and Fijian Methodists in the 1930s

The impetus for establishing a self-governing church forced the Methodist mission's leadership to continually re-evaluate their views of Fijian and Indo-Fijian abilities and capacity for self-rule, yet the obstacles that the mission still placed in the path of non-European leaders were starting to cause friction.[1] Within a global context of growing anti-colonial discontent, the delegates of the International Missionary Council (IMC), who came from all of the far-flung corners of the globe, were similarly responding to anti-colonial movements. The ideas circulating at their conferences and in their publications had already inspired a reflexive approach and the acculturation of Christianity in Fiji. These were increasingly necessary as non-European church members voiced their dissatisfaction with their exclusion from positions of authority. This chapter focuses on the missionaries' efforts to come to grips with their identity as colonisers and to respond to the antagonism that was building against them. It follows the careers of key figures — both Indo-Fijian and Fijian — who were stepping into leadership roles and challenging European hegemony. It also follows the means devised used by European missionaries to respond to these challenges. Some followed the IMC's directions to ensure self-support, self-government and self-propagation. Following the ideas of the General Secretary of Methodist Foreign Missions, the Reverend John W Burton,

---

1   A Porter, '"Cultural imperialism" and Protestant Missionary Enterprise, 1780–1914', *Journal of Imperial and Commonwealth History*, vol. 25, no. 3, 1997, p. 387.

we can trace the discourses circulating about 'native' governance throughout the 1930s. While Burton's writings offer a gauge of the racialist thinking that existed within Fiji's Methodist mission, the actions of indigenous Methodists spoke in equal volume and projected back on to these colonial structures. Burton discussed the 'three selves' concept at length, but in practice it was manipulated to make sure that European hegemony remained intact.[2] What the missionaries viewed as humanitarian efforts to address the cultural needs of Fijian and Indo-Fijian peoples were identified by non-European ministers as the institution of racialised barriers.

To illustrate the reinforcement of European hegemony through habitual colonial exclusion, this chapter presents snapshots in the careers of two of the mission's workers, with case studies of the Reverend Aseri Robarobalevu, who was appointed as assistant superintendent of Bua Circuit in 1930, and Ramsey Deoki, who became the first Indo-Fijian minister when he was ordained in 1939. While focusing on critical moments of tension, these case studies demonstrate the extent of ethnicised exclusion practised within the mission, which crystallised and became most visible at times when they were challenged.[3] These events are then positioned within the context of the continuing discussions between missionaries — particularly the chairmen, Richard McDonald and Charles O Lelean — and John W Burton during this decade. As Mamdani identified in his studies of governance under indirect rule, missionaries were responding to difference and this, in turn, coaxed their establishment of a racially segregated organisation. Distinctions between communities were not only racial, but hierarchies were also established between and within them. Each branch had unique challenges due to their segregation from one another and the different processes and paces of acculturation in each, but there were commonalities in the ways that missionaries simultaneously exacerbated the differences between peoples while trying to understate, in their rhetoric, the racial nature of the Methodist mission. At the same time, non-European ministers were increasingly articulating their dissatisfaction with the inequity of the mission's structure. This chapter reveals both the structural inequities embedded within the mission while showing the ways in which they were starting to fracture.

---

2   A Walls, 'Foreword: A Salute to Lamin Sanneh', in A E Akinade (ed.), *New Day: Essays on World Christianity in Honor of Lamin Sanneh*, New York, P Lang, 2010, p. xi.

3   L Manderson and M Jolly, *Sites of Desire, Economies of Pleasure: Sexualities in Asia and the Pacific*, Chicago, University of Chicago Press, 1997, p. 9.

In 1930, the effects of the Wall Street Crash hit Fiji hard, leading to a rise in unemployment and downturn in business.[4] Missionaries Lewis Barnard and L I Linggood were retrenched after only a few months in the colony.[5] Barnard had been stationed at Bua Circuit and, loath to leave this important station unattended, the synod decided that it was the right time to try a system of self-governance, which was to commence on 1 November 1930.[6] Until this point, only European missionaries had been appointed as circuit superintendents, charged with overseeing the payment of ministers' wages and distributing discipline when it was deemed necessary, so the decision to employ a *talatala* (Fijian minister) as superintendent was groundbreaking.[7] The mission had a policy of paying *talatala* considerably less than European missionaries, so the replacement of European missionaries with a *talatala* would ease financial pressure.[8] As discussed in Chapter Two, the mission had instituted a hierarchy in their wage scheme, which was allocated according to race. In 1919, stipends were increased, with European missionaries paid £230 per annum, but the wage hierarchy was still intact in 1930.[9]

The synod sought a *talatala* 'of outstanding ability and worth' to assume the position of 'Assistant of the Superintendent missionary', a title that flagged the hesitation Europeans felt about admitting *talatala* to this position of prestige and responsibility. The synod nominated Aseri Robarobalevu, the son of a minister and not of notable chiefly rank, to the position.[10] Robarobalevu was described as 'one of the outstanding men in the native ministry', 'of choice gifts and ability', with 'commendable zeal and patience'.[11] Filling Barnard's position, Robarobalevu was to minister the Nabouwalu congregation, including government officials, two boys' schools, and a hospital. He was also to train teachers and pastors at the local training institution, where between 20 and

---

4   'The Innocents Abroad: "Sorry to stow away": Some Sidelights on Suva', *Western Mail*, Perth, 14 August 1930, p. 16.

5   Barnard recalled his arrival in Fiji and meeting Linggood. L Barnard, 'Experiences by Land and Sea', 30 Aug 1929 – 11 Feb 1930, Nabouwalu Fiji, Reports and photographs from the Methodist Mission in Fiji, 1929–1930, PMB 1325, NLA, p. 4.

6   A Thornley, 'Custom, Change and Conflict: Fijian Wesleyan Ministers, 1835–1945', in R J May and H Nelson (eds), *Melanesia: Beyond Diversity*, Canberra, Research School of Pacific Studies, The Australian National University, 1982, p. 136.

7   L Wallace has written about missionary wives and surveillance, focusing mainly on the lack of privacy brought about by the need to use the compound 'as a stage for domestic spectacle': L Wallace, 'A House is not a Home: Gender, Space and Marquesan Encounter, 1833–34', *Journal of Pacific History*, vol. 40, no. 3, December 2005, p. 279; See also W Fife, 'Creating the Moral Body: Missionaries and the Technology of Power in Early Papua New Guinea', *Ethnology*, vol. 40, no. 3, 2001, pp. 256–57.

8   Report, Commission to Fiji 1907, CY3465, MOM 238, ML.

9   Annual Synod, 20 October 1919, Annual Synod Minutes and Journals, 1854–1945, together with Miscellaneous Correspondence, 1869–1899, Methodist Church of Fiji, PMB 1138, reel 2, p. 474.

10   'Particulars of the first native minister appointed to a circuit in Fiji formerly worked by a European missionary', F/1/1930, NAF; A Thornley, personal communication, 18 March 2013.

11   R A Gibbons, 1930 Macuata-Bua circuit report, F/6/1926/31, DD/38.

30 students studied at any one time, and oversee other *talatala*, travelling regularly throughout the circuit.[12] McDonald reported to Robarobalevu's benefactor, Robert Smith:[13]

> He has a difficult task and the eyes of Fiji are on him. Should he succeed, then having shown what the present-day Fijian can do, the way is open for others to similar stations, so we shall gradually reach the goal of a self-dependent, self-propagating, indigenous church in Fiji.[14]

The Reverend R A Gibbons inducted Robarobalevu to his new elevated office.[15] When the two men arrived at Bua, they were greeted with a ceremony held in Robarobalevu's honour. Gibbons made a speech, declaring this an 'epoch in the history of the Methodist Church of Fiji'.[16] Chiefs and *talatala* based in Bua also expressed 'gratitude and pride, professing their faith in Robarobalevu'.[17] According to Gibbons, there was overwhelming enthusiasm in the community for the new appointment. Gibbons described Robarobalevu as being overjoyed and comforted by the words of his colleagues and 'the assurances of loyalty', knowing the weight of his responsibility.[18] Ministers from the eastern islands had requested greater involvement in higher levels of the mission throughout the previous 95 years and it was finally coming to fruition.[19] However, it quickly became evident that Robarobalevu would not share the symbolic markers of status afforded their European colleagues.

The anxiety about *talatala* ability to manage finances was evident from the outset, with special arrangements made to minimise Robarobalevu's involvement in taking care of mission money. While Robarobalevu would be appointed to the circuit, he would be paid a lower rate than European superintendents, with money drawn from the balance of missionary contributions and circuit grants held in each circuit's funds. He would not be responsible for circuit finances, with the circuit's funds to be held in reserve. Synod would take responsibility for its expenditure.[20]

---

12   'Particulars of the first native minister appointed to a circuit in Fiji formerly worked by a European missionary', F/1/1930, NAF.
13   A Thornley, personal communication, 18 March 2013.
14   'Particulars of the first native minister appointed to a circuit in Fiji formerly worked by a European missionary', F/1/1930, NAF.
15   Gibbons to McDonald, 22 July 1930, F/1/1930, NAF.
16   Ibid.
17   Ibid.
18   Ibid.
19   A Thornley, '"Through a glass darkly": Ownership of Fijian Methodism, 1850–80', in P Herda (ed.), *Vision and Reality in Pacific Religion*, Canberra, Pandanus Books, 2005, pp. 147–50.
20   District meeting minutes, 1929, CY3040, ML.

Figure 5: 'Native Ministers, Nabouwalu, Welcome to Us'.

Source: Reverend Lewis Barnard, 'Reports and photographs from the Methodist Mission in Fiji', PMB MS 1325. Published with permission of Koraline Killeen.

Figure 6: Inside of mission house, Nabouwalu.

Source: 'Welcome to Us', Reverend Lewis Barnard, 'Reports and photographs from the Methodist Mission in Fiji', PMB MS 1325. Published with permission of Koraline Killeen.

Figure 7: 'Front verandah'.
Source: Reverend Lewis Barnard, 'Reports and photographs from the Methodist Mission in Fiji', PMB MS 1325. Published with permission of Koraline Killeen.

European superintendents typically resided in mission houses in relatively central locations within their designated circuit. This house, often referred to as 'the compound', acted as a base from which to travel and visit congregations.[21] The Reverend Robert H Green, stationed on Bau throughout the late 1930s, wrote that only European missionaries and chiefs were allowed to enter the compound through the front gate, 'while commoners climbed the rough back track up the elevated end of the island'.[22] If a commoner used the gate, their church membership was suspended for three months.[23] There were thus both racial and class boundaries, exemplified by who could or could not enter mission compounds, dictated who could and could not inhabit certain spaces, and how access to these spaces would be gained.

Robarobalevu, who was not European or of chiefly background, would have to go against similar protocol to enter the property at Bua. Fijians were generally excluded from the mission quarters except when invited or when working as domestic labour.[24] In both branches of the Fiji Methodist mission, non-European

---

21 A similar situation was employed in Papua New Guinea, see W Fife, 'Creating the Moral Body: Missionaries and the Technology of Power in Early Papua New Guinea', *Ethnology*, vol. 40, no. 3, 2001, p. 253.
22 R H Green, *My Story: A Record of the Life and Work of Robert H Green*, Melbourne, 1978, p. 188.
23 Ibid.
24 H Cato, stationed on Kadavu, had two boys and two girls working in their home. H Cato, *The House on the Hill*, Melbourne, The Book Depot, 1947, p. 25.

people were employed for domestic work. Missionaries working in the Indo-Fijian mission had wages for domestic labourers incorporated into their pay. This was not a cost incorporated into the wage for non-European ministers — they were expected to do the cleaning themselves or have another type of arrangement.[25] According to the Reverend Robert Green, people on Bau had believed that a European could not 'soil his hands with manual or dirty work'.[26] More aptly, historian David Hilliard's work on the Anglican Melanesian mission depicted the typical 1930s mission residence as 'a self-conscious European outpost, with house-girls, schoolboy servants and a closely observed routine for work and leisure, to which Melanesians were rarely admitted as equals'.[27] Colonial identity was crafted thusly in mission houses.

Robarobalevu had to negotiate the changes to this essentialised hierarchy at Bua. He was not invited to live in the mission house at Nabouwalu. This surprised the local chiefs and *talatala*. Gibbons relayed their reaction to McDonald and requested that Robarobalevu be allowed into the compound, unless the mission wanted a battle on their hands.[28] The earlier euphoria about what seemed like progress towards indigenous governance dissipated when the barriers to equality were realised. While willing to concede the circuit to Robarobalevu's oversight, domestic spaces remained a symbol of European status and privilege that needed to be redefined, spaces that continued to define racial difference, status and prestige.[29] This case study illuminates a moment in which missionaries' visions of mission homes as exemplary models of domesticity and ministry were unsettled.[30] By not allowing Robarobalevu to live in the mission house, missionaries enacted a social convention of exclusion and colonial culture, which highlighted the disparity between the mission's policy for devolution

---

25   R H Green, *My Story: A Record of the Life and Work of Robert H Green*, Melbourne, 1978, p. 250.

26   Ibid., p. 188.

27   D Hilliard, *God's Gentlemen: A History of the Melanesian Mission, 1849–1942*, St Lucia, University of Queensland Press, 1978, p. 272.

28   R A Gibbons to R L McDonald, 22 July 1930, F/1/1930, NAF, p. 4.

29   M Rodman, *Houses Far from Home: British Colonial Space in the New Hebrides*, Honolulu, University of Hawai'i Press, 2001, p. 3; J Rensel and M Rodman, *Home in the Islands: Housing and Social Change in the Pacific*, Honolulu, University of Hawai'i Press, 1997, pp. 7, 14; J Lydon, '"Our sense of beauty": Visuality, Space and Gender on Victoria's Aboriginal Reserves, South-eastern Australia', *History and Anthropology*, vol. 16, no. 2, 2005, p. 212; I Baucom, *Out of Place: Englishness, Empire and the Locations of Identity*, Princeton, Princeton University Press, 1999, p. 4.

30   D Gaitskell, 'Rethinking Gender Roles: The Field Experience of Women Missionaries in South Africa', in A Porter (ed.), *The Imperial Horizons of British Protestant Missions, 1880–1914*, Grand Rapids, Michigan, William B Eerdmans Publishing Company, 2003, p. 139; L Wallace, 'A House is not a Home: Gender, Space and Marquesan Encounter, 1833–34', *Journal of Pacific History*, vol. 40, no. 3, December 2005, p. 279.

and its imperial tendencies. This was similar to exclusionary practices enacted in other colonies throughout the world, which had become part of the protocols of colonialism, a defining feature of the lifestyles of expatriate communities.[31]

Chiefs were important in the renegotiation of the mission's spaces, with the chiefs at Bua pressuring Gibbons to make a complaint. McDonald had been relieved to hear from a chief who was an assistant district commissioner based in Nabouwalu, where Robarobalevu was working. This 'young chief' was in Suva, and he spoke highly of Robarobalevu's work and influence.[32] Consultation with chiefs was still highly valued, despite the lack of chiefs in the ministry, with the mission's chairman consulting privately with chiefs whenever possible. Chiefs acted as intermediaries between the colonial administration, the mission, and the villages. In this instance, chiefs provided support for their *talatala* in ensuring that he was not disadvantaged.

Sufficient evidence is not at hand regarding the outcome of the dispute over access to the mission compound. It was never discussed in the mission's synods. However, there are hints that there were changes made after this incident. The Reverend Robert Green believed it took 'more than a century to quite remove this class distinction that crept into the standing of a missionary, a chief or a European'.[33] Non-European ministers, both Fijian and Indo-Fijian, were all theoretically allowed to move into mission compounds as they became superintendents in the 1940s, yet the Reverend Harold Bock was reluctant to have a *talatala* stay in the mission house at Nailaga, Ba, while he was absent.[34] While it was unclear how this system unravelled, there were certainly still examples of missionaries having indigenous domestic workers clean their homes in the late 1940s.[35] Robarobalevu's appointment was a significant step in moving *talatala* toward a more equal footing with their European counterparts and allowing them greater access to mission spaces.

Despite Gibbons' correspondence in 1930 suggesting that Robarobalevu was receiving considerable support from the chiefs at Bua, he clung to essentialist ideas about the relationship between chiefs and commoners, arguing in his report that year that the chiefly system hindered the 'native ministry':

---

31   U S Mehta, 'Liberal Strategies of Exclusion', in F Cooper and A L Stoler (eds), *Tensions of Empire: Colonial Cultures in a Bourgeois World*, Berkeley, University of California Press, 1997, p. 60; A L Stoler, 'Sexual Affronts and Racial Frontiers: European Identities and the Cultural Politics of Exclusion in Colonial Southeast Asia', in A Brah and A Coombes (eds), *Hybridity and its Discontents: Politics, Science, Culture*, London, Routledge, 2000, pp. 22–23.

32   R L McDonald to R Smith, 25 September 1930, F/1/1930, NAF.

33   R H Green, *My Story: A Record of the Life and Work of Robert H Green*, Melbourne, 1978, p. 188.

34   H Bock to W Green, 2 January 1943, F/1/1944, NAF.

35   D Telfer, *Of Love and Privilege*, Fullarton, South Australia, Colin Telfer, 2009, p. 50.

Though the power of the Fijian chief is diminishing today, he is still an important power in Fijian Society to be reckoned with. However able and reliable a native minister may be, he must respect and carry out the wishes of the chief and all Fijian chiefs are not enlightened nor are they all good men. To antagonise the chief may be to alienate his people also. Hence the difficulty of appointing a native minister to an office in which he must exercise spiritual and moral authority. It is difficult for a Fijian to take care of money even sacred Church monies. A native finds it difficult to refuse a 'kerekere' (a request) made by a chief or a friend.[36]

Gibbons' comment highlighted again the issue of financial responsibility and the implications of kerekere — of having to share their income with their families — for the Methodist community. The responsibilities to their families, chiefs and villages weighed heavily on talatala, and made budgeting difficult. When it was a question of chief or church, the chief often won out.

Gibbons' concerns came from what he had witnessed while working in Fiji. These were real concerns about the continuation of cultural practices. He voiced these at the same time as Indo-Fijian and Fijian Methodists, such as Robarobalevu, gained support from their communities to combat the colonial culture within the mission. Anti-colonial feeling was fed by concurrent discussions held within the colony about political representation for Indo-Fijians in the Fijian legislative assembly.[37] European missionaries clung to the symbols of their prestige, their authority being too entrenched to simply vanish in an instant. Their concerns about the real difficulties in transitioning to self-governance were muffled as a result. Racialist thinking ran alongside missionaries' concern about culture, and both were used to maintain their control. Yet the racialist nature of the mission's systems and the infantilising discourse employed by missionaries increasingly irritated non-European ministers, who were developing their own race consciousness.[38]

The political atmosphere demanded increased responsibility for non-European peoples in all colonial institutions, and the mission used the colonial administration as a benchmark for its own progress, as Fijian roles within the colonial administration were changing at the same time. Ratu Sukuna, who was educated at Oxford, was the only indigenous Fijian in the upper echelons of Fiji's colonial administration by 1930, despite the administration's efforts to

---

36   R A Gibbons, 1930 Macuata-Bua circuit report, F/6/1926/31, DD/38.

37   M Kaplan and J Kelly, 'On Discourse and Power: Cults and Orientals', American Ethnologist, vol. 26, no. 4, 2000, pp. 855–56.

38   Missionaries created their own discourse to infantilise indigenous peoples and perpetuate their position of authority. A L Stoler, Race and the Education of Desire: Foucault's History of Sexuality, Durham, Duke University Press, 1995, p. 6; U S Mehta, 'Liberal Strategies of Exclusion', in F Cooper and A L Stoler (eds), Tensions of Empire: Colonial Cultures in a Bourgeois World, Berkeley, University of California Press, 1997, p. 60.

increase Fijian leadership.[39] McDonald argued that the mission should also move slowly, as it would be difficult to retract autonomy 'once bestowed', and so they had better 'make no mistake when finally we relinquish the reins of authority'.[40]

McDonald continued to find ways to 'indigenise' the mission that did not necessitate handing power to his indigenous colleagues, which meant that he still appeared to be working towards the 'three selves' church policy. As mentioned in Chapter Three, McDonald was interested in the process of embedding the church within the chiefly system by having the institution's structure mirror that of the chiefly society. This meant, ultimately, that there would be strong leadership from the top. According to McDonald's 1931 District Report, this did not require significant change to the existing mission structure. Even though he thought a British-styled Methodist structure had been implanted into Fiji, he believed that it was a 'natural' extension of the Fijian governance system, with the 'head station at the chiefly centre and the subordinate and dependent sections either clustered round in island groups or stringing away along the coasts or following the waterways to the hill districts'.[41] Villages in the hills of Fiji were dependent on chiefly centres to make decisions: 'They are the weaker members of the tribe … and they are financially dependent.'[42] He believed that 'the system of self-support must be laid down along the lines that fit in with the conditions of life and the people'.[43] McDonald then described the mission circuit in a similar fashion. Its outlying stations were dependent on superintendents, who were in turn dependent on the chairman in Suva. The parallels between the mission and the chiefly social structure meant that Methodism was already, in a way, indigenised — it was installed in a pattern familiar to Fijian culture.

The processes of indigenisation and the 'three selves' church concept were central to mission thinking during this period of heightened political awareness around race. Racial exclusivity was a crucial point of contest in the Indo-Fijian branch during the 1930s. Ramsey Deoki, who we met in the previous chapter, had been back in Fiji for three years by 1932, fully trained in Australia for missionary duties, but still not ordained. The mission was faced with the question of where to train Indo-Fijian catechists for ordination, if they were not allowed to attend the Davuilevu theological school. In 1933, the synod finally responded to requests to open ministerial training to Indo-Fijians. Shortly afterwards, three-year courses for Indo-Fijian theological students commenced; students would follow the course with a year as circuit assistants and culminate in a four-

39 R McDonald, Chairman's report, 1931, F/6/1926–31, DD/40.
40 Ibid.
41 Ibid.
42 Ibid.
43 Ibid.

year probation period before ordination.[44] While the path to ordination became clearer for Deoki, he started to wonder how his career would look if he were not to be allocated the same degree of authority or pay as his European colleagues.

Figure 8: 'Esau's/Native Minister's house', Nabouwalu.
Source: Reverend Lewis Barnard, 'Reports and photographs from the Methodist Mission in Fiji', PMB MS 1325. Published with permission of Koraline Killeen.

Signs of Deoki's discontent were obvious when he turned his back on the Methodist mission and joined the Gospel Hall resistance movement that had emerged in Levuka. The Gospel Hall united Indo-Fijians from several Christian denominations who were disaffected with the existing mission. Mr Sperber, described by Burton as a 'religious wanderer', assisted its members.[45] In January 1934, Indo-Fijian Methodists who had attended the Toorak Methodist Church in Suva left to join the Gospel Hall movement and push for self-representation. They may have been attracted to the Gospel Hall because of its rousing hymns, clarity through fundamentalism, or family connections, but it was also clear that they did so primarily because they were frustrated with the Methodist mission's racialist nature, and their frustration was developing into an articulation of anti-colonial feeling. While the Gospel Hall movement was at its height, so too was agitation from Indo-Fijian leaders who wanted self-representation in the

---

44   R H Green, 'Fiji Synod 1933', *The Spectator*, 11 April 1934, p. 301.
45   J W Burton, diary, Visit to Fiji, 11 May 1933, MLMSS 2899 Add On 990, ML.

Legislative Assembly.[46] The Toorak congregation signed a petition demanding to be represented by Indo-Fijian rather than European missionaries, an explicit request for self-representation.[47] That year, despite there being 11 European missionaries and four Indo-Fijian representatives in synod, Europeans still held all the superintendent positions and maintained power in the Indo-Fijian branch. At the very least, Indo-Fijian Methodists in the Gospel Hall movement wanted an Indo-Fijian ministry, with equal numbers of Indo-Fijian and European members in the Indo-Fijian synod. Burton initially dismissed the request. The Reverend W Rex Steadman, leader of the Indo-Fijian branch, was frustrated. He had spoken with numerous members of the movement — Taluri Yohan, Phulkuar, Ram Padarath, and Ishwari Prasad, who was then severely ill — and they had all urged him to speak with Deoki who, discouraged by Burton's response, had remained with the Gospel Hall movement.[48] Steadman reported: 'Ishwari has recently been a strong advocate of reunion ... Ishwari begged me to see Ramsey [Deoki], and said he thought the present position revealed a God-given opportunity for reconciliation.'[49] Steadman sympathised with Deoki's demands. He wrote to Burton:

> The delay in finding an appointment for Ramsey is to them a notable example of our reluctance to appoint Indian preachers to the work. Among ourselves as European members of the staff we maintain that it was financial considerations that prevented an appointment for Ramsey as a preacher, but we have not been able to convince our Indian brethren on this point.[50]

Members of the 'Indo-Fijian branch' rallied in Deoki's defence, unhappy with the limitations imposed upon him and his elevation in the ministry. Burton was intent on downplaying race as an issue, but this grew increasingly difficult as the Gospel Hall members put forward their case.

---

46   M Kaplan and J Kelly, 'On Discourse and Power: Cults and Orientals', *American Ethnologist*, vol. 26, no. 4, 2000, p. 855. J Garrett described the Gospel Hall movement as a sign of dissent from the Methodist Mission. J Garrett, *Footsteps in the Sea: Christianity in Oceania to World War Two*, Suva, University of the South Pacific in conjunction with the World Council of Churches, 1992, p. 396.

47   G H Findlay, 'A Missionary Problem in Fiji', *The Spectator*, 13 January 1932, p. 33; 'India in Fiji', *The Spectator*, 9 June 1920, p. 422; A H Wood, *Overseas Missions of the Australian Methodist Church: Fiji-Indian and Rotuma*, vol. 3, Aldersgate Press, Melbourne, 1978, pp. 63–64.

48   W R Steadman to J W Burton 22 January 1934, Fiji 1934 folder, MOM 524, ML, p. 1.

49   Ibid.

50   Ibid., pp. 1, 3.

Figure 9: 'Mr and Mrs Deoki'.

Source: Photo by R H Rickard and others for the Methodist Church of Australasia, Department of Overseas Missions, 'Series 01: Photographic prints of missionaries and Indigenous people in the Northern Territory, Papua New Guinea, Fiji, Samoa and India, ca 1885–1938', PXA 1137, 490-535, pic acc 7061, neg 21, Mitchell Library, State Library of New South Wales. Published with permission of Uniting Church of Australia.

In June 1934, the Gospel Hall movement again articulated requests for Indo-Fijian representation.[51] South Australian missionary Arthur H Blacket had recently commenced work in the Indo-Fijian mission in 1933 after spending three years at the Methodist mission in Azamgarh, India.[52] He claimed that no one had wanted theological training, but he felt that:

> one of the surest ways to happiness and efficient service in the Indian church is the training of its own ministers here. The great barrier in the way of advance is distrust, and it is only as the future leaders of the Church work and study closely with us that they will gain our confidence, and we theirs.[53]

Building trust was going to be a long and arduous process, and Steadman heeded the advice from other Indo-Fijian Methodists that Deoki would be the key to reconciliation. He maintained in August that Deoki was the 'pioneer of our locally trained ministry in Fiji', a man of 'patience and restraint' who had won the confidence of the congregation.[54] He was a 'good preacher both in English and Hindi', and 'very keen and industrious in his work'.[55] His beliefs were described as 'fundamentalist', which was in line with the Gospel Hall's principles, but he was still receptive to a breadth of opinion.[56] Steadman considered Deoki 'the most promising man that has appeared so far in the history of our work here'.[57] While Steadman tried to smooth the situation, Burton exacerbated tensions, making it clear that racial parameters would be applied if Deoki offered for ordination. Burton wrote to McDonald: 'If Ramsey [Deoki] offers as a candidate for the ministry he offers for the ministry in Fiji just as the Fijian minister does ... His salary too will be fixed on the basis of an Indian minister.'[58] Burton warned that a racially determined pay scale would remain in place: Europeans would continue to receive one rate of pay, Fijians another, and Indo-Fijians another rate again.

One of the main points discussed by Burton, McDonald, Deoki and Steadman was Deoki's efforts to be treated as equal to his European colleagues. Deoki had made it clear that he was not happy with the lack of opportunity afforded to him in Fiji. Since 1930, Deoki had wondered whether he would have to return to Australia for further education in order to obtain equal status with European

---

51   W R Steadman to J W Burton, 7 June 1934, Fiji 1934 folder, MOM 524, p. 4.

52   A H Wood, *Overseas Missions of the Australian Methodist Church: Fiji-Indian and Rotuma¸* vol. 3, Aldersgate Press, Melbourne, 1978, p. 98.

53   A Blacket to J W Burton, 18 June 1934, Fiji 1934 folder, MOM 524.

54   W R Steadman quoted in letter from J W Burton to R McDonald, 17 August 1934, Fiji 1934 folder, MOM 524, ML, p. 2.

55   Ibid., p. 1.

56   Ibid.

57   Ibid., p. 2.

58   J W Burton to R L McDonald, 17 August 1934, Fiji, 1934, MOM 524, ML, p. 2.

missionaries.[59] By October 1934, Burton had made it clear that Deoki's ordination would not secure his equality with his European colleagues in Fiji or Australia. He elaborated on this point by discussing the various potential developments that might occur if Deoki were to seek work elsewhere. Australia's immigration policy would make it difficult for Deoki to move there, so Burton suggested that he look to New Zealand where he might have more opportunities. Burton elaborated:

> We could not imagine Ramsey with his wife and Indian children being settled in any of our [Australian] circuits, and in any case the Immigration act would make it impossible, and the best we could do would be to get a permit to reside in Australia from year to year for educational purposes.[60]

Burton suggested that Deoki follow in the footsteps of the Reverend Raymond Dudley, who had been taken by Hannah Dudley and raised in New Zealand, where he undertook theological training.[61] Despite receiving the same training as his Australian colleagues, the mission board in Sydney felt that 'there was not the slightest hope of Ramsey being accepted as a candidate on the same basis as a candidate in Australia, that is, having the right to a circuit in New South Wales and all other particular privileges of a minister here in this stage'.[62] The 'White Australia' policy shaped Burton's response to Deoki — a reality over which neither Burton nor Deoki had any control. Yet it was evident that the national immigration policy equated with Burton's own racial thinking. Burton compared Deoki with Raymond Dudley.[63] Burton wrote: 'Raymond Dudley is an Indian only by birth, and by education and association is an Englishman. This cannot be said of Ramsey.'[64] Burton's comparison between Dudley and Deoki revealed the distinction he drew between culture and race. In Burton's thinking, a person raised within European culture could pass as a European, despite being born an 'Indian'. Christianity, from Burton's perspective, was not a prerequisite for acceptance, and race trumped any evidence of cultural change. Burton's ideas about race and culture, shaped by his experience of Australian politics and policies, his knowledge of anthropology, and his time in Fiji, influenced the Methodist mission board's approach to the challenges in the Indo-Fijian branch.

59   A H Wood, *Overseas Missions of the Australian Methodist Church: Fiji-Indian and Rotuma*, vol. 3, Aldersgate Press, Melbourne, 1978, p. 81.
60   J W Burton to R L McDonald 16 October 1934, Fiji 1934 folder, MOM 524, ML, p. 1.
61   R Dudley became President of New Zealand's Methodist Church in 1956. For further information, see M Sidal, *Hannah Dudley: Hamari Maa: Honoured Mother, Educator, and Missioner to the Indentured Indians in Fiji, 1864–1931*, Suva, Fiji, Pacific Theological College Press, 1997, p. 72.
62   J W Burton to R L McDonald 16 October 1934, Fiji 1934 folder, MOM 524, ML, p. 1.
63   M Sidal, *Hannah Dudley: Hamari Maa: Honoured Mother, Educator, and Missioner to the Indentured Indians in Fiji, 1864–1931*, Suva, Fiji, Pacific Theological College Press, 1997, p. 95.
64   J W Burton to R L McDonald 16 October 1934, Fiji 1934 folder, MOM 524, ML, p. 2.

Despite Burton's opinion, the synod accepted Deoki as one of the two first Indo-Fijian candidates to stand for the ministry in 1934. The other candidate was George Prakash.[65] The synod attendees declared that Deoki's candidacy marked 'the Indianisation of our church in Fiji', a step towards awarding 'a greater share in the Government and development of the church' with Indo-Fijian adherents.[66] Prakash later withdrew his candidacy, leaving Deoki to forge this new path in the ministry alone. It was not considered necessary for him to go through the entire theological training at Davuilevu, and he went in to his probation straight away under the guidance of the Reverend W Rex Steadman at Lautoka, who was still the head of the Indo-Fijian branch.[67] This was the same style of training provided to catechists in the Indian mission at Azamgarh.[68] Steadman and Deoki discussed the racial issues at length, with Steadman reporting to McDonald by November that Deoki disliked 'the distinctions in the ranks of our ministry made merely on racial grounds', that they were 'undesirable and unfair … they should have equal standing and status with other ministers in the church'.[69] Steadman also corresponded with Burton on this point, but to no avail — the status of Indo-Fijian mission workers was fixed for the time being.[70]

During the early 1930s, Burton's approach was increasingly informed by the work of Adolphus Peter Elkin, an ordained Anglican priest who by 1934 was employed as an anthropologist by the University of Sydney.[71] Burton met Elkin at various missionary conferences and through their work on the National Missionary Council. Elkin published widely on matters relating to Australia and the Pacific on the cultural change in indigenous communities that had resulted from colonialism. Elkin's publications had influenced mission policies in the Pacific, and his theories did not require a great shift in Burton's thinking — both presented cultural change as part of progressive social evolution.[72] In Australia, Elkin suggested that 'civilising agents' such as missionaries were

---

65   District meeting minutes, 1934, Shot 48, MOM 202, CY 3045, ML, p. 35

66   Indian session of Synod, 10 October 1934, Shot 52, p. 39; A H Wood, *Overseas Missions of the Australian Methodist Church: Fiji-Indian and Rotuma*, vol. 3, Aldersgate Press, Melbourne, 1978, p. 81.

67   For example minutes of district meeting, 1937, MOM 270 CY3286, ML; A H Wood, *Overseas Missions of the Australian Methodist Church: Fiji-Indian and Rotuma*, vol. 3, Aldersgate Press, Melbourne, 1978, p. 81.

68   A H Wood, *Overseas Missions of the Australian Methodist Church: Fiji-Indian and Rotuma*, vol. 3, Aldersgate Press, Melbourne, 1978, p. 81.

69   W R Steadman to R L McDonald, 26 November 1934, F/1/1934, NAF.

70   W R Steadman to J W Burton, 22 January 1934, Fiji 1934 folder, MOM 524, ML, p. 1.

71   G Gray, 'From Nomadism to Citizenship: A P Elkin and Aboriginal Advancement', in N Peterson and N Sanders (eds), *Citizenship and Indigenous Australians: Changing Conceptions and Possibilities*, Cambridge, Cambridge University Press, 1998, p. 56; R McGregor, 'From Old Testament to New: A P Elkin on Christian Conversion and Cultural Assimilation', *Journal of Religious History*, vol. 25, no. 1, 2001, p. 39.

72   T Wise, *A P Elkin: The Self-made Anthropologist*, Sydney, George Allen and Unwin, 1985, p. 135; see Burton's rhetoric in 'Native races: Problems of the Pacific. Rev J W Burton's address', *The Sydney Morning Herald*, 19 February 1935, p. 8; G Gray, 'From Nomadism to Citizenship: A P Elkin and Aboriginal Advancement', in N Peterson and N Sanders (eds), *Citizenship and Indigenous Australians: Changing Conceptions and Possibilities*, Cambridge, Cambridge University Press, 1998, p. 58.

to 'preserve and modify or supplant the aboriginal view of life and the rites and practices arising from it, that primitive man may still feel at home in the universe'.[73] Burton used Elkin's studies to think through the anti-colonialism in the Pacific. This was evident in a speech he made in 1935, as questions about the inclusion of Indo-Fijians in the Legislative Assembly were debated at length in Fiji's colonial administration:[74]

> The growth of nationalism, with its eager cries of 'Fiji for the Fijian!', 'India for the Indians', had brought with it a reaction against European control. This should be met, not with a dominating, masterful spirit, but on lines of human brotherhood and comradeship. The ideal to be striven for was an indigenous church, self-propagating, self-supporting, self-governing. The missionary motive, although ever the same, must express itself in ways to meet today's needs.[75]

This speech signalled a considerable shift in Burton's thinking. He had moved from a belief in the need to have European missionaries in the field to oversee and guide non-European peoples through social change, to a position that encouraged a more equitable relationship between European missionaries and 'native' ministers. The messages of discontent from the mission field likely pushed Burton to question the paternalism of earlier decades. Burton was reconsidering his approach to the 'three selves' church model, but his interpretation of what 'today's needs' were and how indigenous people might be prepared for them still centred on industrial education. He hoped to ensure that non-European peoples were 'fit' for the 'oncoming of civilisation'.[76] If missionaries were to protect indigenous peoples from the evils of civilisation, they had to teach 'natives to be peasant proprietors in their own right, to use to the best advantage the tools which were obtainable in their own villages'.[77]

The tensions that surrounded discourses of labour and land were also addressed at the Davuilevu theological school. With Indo-Fijian catechists now able to enrol at Davuilevu, changes were made to the theological curriculum to incorporate church history and contemporary religion, the latter including Hinduism and Islam. The idea was to make education more inclusive for all attendees. A H Blacket taught this subject when Robert Green was principal, believing that increased understanding and awareness of other religions would 'help lessen the pressures that were growing between the races as the Indians

---

73 A P Elkin, 'Civilised Aborigines and Native Culture', *Oceania*, vol. 6, no. 2, 1935, p. 145.

74 D Scarr, *Ratu Sukuna: Soldier, Statesman, Man of Two Worlds*, London, Macmillan Education for the Ratu Sir Lala Sukuna biography committee, 1980, pp. 110–11.

75 'Missionary Difficulties. Rev J W Burton's Analysis', *The Advertiser*, South Australia, 25 May 1935, p. 15.

76 'Missionary Work', *The West Australian*, Perth, 9 June 1934, p. 14.

77 Ibid.

were already showing signs of becoming the dominant race in Fiji', which Green referred to as an 'alien intrusion'.[78] 'We brought these wide awake Asians to the Pacific', he quipped, 'who through suffering have won through to success'.[79]

Despite the persisting racial system, Deoki returned to work in the mission and was given increasing levels of responsibility. By 1937 he was working in the Penang circuit of the Indo-Fijian branch, at Rakiraki. He answered directly to the mission's chairman in a similar fashion to his European colleagues who were appointed as superintendents.[80] In 1938 he was paid £180 per annum, and was permitted to employ Ishwari Prasad, an Indo-Fijian catechist, as a supernumerary for £2 per week.[81] He was slowly receiving greater responsibility and financial reward for his work.[82] In 1939, as the decade drew to a close, celebrations were organised for his ordination. It was a monumental accomplishment after a drawn-out battle for equal training and status.

While it seemed that the Fijian membership had more opportunities for leadership than the Indo-Fijian Methodists, the Reverend Charles Oswald Lelean, who in 1939 was acting chairman as McDonald had left the mission field, reflected pessimistically on the process of installing Fijian ministers to superintendent posts. A self-proclaimed 'conservative die-hard', Lelean was dubious about implementing circuit independence, citing financial matters as the principal problem that would delay the transition to self-support. When Fijian self-support had been trialled previously, he said that *talatala* had starved: 'a pitiable story which I suppose will never be told'.[83] He had been making the argument that laymen would struggle to manage circuit finances for 30 years, and believed that making circuits self-supporting would result in the 'misappropriation of church funds'.[84] He wrote:

> I am not mentioning this by way of disparaging the moral character of the Fijian. We must make every allowance for his psychological peculiarities. But we must accept the fact of his lack of financial exactness. Even the average Native Minister today is incapable of managing the finances of his section.[85]

78   R H Green, *My Story: A Record of the Life and Work of Robert H Green*, Melbourne, 1978, p. 243.

79   Ibid.

80   Minutes District Meeting, 1937, CY3286, MOM 270, ML.

81   Prasad died in 1940. The obituary in the mission's minutes said that he was born in Sanjaharpur, Uttar Pradesh, India, in 1871. His parents had been Christian, and he was speaking at revivals by the age of 18. He went to Bareilly College and was head catechist at CMS Calcutta during his 20s, before working at the Methodist mission at Azamgarh. In 1913 he had offered for work in Fiji. Indian ministerial session 1938, PMB 1138, reel 2, p. 1.

82   Ibid.

83   C O Lelean to J W Burton, 19 July 1939, Fiji district correspondence regarding constitution, MOM 386, ML.

84   Ibid., p. 3.

85   Ibid.

Charles Lelean believed that the mission needed a 'better type of Native Minister', equal or superior to Fijian teachers and government administrators.[86] However, in an institution where class and prestige mattered, Charles Lelean wondered what relationship a superior minister would have with his European colleagues or the 'older type' of *talatala*, and suspected they would not be paid the same as their European colleagues, but rather remuneration 'approximate to that of the trained teacher or other government employee'.[87] He described a system of self-governance that he felt would work best, suggesting that a Fijian superintendent be sent to each province, with oversight of the 'old type' of ministers, with European missionaries retained as deputy chairmen to manage the circuit finances.[88]

Charles Lelean did not explicitly connect financial incompetence with the communal system or the chiefs, but he urged the mission to continue to recognise chiefly power, which was:

> supposed to be waning, but it is still a power to be reckoned with. Each new missionary going to Fiji should be willing to jettison some of his democratic ideas, and make allowances for the authority of the chiefs. We divide our church at home into ministerial and lay. But in Fiji there is a third element — the chiefs.[89]

Charles Lelean was aware that endorsing chiefly authority challenged missionaries who sought a more egalitarian structure, and that chiefs were still associated with the idea of 'primitive' societies. Missionaries still wondered how the Indo-Fijian branch of the church would overcome its own internal social stratification.

The events of the 1930s forced missionaries to extrapolate and explain their reasons for supporting an organisation designed on race, culture and class. There were numerous practicalities to consider, but both the missionaries and non-European Methodists were increasingly aware of the racial dynamic that shaped their working lives. The protocols around who could access certain public or private spaces, and who could hold positions of authority and status were reassessed. Racial theories and colonial culture continued to reinforce European hegemony, but Methodist communities throughout Fiji, in both the Fijian and Indo-Fijian branches, consistently pushed the boundaries.

Australian anthropology, popular with John W Burton, was used to support the proliferation of separate spheres within the mission. Anthropological theories filtered into the Fiji mission field through his publications, and his concepts of

---

86   Ibid.
87   Ibid.
88   Ibid., p. 4.
89   Ibid.

culture and race that informed discussions in the ecumenical movement for the development of native churches. As in earlier decades, missionaries hoped that they could assuage anti-colonial sentiment by fostering the positive elements of emerging nationalisms in the colony.[90] Missionaries used the promise of devolution, especially the promise of self-government, to abate virulent new nationalisms, but were not necessarily ready to see authority pass out of European hands.

---

90   D Wetherell, *Charles Abel and the Kwato Mission of Papua New Guinea 1891–1975*, Melbourne, Melbourne University Press, 1996, p. xvi.

CHAPTER SIX

Colonialism and Culture Throughout the Pacific War

Theories about culture, combined with the missionary imperative to produce 'native' churches, had led to the creation of a racial hierarchy within the mission by the 1940s. While the mission increasingly included Fijian and Indo-Fijian ministers into its spheres of government, there were still modes by which missionaries distanced themselves from their non-European colleagues and projected their own seniority.[1] Fijian-born ministers were increasingly frustrated by the racialist system and were finding new ways to articulate their disaffection. To appease them, the mission board, still led by General Secretary John W Burton, continued to push the 'three selves' church policy, trying to increase, in controlled ways, greater non-European representation in leadership positions. However, just as had been the case between Burton and the previous chairman, Richard McDonald, there were tensions with the new chairman, the Reverend William Green, from 1938 to 1947.[2] This chapter looks at missionaries' continued efforts to understand and manage the mission's colonial culture, from commissions to providing missionaries with anthropological training. Functional anthropology still prompted missionaries to question the morality of colonialism. Accusations of racism from ministers in Fiji could

1   A L Stoler, 'Sexual Affronts and Racial Frontiers: European Identities and the Cultural Politics of Exclusion in Colonial Southeast Asia', in A Brah and A Coombes (eds), *Hybridity and its Discontents: Politics, Science, Culture*, London, Routledge, 2000, pp. 22–23.
2   William Green had previously worked in Papua, R H Green, *My Story: A Record of the Life and Work of Robert H Green*, Melbourne, 1978, p. 184; A H Wood, *Overseas Missions of the Australian Methodist Church: Fiji*, vol. 2, Melbourne, Aldersgate Press, 1978, p. 391.

no longer be ignored, nor could the grumblings from the broader Methodist community.[3] It was during these war years that earlier bids to challenge European hegemony crystallised in moments of polite confrontation.

Throughout this period, international mission networks still influenced the Methodists in Fiji, prompting its leaders to regularly consider the processes by which the mission could develop into a fully fledged church. The mission sent its first non-European representative to the 1938 International Missionary Council Conference, held in Madras, India. This was the Rotuman minister, the Reverend Wilisoni Inia, who travelled to the conference with the Reverend Arthur Blacket, a European missionary who was representing the Indo-Fijian mission branch.[4] Conference delegates at Madras reiterated the need to encourage 'younger', 'native' churches to develop and to transfer governance to indigenous ministers.[5] The conference was charged with idealism. With such a vast array of mission fields represented, it was not easy to prescribe a model for devolution that would suit all situations. However, one important concept was discussed at this particular conference that was subsequently adopted in the Fijian mission field. This was the 'indigenisation' of Christianity. Until then, missionaries at these conferences had referred to the burgeoning churches as 'younger' or 'native' churches. They now started to think about 'indigenous' churches, and the 'indigenisation' of Christianity. The process of 'indigenisation', discussed at the 1938 mission conference in Tambaram for example, offered something slightly new, a progression in the belief that the churches had to be transformed to fit within their local cultural context.[6] The term 'indigenisation' came to sum up the 'three selves' church concept; the ideal of self-support, self-propagation and self-governance was increasingly linked to a broader effort to acculturate Christianity.

The Madras conference delivered the message that indigenous churches should not be 'copies of the Churches in the West in economic, social and cultural matters'.[7] If western powers were to leave their colonies, as delegates suspected might occur in the near future, indigenous missions needed to rely on their own financial systems. Evidently, the ethnicised and hierarchical system of wage allocation that had been adopted in Fiji throughout previous decades had

3   A L Stoler, 'Sexual Affronts and Racial Frontiers: European Identities and the Cultural Politics of Exclusion in Colonial Southeast Asia', in A Brah and A Coombes (eds), *Hybridity and its Discontents: Politics, Science, Culture*, London, Routledge, 2000, p. 19.
4   See A Howard, *Hef Ran Ta (The Morning Star): A Biography of Wilson Inia, Rotuma's First Senator*, Suva, Institute of Pacific Studies, 1994.
5   B Stanley, *The World Missionary Conference, Edinburgh 1910*, Grand Rapids, Eerdmans, 2009, p. 309; 'Confirms Unity of the Church: Madras Conference Opens Today', *The Advertiser*, South Australia, 12 December 1938, p. 22; 'Mission Conference, World Meeting at Madras', *The West Australian*, Perth, 29 November 1938, p. 3.
6   E J Schoonhaven, 'Tambaram 1938', *International Review of Missions*, vol. 67, 1978, p. 306.
7   Ibid., p. 313.

been used in other mission fields. The rate of ministers' pay had often been decided based on the assumed living standards of their cultural practices. Conference delegates also suggested that self-support models 'should not be judged by western norms', and that 'the cultural identity of these peoples will have to show itself also on the economic and social level'.[8] Henry Venn, who is widely considered the father of the concept of the 'three selves church' idea, had believed that native ministers should be paid a wage similar to that earned by members of their congregation, so that there would not be a gulf created between ministers and their congregations.[9] However, the stratified wage system was progressively more problematic as race consciousness increased. European assumptions about culture had been used as the framework for the mission's administration and pay schemes, because this was the policy pulsating from the heart of the global mission movement. Non-European ministers in the field increasingly detested its racial undertones.

European missionaries still had a degree of autonomy and could address the 'indigenisation' process as they saw fit. Harold Bock replaced Arthur Lelean as superintendent at Nailaga. He arrived in Fiji in 1936, stationed first at Lau, and then moving to Nailaga in Ra circuit. Unlike many missionaries before him, Bock did not see Fijian and Indo-Fijian cultures as irreconcilable, or believe that the mission should be so separate. He was appointed to serve in the Fijian branch of the mission, yet in 1939 he was anxious to start learning Hindi, thinking it would be helpful around the north-west of Viti Levu, which was home to a large part of the Indo-Fijian population.[10] Racial boundaries had been constructed around language difference in the past, and Bock believed that it was important to continue preaching in Fijian and Indo-Fijian languages, but that the mission's workers should transcend those linguistic boundaries and speak all of the colony's dominant languages.

Another minister who was to be instrumental in challenging the existing boundaries within the mission arrived on Suva Wharf in 1941. The Reverend Maurice Wilmshurst met the Reverend Alan Tippett and his family at the wharf. He escorted them in a taxi, and they passed through the 'Indian section' of Suva and along 'All Nation's Street' to the Toorak mission compound, where they spent their first night, before travelling to the Nadroga mission circuit house at Cuvu.[11] From his first day in Fiji, Tippett was aware of the segregated nature of Fijian society, and was watchful of World War II's impact on the colony. Tippett had arrived in Fiji just six months before Japan's military bombed the

---

8   Ibid.
9   P Williams, *The Ideal of the Self-Governing Church: A Study in Victorian Missionary Strategy,* Leiden, E J Brill, 1990, pp. 6–7.
10   H Bock to W Green, 16 February 1939, F/1/1939, NAF p. 2.
11   A R Tippett to friends and family, 16 May 1941, TIP 70/39/1/3, p. 2.

American base at Pearl Harbour. There was already a military presence in the colony. Troops had already been stationed on the west side of the island at Nadi, and a military camp established at Dilkusha, the Indo-Fijian mission station at Nausori.[12]

The mission mirrored the colonial administration's bids to safeguard Fijian interests, continuing to acquire land through negotiation with *mataqali* landowners — according to the protectionist land tenure system, for example.[13] While missionaries supported Fijian land access, they also occasionally represented the Indo-Fijian community in land negotiations. For example, William Green and W Rex Steadman visited Fijian land owners to negotiate land use for the Indo-Fijian mission station at Penang, 'and ask them "*vaka-Viti*" [in the Fijian way] to lease the land to us'.[14] In this instance, missionaries acted in a triumvirate with the colonial administration and Fijian landowners to negotiate the terms on which Indo-Fijians would use the land, enhancing the sense that Indo-Fijians were on the outer, separate and isolated.

Although European missionaries tended to give Fijian interests precedence in the mission, Fijians still resisted European hegemony. The farmers from Toko articulated their desire for a national Fijian church. During the Fijian session of the 104th Annual Methodist Fiji District Synod, which opened on 13 October 1941, the Toko farmers approached the mission's chairman, William Green, who was seated with Maurice Wilmshurst, then superintendent of the Suva Indo-Fijian circuit, and the Reverend Robert Green, principal of Davuilevu. The farmers presented 118 *tabua* (whale teeth), collected from chiefs throughout the islands, and £500.[15] The presentation involved a lengthy speech, done in customary fashion. Seated in the prime position to oversee proceedings, the chairman witnessed the changing tide — the sands were shifting under the feet of the European ministry. The farmers asked William Green to fulfil the promise of self-government and self-support.[16]

Ratu Nacanieli Rawaidranu and the Reverend Arthur Lelean had been instrumental to this petition. In 1936, the year that Arthur Lelean left the circuit and returned to Australia, the farmers pledged to work towards a separate Fijian church conference. Many details remain obscured as to who initially came up with the idea to appeal for a Fijian church. Under Rawaidranu's leadership, wages

12   Ibid.; B V Lal, *Broken Waves: A History of the Fiji Islands in the Twentieth Century*, Honolulu, University of Hawai'i Press, 1992, p. 113.

13   J Overton, 'The Limits of Acculturation: Changing Land Tenure in Fiji', *Journal of Peasant Studies*, vol. 19, no. 2, 1992, p. 328.

14   W Green to H Bock, 23 March 1939, F/1/1939, NAF, p. 1.

15   'Methodist Mission 104th Annual Synod', *Fiji Times and Herald*, 15 October 1941, p. 5.

16   M Tomlinson, 'Passports to Eternity: Whale's Teeth and Transcendence in Fijian Methodism', in L Manderson, W Smith and M Tomlinson (eds), *Flows of Faith: Religious Reach and Community in Asia and the Pacific*, Melbourne, Springer, 2012, p. 223.

were collected from the farmers and put towards credit at Morris Hedstrom for labourers and their families, as well as the fund for a self-supporting church.[17] The farmers were aware of the mission's debt of £4,658, and though they could not pay it, they hoped to raise funds in Australia and Fiji to pay off the debt, so as to 'achieve our goal'.[18] They wanted an autonomous church, 'for it is a sign of weakness to be leaning on others and not making decisions for ourselves'.[19] The farmers believed the church provided an avenue through which to display the strength of the *vanua* — Fijian people, culture and land.

The decision to take *tabua* to the 1941 synod was deliberate. By presenting both *tabua* and money, the farmers enlisted both indigenous and colonial cultural capital. The *tabua* — yellowed, riveted and linked at each end to rough roped sennit — at once symbolised the connection between the giver and receiver, and embodied 'everything that is chiefly in nature, including chiefly behaviour and socially valued chiefly qualities'.[20] It catered to the chiefly factions in the church and the European missionaries' understanding of the ongoing pre-eminence of chiefly opinion in the church.[21] The Toko farmers had collected the *tabua* through the *vakaturaga* practice, through appealing to chiefs, suggestive of a pan-Fijian chiefly alliance in support of the request.[22] The *tabua* were material symbols that marked the connectedness of the *vanua*.[23] As Gosden and Marshall have demonstrated, *tabua* reflect a link between the past and the present through their biographies, handed from person to person in constant transition. While the biographies of the *tabua* were important in recognising the longevity of the desire for self-governance within the mission, they also bore the future imaginings of the mission. A presentation of *tabua* also suggested dissatisfaction with the trajectory the community seemed to be on, recognition that transformation was needed to transcend the 'entanglements of the *vanua*'.[24]

---

17   K Close, field notes, Yaladro, 2010; *Talanoa*, Senivalati Toroki and Emosi Tabumasi, nephews of N Rawaidranu, June 2013.

18   M G Wilmshurst to C F Gribble, 12 Sept 1949, File 1949, Movement for independent conference in Fiji, MOM Correspondence and papers, Fiji 1905–1953

19   Ibid.

20   M Tomlinson, 'Passports to Eternity: Whale's Teeth and Transcendence in Fijian Methodism', in L Manderson, W Smith and M Tomlinson (eds), *Flows of Faith: Religious Reach and Community in Asia and the Pacific*, Melbourne, Springer, 2012, pp. 219, 221; A D Ravuvu, *The Fijian Ethos*, Suva, Institute of Pacific Studies, University of the South Pacific, 1987, pp. 22–23, as cited in A Arno, 'Cobo and Tabua in Fiji: Two Forms of Cultural Currency in an Economy of Sentiment', *American Ethnologist*, vol. 32, no. 1, 2005, p. 54.

21   Ibid.

22   A D Ravuvu, *The Fijian Ethos*, Suva, Institute of Pacific Studies, University of the South Pacific, 1987, p. 324.

23   C Gosden and Y Marshall, 'The Cultural Biography of Objects', *World Archaeology*, vol. 31, no. 2, 1999, p. 170.

24   M Tomlinson, 'Passports to Eternity: Whale's Teeth and Transcendence in Fijian Methodism', in L Manderson, W Smith and M Tomlinson (eds), *Flows of Faith: Religious Reach and Community in Asia and the Pacific*, Melbourne, Springer, 2012, p. 227.

The *tabua* carried the farmers' hopes for the future; by transferring the *tabua* to the hands of William Green, they hoped that he would consider their request and enact their plan for self-governance.[25]

The farmers wrote a letter, entitled 'The new way in which advance may be sought', that outlined their aims and wants.[26] The farmers wanted to be 'partners in establishing the Methodist Church'.[27] They did not expect that the mission would become independent for a number of years, and did not hope to separate from the Australian General Conference, or for the European staff to leave the colony.[28] They wanted European missionaries to 'lead us or teach us until the time they think that we can be left to ourselves and if it is approved, some of our youths be trained in Theological Institutions in Australia'.[29]

The scheme relied on chiefly networks to levy support in the broader Fijian community.[30] The farmers had intended to go to the Council of Chiefs and explain the scheme to gain support, believing that the chiefs would 'not be able to neglect it for the Church and land is theirs'.[31] The rhetoric of exclusion, tradition, chiefs (*turaga*), *lotu* and *vanua* were adopted to describe the aims of the farmers — this was a Fijian movement for a Fijian church. The synod accepted the money and placed it in a trust. By accepting the *tabua,* the chairman signalled his acceptance of responsibility to fulfil the farmers' request.[32] Wilmshurst wrote that the 'the upshot of the discussion' was that synod had been given the money and yet were left to define the timing of the transition to independence.[33] Robert Green's 1943 article in *The Spectator* offers another perspective on the outcome of the conversation. He suggested that the post-war period would be a time of true reconciliation in the mission, one that required further planning, in which international church bodies would be the main driving force behind a movement to stop 'misunderstanding and falsehood and prejudice and racialism'.[34] The main message was that the mission was not yet ready for devolution. When the matter was reconsidered in 1948, synod decided that the mission should work to clarify and develop the Toko farmers'

---

25   V Cretton, 'Traditional Fijian Apology as a Political Strategy', *Oceania*, vol. 75, no. 4, 2005, pp. 406–7.

26   M G Wilmshurst to C F Gribble, 12 Sept 1949, Movement for independent conference in Fiji, MOM Correspondence and papers, Fiji 1905–1953, File 1949.

27   Ibid.

28   Ibid.

29   Ibid.

30   Ibid.

31   Ibid.

32   For more recent examples of *tabua* presentation in the Fijian Methodist church, see J E Bush, 'Land and Communal Faith: Methodist Belief and Ritual in Fifi [sic]', *Studies in World Christianity*, vol. 6, no. 1, 2000, p. 30; J W Turner, 'Blessed to Give and Receive: Ceremonial Exchange in Fiji', *Ethnography*, vol. 26, no. 3, 1987, p. 212.

33   M G Wilmshurst to C F Gribble, 12 Sept 1949, Movement for independent conference in Fiji, MOM Correspondence and papers, Fiji 1905–1953, File 1949, ML.

34   R H Green, *My Story: A Record of the Life and Work of Robert H Green*, Melbourne, 1978, p. 265.

plans. Wilmshurst suggested that this 'movement has come and will grow and it requires that we think with them and guide them. This does not mean immediate independence for the Fijian Church but that we now assume the lead.'[35]

Rawaidranu died in 1941. Neither he nor Arthur Lelean were able to attend the presentation at the 1941 synod. Samisoni Lalaqila, Rawaidranu's nephew, led the farmers after Rawaidranu's death and helped to establish the Toko auxiliary, a formal organisation that represented the farmers. Noticing that change was not immediate, Lalaqila tried to find out what had happened to the farmers' money, corresponding with William Green and Arthur Lelean. Wilmshurst corresponded with Arthur Lelean about the Toko farmers' finances after their secretary, Akarifa Aravure, made enquiries in 1948.[36] In his response, Arthur Lelean recalled the intimidation that the farmers had experienced:

> ... native farmers would just be about to plant a crop on soil prepared by great effort — often by moonlight — and an officer would appear with demands for 1 pound per head for Government, tax, *soli* ... and absence from Town Duties. The money was always available from Ratu Naca [Ratu Nacanieli Rawaidranu], who carried pencil and paper with him, and a messenger or two for a sprint to Nailaga Ba. But the 'catch' was to catch the men before the messengers would make a book, and he was only one. Other opposition was just as acute later ...[37]

The *galala* sites had been monitored closely.[38] While historian Timothy Macnaught argued that the communities had enjoyed a short burst of enthusiasm before 'going to sleep', the mission archives and recollections of the farmers' families show that while the Navatu company might have stalled in 1938 when the 10-year lease ended at Toko, the farmers continued to function as an auxiliary group, to pursue their hopes for a Fijian *Lotu Wesele*.[39]

---

35 M G Wilmshurst to C F Gribble, 12 Sept 1949, Movement for independent conference in Fiji, MOM Corr and papers, Fiji 1905–1953, File 1949. Garrett noted that missionaries accepted the need to change but that it did not necessarily occur in a manner that the farmers expected. J Garrett, *Where Nets Were Cast: Christianity in Oceania since World War Two*, Suva, Institute of Pacific Studies, University of the South Pacific in association with the World Council of Churches, 1997, p. 392.

36 M G Wilmshurst to A D Lelean, 18 May 1948, F/3/1947–8m, NAF; W Green to A D Lelean, 31 Oct 1948, F/3/1947–8m, NAF. It is unclear from these letters what finances Aravure was inquiring about, whether it was funds donated to the church or something to do with the Navatu company.

37 A D Lelean to M G Wilmshurst, 10 July 1948, F/3/1947–8m, pp. 1–2.

38 T Macnaught, 'Chiefly Civil Servants? Ambiguity in District Administration in the Preservation of the Fijian Way of Life, 1896–1940', *Journal of Pacific History*, vol. 9, 1974, p. 14; T Macnaught, *The Fijian Colonial Experience: A Study of the Neotraditional Order Under British Colonial Rule Prior to World War II*, Canberra, ANU Press, Pacific Research Monograph Number 7, 1982, p. 140.

39 T Macnaught, 'Chiefly Civil Servants? Ambiguity in District Administration in the Preservation of the Fijian Way of Life, 1896–1940', *Journal of Pacific History*, vol. 9, 1974, p. 14; K Close-Barry, *talanoa*, Senivalati Toroki and Emosi Tabumasi, nephews of N Rawaidranu, June 2013.

Having heard the farmers' demands, European missionaries conceded that the time had come to accelerate efforts to decolonise the mission. Burton demanded better missionaries and administrators for the Pacific, advocating for missionaries and administrators to train in anthropology, and for government anthropologists to be appointed in mission fields. His ideas echoed Elkin's treatise for missions from nearly 10 years prior.[40] Burton's critique of missionary efforts had offended several missionaries still in the field. William Green wrote to Bock in 1944 quoting some of the mission board's minutes: 'Some things are becoming clearer in regard to the missionary effort. The first is that we must obtain a more capable and better equipped type of missionary.'[41] Green was so aggrieved by the insinuation that current mission workers were doing a poor job that he threatened to leave the mission, believing that the board sought an opportunity to replace him. Bock consoled him and managed to soothe Green's wounded ego.[42]

It was clear that industry was bringing swift changes to the Pacific, and Burton was convinced that less educated missionaries would struggle to keep pace with the modern era. The war brought new job opportunities and the colonial administration alleviated some of the strict labour legislation of earlier decades, raising hopes that the mission would receive higher financial contributions from its membership. In 1940, Bock assessed how the increasing industrialisation of Viti Levu's north-west was impacting the mission's finances and found that, despite the increase in personal incomes for Fijian families, the mission's revenue was falling. Some sections of the circuit raised their quota year after year, and built new churches, he reported, but others dwindled.[43] He blamed the 'utter weakness of some of the *talatala*, who could succeed under the old conditions, or still in a place like Lau'.[44] He noted the differences between Ra and Lau. The '[e]normous foreign population and its industries' was robbing 'the Fijian … of his former simplicity and most of our *talatala* are failing to influence the modern Fijian. My balance sheet shows where the weak men are.'[45] Green said that while many Methodists had found work in the gold mine at Tavua, the 'influence of the gold mines must have a serious effect on the general attitude of the Fijian in regard to *Vakamisioneri*'.[46] He agreed that Bock was carrying 'too many passengers' — men who were 'not pulling their weight'.[47] While European missionaries were being trained in anthropology in preparation for 'managing' social change in industrialising colonies, *talatala*

---

40 'Message of the Church: "Strategy in missions"', *Advocate*, Tasmania, 10 June 1943, p. 4.
41 W Green to H Bock, 2 June 1944, F/1/1944, NAF; W Green to H Bock, 16 May 1944, F/1/1944, NAF, p. 3.
42 Ibid.
43 H Bock to W Green, 15 March 1940, F/1/1940, p. 2.
44 H Bock to W Green, 25 Sept 1940, F/1/1940, pp. 1–2.
45 Ibid.
46 W Green to H Bock, 28 Sept 1940, F/1/1940.
47 Ibid.

were not receiving equivalent training at the Davuilevu theological school. The effect of Burton's training scheme for European missionaries had increased the disparity between European and indigenous mission staff, with the training each group received being designed for different purposes.

In the south-east of the island, Methodist Fijian and Indo-Fijian students studied together at Davuilevu theological school, but racial tensions flared when 21 Indo-Fijian students left the Methodist teacher training school in 1941. They had allegedly complained about food and the general conditions at the institution. Harold Wood attests that the students walked out, but newspapers at the time said that the students were dismissed.[48] The Hindu nationalist group the Arya Samaj used this opportunity to point to the colonial nature of the mission.[49] The Arya Samaj leader Pundit Motichand held meetings in Ra and demanded that the colonial administration take action against the Methodists. Richard Piper, still working in the Indo-Fijian branch, reported on the situation to Green and said that Indo-Fijian Methodists had 'stood by very loyally and done their best to combat the horrible lies which were sent out against us'.[50] However:

> One or two [of their members] have chosen to stand for racial interests rather than for Christian principles, and have dropped away from the church, but our leaders in the Indian church are going to be the stronger for the testing.[51]

Piper stated that 'when the students realised that they had been sacrificed to the god of racialism and political agitation they were most distressed'.[52] The Arya Samaj had only been fleetingly successful in rallying supporters from the Methodist community, persuading only a few people to break away. In the end, the colonial administration became involved, coming down on the mission's side and deeming the students' expulsion to be fair.[53]

Despite not having formal anthropological training, Alan Tippett was interested in the question of cross-cultural encounters.[54] At his station at Nadroga, Tippett worked with eight ordained Fijians, 48 catechists, 18 village teachers, and 398 local preachers within a 700-mile area.[55] At the start, Tippett was at odds

---

48   A H Wood, *Overseas Missions of the Australian Methodist Church: Fiji*, vol. 2, Melbourne, Aldersgate Press, 1978, p. 51.

49   'Indian Education', *Fiji Times Herald*, 15 July 1941, p. 8.

50   R Piper to W Green, 20 August 1941, CY 3465, MOM 238, ML; B V Lal, *A Vision for Change: A D Patel and the Politics of Fiji*, Canberra, ANU E Press, 2011, p. 49.

51   R Piper to W Green, 20 August 1941, CY 3465, MOM 238, ML.

52   Ibid.

53   A H Wood, *Overseas Missions of the Australian Methodist Church: Fiji*, vol. 2, Melbourne, Aldersgate Press, 1978, p. 51.

54   C H Kraft and D D Priest, Jr., 'Who Was This Man? A Tribute to Alan R Tippett', *Missiology: An International Review*, vol. 17, no. 3, 1989, p. 271.

55   Ibid.

with the colonial mentality and practices alive within the Methodist mission.[56] He observed that the balance of power remained with his European colleagues, with whom he was expected to collaborate on the practice of disciplining native ministers, including the withholding of wages.[57] He was also initially perturbed by the extent to which chiefs exerted power within the mission, writing to William Green that he held 'the decisions of the synod as considerably more important than the wishes of the chiefs'.[58] Chiefs were consulted and their opinions valued on ministerial appointments, but Tippett saw the need to give greater heed to the opinions of *talatala* and European missionaries. Though interested in Fijian culture, Tippett did not believe it necessary to incorporate chiefly power into Methodism, seeking a more democratic system.

Tippett focused his attentions on training *talatala*. The mission had tended to seek out 'middle class' chiefs for the ministry, and by the 1940s they had noticed one man in particular who fitted this description and had leadership potential. The Reverend Setareki Tuilovoni had grown up on Matuku island, in Natokalou village in the Lau island group. His parents were Akeai Koroi and Ro Mere, his mother was a descendent of the Tui Matuku (chiefs of Matuku).[59] Being both a chief and a *talatala* meant that Tuilovoni could assert considerable authority. In 1941, while he was employed as a teacher for the mission school on Bau, the mission sent him to Australia on deputation work. Despite his heritage, Tuilovoni was critical of the chiefly system. Delivering a speech at Ulverstone Methodist Church in Tasmania in 1941, he told the congregation that, prior to Christianity, Fiji 'was under the domination of a dictatorship. The chief was as Hitler in Europe.' He likened pre-Christian Fiji to Nazi Germany:

> To-day, democracy was challenged by the common enemy — Hitler. In Hitler's work, power, purposes and purges, the Fijian saw a typical example of Fiji under the chiefs. His will was absolute and final. And it was the common people who had most to suffer under the chieftain dictator. One chieftain visiting another's island kingdom would have his visit attended by the gift of the death of a score of common people. When the visit was reciprocated, as an act of courtesy, the number of deaths would be increased to make a good impression. Consequently, the common people had more to gain from Christianity.[60]

56 Ibid.
57 H Bock to W Green, 20 June 1942, F/1/1942, NAF.
58 A R Tippett to W Green, 25 November 1941, F/1/1941, NAF, p. 1.
59 T Baleiwaqa, 'Setareki Akeai Tuilovoni and the Young People's Department of the Methodist Church in Fiji (1951–1957)', Bachelor of Divinity thesis, Pacific Theological College, 1987, p. 6; Reel 3, PMB 1072, p. 1.
60 'Message from the Church: What Fiji Owes to the Church', *The Advocate*, Tasmania, 13 October 1941, p. 2.

Figure 10: Setareki Tuilovoni.
Source: GCAH collection.

His speech reflected the wartime context in which it was delivered, but Tuilovoni's words signalled a bid to demonstrated modernity. In his critique of pre-Christian chiefs, Tuilovoni focused on the changes Christianity delivered to Fijians, depicting the moderation of chiefly power as beneficial. He argued that

Christian missions had 'laid the foundations of civilisation', and missionaries had prepared Fiji for 'the wiles of western civilisation'.[61] This comment indicated Tuilovoni's engagement with concepts of 'primitive' and 'civilised' societies, depicted indigenous culture as liminal, with Christianity operating as a linking element that carried Fijian culture from one stage to another in the path toward 'civilisation'. When he referred to the *vanua*, Tuilovoni suggested that Fijian land had 'not been taken from them, because Christianity preceded civilisation'.[62] There was a racial undercurrent through his speech that linked back to the anxieties about the *vanua*.

Confident that Tuilovoni's profile was on the rise, Burton challenged the existing structure of the mission in mid-1941, calling for the elimination of the European synod. 'I think your District is the only place in the World where such a thing exists', Burton told William Green, 'It is one thing to have a European committee … but I can see very grave dangers in the future in having a specifically European session'.[63] Burton sent Green a sample of the New Guinea mission constitution as a guide for changes to the Fijian constitution. He wanted the European synod to be dismantled, but maintained that 'separate committees for the Indian and Fijian work' needed 'to be endorsed by the Synod as a whole'.[64] William Green argued that closing the European synod would not eradicate racial tensions, but would further separate the Fijian branch from the Indo-Fijian branch of the mission.[65] In Green's opinion, the European synod acted an essential point of contact between the mission's branches.

Burton was heavily critical of the European synod. The previous year, the Indo-Fijian branch had 296 full members and 196 adherents, compared with 98,255 adherents in the Fijian branch.[66] He designed a questionnaire to assess the 'state of Indian work in Fiji' in August 1941 and sent it to people working in both branches of the mission.[67] Bock was amongst the first to reply, voicing his concern about the 'nationalistic' attitude, resulting from the continued practice of the 'customs and faiths of Mother India'.[68] Bock felt that this contributed

---

61   Ibid.
62   Ibid.
63   J W Burton to W Green, 14 August 1941, Fiji District correspondence — some regarding constitution, MOM 386, ML.
64   J W Burton to W Green, 17 Sept 1941, Fiji District correspondence — some regarding constitution, MOM 386, ML.
65   W Green to J W Burton, 3 Sept 1941, Fiji District correspondence — some regarding constitution, MOM 386.
66   1940 Indian statistics, reel 3, 1937–1945, PMB 1138.
67   J W Burton to W Green, 15 August 1941, Questionnaires were sent out regarding state of Indian work in 1941, item 8, MOM 238, ML.
68   H Bock to J W Burton, 13 October 1941, Questionnaires were sent out regarding state of Indian work in 1941 — J W Burton to W Green, 15 August 1941, item 8, MOM 238, ML.

to the Indo-Fijian communities' separation from the rest of Fijian society, and spurred derision amongst the Indo-Fijians for Fijians, who he believed were 'in some respects inferior and in some respects superior to the Indians'.[69]

Bock believed that Europeans were disliked because they had pushed Indo-Fijians into a position of 'dependence in both rule and finance'.[70] He considered it 'a psychological fact that the Indians, as with some of our own people, they dislike most those from whom they receive most assistance, because of the feeling of dependence and inferiority which that assistance engenders'.[71] In an effort to combat the sense of inferiority, Indo-Fijians 'imitated' Europeans, yet professed 'to despise European philosophy, customs, and civilisation'.[72] Bock believed that moving the mission towards self-support would subdue opposition to colonial rule, and increase in the Indo-Fijian staff's responsibilities. A commitment to self-support and self-governance would result in 'increased zeal' in the Indo-Fijian branch.[73] Institutionalised evangelism had failed, and evangelism had to be 'properly tried' outside of the mission's institutions, or there would be no rapid progress among Indo-Fijians, 'for they are an exceedingly difficult people'.[74]

Several responses to Burton's questionnaire referred to European prestige. There was a perception among Indo-Fijians that European missionaries were living more comfortably than the majority of the Indo-Fijian community and this created a barrier between the missionaries and potential converts. Missionary A Cyril Cato suggested that European missionaries related well with members of the Indo-Fijian community, but that they 'necessarily' lived above the standard enjoyed by some members of the Indo-Fijian community. He did not consider this to be a sign of racial exclusivity, as some Indo-Fijians enjoyed a better standard of living than European missionaries.[75] Alice Inez Hames, a mission sister, echoed this assertion. She had arrived in Fiji in 1920 and had worked in both the Indo-Fijian and Fijian mission branches.[76] Dr Dorothy Delbridge, a Methodist medical missionary working at Ba hospital, believed that accusations of racism were unavoidable in Fiji. While 'a missionary may try

---

69   Ibid.
70   Ibid.
71   Ibid.
72   Ibid.
73   Ibid.
74   Ibid.
75   A C Cato to J W Burton, 4 Oct 1941, CY3465, MOM 238, ML.
76   A H Wood, *Overseas Missions of the Australian Methodist Church: Fiji*, vol. 2, Melbourne, Aldersgate Press, 1978, p. 105.

to avoid racial discrimination, it cannot be wholly eliminated'.[77] She declared: 'The Indian is very sensitive to any suggestion of inferiority or of subservience to the European.'[78]

Their responses illuminated European conceptions of race in the early 1940s, and the ways it inhibited the mission's progress. The Reverend Norman Wright, superintendent at Lautoka, was not convinced that the board in Sydney fully understood the challenges experienced by missionaries in the field. When speaking on the topic of self-support and self-governance in the Indo-Fijian branch, Wright wrote:

> The Board's ideal of giving the Indians the privilege of selecting their workers and paying them seems to me but to push on to the European missionary the problem of having an Indian colleague who does his work and not know how to pay him because the Indian congregation will not pay. As for selecting workers, I never remember in the last fifteen Synods, the name of an Indian applying for preaching work being voted against by the Indian members, whoever the man or woman may have been.[79]

Issues of pay, competence and racial allegiances were woven throughout Wright's comment. On the topic of self-governance, Dorothy Delbridge argued that the time had not yet arrived to give greater control to Indo-Fijian church leaders: 'There are possibly a few capable of running some of the institutions, but those folk have already fulltime jobs. The Christian constituency is too small to produce men of ability in sufficient numbers for the carrying on of the work.'[80] The small Indo-Fijian membership contributed to the slow pace of devolution. Delbridge revealed the frustrations at the limited success with conversions that in turn had limited the pool of potential Indo-Fijian leaders. Missionaries had assumed that Ramsey Deoki's ordination and increased responsibility would boost the mission's Indo-Fijian membership as well as its financial income, but no significant impact had been noticed.

The process of indigenising Christianity was also discussed in these questionnaire responses. Conversions were also stifled due to missionaries' limited knowledge of Indian languages. The colonial administration in Fiji had recognised Urdu, Tamil and Teluga languages, but the mission's sermons were delivered only in Hindi. Piper was again attuned to how this was perceived, believing that '[t]he Moslems and the South Indians construe this as a sign of lack of sympathy on the part of the mission'.[81] In addition to the poor efforts

---

77 D Delbridge, response, Questionnaires regarding state of the Indian work, CY 3465, MOM 238, ML, p. 3.
78 Ibid.
79 N Wright, Response, Questionnaires regarding state of the Indian work, 20 January 1942, CY3465, MOM 238, ML, p. 3.
80 D Delbridge, response, Questionnaires regarding state of the Indian work, CY 3465, MOM 238, ML, p. 3.
81 Extract from letter of J Bairigi to R Piper, 26 June 1943, CY3465, MOM 238, ML, p. 2

made with language, Dorothy Delbridge felt 'too much emphasis has been placed upon Christian customs or European customs rather than adapting Christianity to Indian life', listing singing, marriage, funerals, christenings and worship as areas that could be altered.[82] She spoke of the power of the European missionary, referring to the discipleship of the Indo-Fijian Methodists not to God, but to European culture; the Indo-Fijian mission was 'a pale imitation of our Western churches', with 'no true Indian flavour in it at all'. She mourned that the 'vestige of the beautiful Indian symbolism has dropped out … The Indian spirit is not in the Indian church'.[83] Delbridge finished with this potent comment that echoed Hannah Dudley's observations from 40 years before:

> It seems to the outside Indian that to join the Indian church is to turn his back upon his own race and culture and to become a religious disciple of the white man. Therefore we must let the Indian Church be Indian, and that will not be while we are prominent in it.[84]

Delbridge hoped for renewed efforts to 'Indianise' the church as a way to combat public perceptions of the church, so much affiliated with colonialism.

Burton sought input from Indo-Fijian staff as well as European mission workers. Deoki's response was lengthy. He claimed that the church had failed to bring Indo-Fijian Christians into 'the higher light, the higher morality in Christ Jesus'.[85] He said that:

> The greatest drawback is the introduction of the 'white caste'. Every Indian especially every educated Indian feels it most keenly. Instead of the missionary showing the Christian way to these Indians that we are really all one — he has kept alone from the people — he has not mixed freely with the Indian — and this has been the chief excuse of Christian failure.[86]

He said that the European synod gave a place to any young European minister 'because he is a European', and that the same opportunities were not available to Indo-Fijian ministers. Deoki felt that despite his best efforts, the odds were always stacked against him due to his race.[87] He wrote: 'It is high time now that the "white prestige" idea be abandoned from our midst, and where there are racial discriminatory measures in our constitution and church, they

---

82   D Delbridge, response, Questionnaires regarding state of the Indian work, CY 3465, MOM 238, ML, pp. 3, 5.

83   Ibid., p. 5.

84   D Delbridge, response, Questionnaires regarding state of the Indian work, CY 3465, MOM 238, ML, p. 5.

85   R Deoki, response, Questionnaires regarding state of the Indian work, CY 3465, MOM 238, ML, p. 11.

86   Ibid., pp. 12–13.

87   Ibid., pp. 14–15.

too should be amended.'[88] European missionaries had developed what Deoki called a 'superiority complex', which limited their ability to identify with the Indo-Fijian community:[89]

> ... the modern missionary would rather spend three or four hours at the typewriter or with some book rather than spend an hour in the home of the Indian! It is a fact that there is better friendship and fellowship between Indians and ordinary Europeans than with missionaries and Indians![90]

Deoki also claimed: 'In most cases the general standard of living of the missionary is too far above the people to whom he is supposed to minister, but not in every case.'[91]

There were degrees to which missionaries admitted to the importance of race in the mission, but Deoki could not have articulated his opposition to its racialisation more clearly. He called for European missionaries to nullify racial categorisation, declaring that a mission defined by race was 'doomed to failure'.[92] This challenged existing notions that an indigenous church had to be linked to a 'national character', for he pointed to how this had promoted racial separation. Deoki questioned the whole notion of an 'Indian church':

> Why should the emphasis on race be so prominent in a cosmopolitan country as Fiji? Specialisation, we read in economics is good, but overspecialisation is bad. It is time also where Church organisation is concerned. Racial divisions for the sake of greater effectiveness is good, but when over emphasis on the racial division is placed then it is certainly harmful.[93]

Deoki believed that the colony was not 'Indo-Fijian' or 'Fijian' but English. He no longer wanted the mission's constitution to refer to Indo-Fijians as a 'native race'.[94] 'It is my own experience', Deoki wrote. 'If my own faith has been sorely tried, what of the ordinary Indian believers. For years I have asked for the Christian treatment to Indians, and it has been denied.'[95]

At the peak of World War II, Indo-Fijian farmers were displaced in Nadi to make way for Allied troops, and the cost of living rose. Workers were being organised by the sugar cane workers' unions, the Kisan Sangh and Akhil Fiji Krishak Maha Sangh (All Fiji Farmers' Association). Against this backdrop of industrial action, Deoki launched his campaign against the racial system of pay within

---

88   Ibid., p. 32.
89   Ibid., p. 28.
90   Ibid., pp. 28–29.
91   Ibid., p. 29.
92   Ibid., p. 25.
93   Ibid., p. 23.
94   Ibid., p. 35.
95   Ibid., p. 36.

the mission.[96] If circuits were to become self-supporting, Fijian and Indo-Fijian ministers would have to be paid from Methodist membership contributions. In 1942, Deoki's ministerial salary was £180 per annum plus allowances, while his European colleagues earned approximately £344 per annum.[97] The chairman paid the European missionaries, who in turn paid the *talatala* and the Indo-Fijian minister. Deoki was working under the supervision of Norman Wright at Nadi, despite being equally qualified. To Deoki, his wage was evidence that he was lower in status than his European colleagues.

Wright was conscious that Deoki considered his involvement in delivering his pay as a slight, however, the hope that the mission would one day be financially self-supporting made raising Deoki's wage seem impossible. They trialled self-support at the Nadi Indo-Fijian circuit, and Wright was worried that the circuit would not raise enough to cover Deoki's current rate of pay, let alone a higher rate. Deoki's additional income might have to come from Wright's own wage. Wright gave personal contributions, but the circuit was still often in debt. Debt was only 'wiped out' when there was no minister stationed there who needed to be paid. Wright suggested that rather than increase Deoki's wage, it should be reduced to ease the financial pressures on the mission at the height of the war. He did not want to be the one to suggest that to Deoki though, hoping that William Green would deliver the message. 'I do not like the arrangement', he said, but 'I do not want the responsibility of a debt later'.[98]

Despite growing concerns, the mission's racial divide was exacerbated in the early 1940s. In 1943, the mission established an entirely separate Indo-Fijian synod, and an Indo-Fijian division.[99] The reasons given were the 'differences of language, culture, civic organisation and the very different standard of Indo-Fijian and Fijian ministerial training'.[100] The explanatory notes in the synod minutes acknowledged that this was 'a racial division, since it is the natural division'. They argued: 'A division on racial lines is harmful only if it is made in a spirit of racialism — and that spirit certainly does not underlie our suggestions

---

96   B V Lal, *Broken Waves: A History of the Fiji Islands in the Twentieth Century*, Honolulu, University of Hawai'i Press, 1992, p. 128; J A Bennett, 'War, Emergency and the Environment: Fiji, 1939–1946', *Environment and History*, vol. 7, no. 3, 2001, p. 264; M Pickering-Bhagwan, 'A Historical Examination of the Indian Synod's Amalgamation into the Conference of the Methodist Church of Fiji and Rotuma', thejournalofaspiritualwonderer. blogspot.com.au/2013/05/a-historical-examination-of-indian.html.
97   W Green to N Wright, 26 February 1942, F/1/1942, NAF. The total amount for wages paid to European ministers working in the Indian branch in 1940 totalled £1377 10s, and there were four European ministers working in the Indian circuit. I divided the total figure by four to approximate their wages, but there would have been some personal variations between each ministers pay based on their family needs, etc. Deoki's pay is listed as £180 per annum plus stipends. 1942 Synod Minutes, PMB 1138, p. 7.
98   N Wright to W Green, 12 February 1942, F/1/1942, NAF.
99   'Explanatory notes on the proposed constitution for a separate Indian district in Fiji', F/3/1945–59D, NAF; A H Wood, *Overseas Missions of the Australian Methodist Church: Fiji*, vol. 2, Melbourne, Aldersgate Press, 1978, p. 66.
100 Ibid.

for a separate Indian district.'[101] Far from eliminating racial distinction within the mission, the mission had elected to push the separation further, but did so while attempting to dissolve, at least in part, the accusations of European hegemony that dogged the European synod.

In 1943, when there were only 140 Indo-Fijian Methodist adherents, Arthur Blacket again called for two separate districts and the end of the European synod, and was supported by Norman Wright, Robert Smith, Ramsey Deoki, Ram Padarath and Donnelly.[102] It was suggested that unity would 'spring from the soul', and did not need to be expressed outwardly. The call for separation was not for 'racial feeling of Indian against Fijian', but it was admitted that there was a 'deep feeling of frustration' at the way that the mission was then structured. Indo-Fijian members of the mission were made to feel excluded, which prevented cooperation.[103] Blacket had suggested the mission needed two chairman — one for each district — but Deoki told Green after this meeting that he felt that it would be best to have just one chairman for one district in Fiji, rather than separate the districts under two different chairmen.[104] Deoki considered the idea of separation to be at odds with the Christian message of unity, an idea he had already begun to form in his response to Burton's questionnaire. His call for cohesion, the first to come from within the mission, sat at odds with European missionaries' efforts to maintain the separation between the Fijian and Indo-Fijian mission work.

Missionaries struggled to create a more inclusive atmosphere, still mindful of the principle of indigenising churches. In 1944, the Reverend Cyril Germon took part in reviewing the Davuilevu curriculum. A comparative religion subject was introduced, including studies of 'Mohammodanism, Confucianism, Hinduism'.[105] Increased awareness of difference was seen as a means by which to bridge the divide between ministers in training and potential converts. Bock and Germon were unsure about their strategy, wondering about the extent to which materials for the comparative religions course should be translated into Fijian. Bock supposed that translation might defeat the purpose of the course, which was to lift the students' awareness of other cultures, not further embed their own. However, as the mission still placed high value on the process of 'indigenising' faith, Bock's hesitation was cast aside and texts selected for translation into a standardised form of the Fijian language, based on the Bauan dialect, including the Reverend Wesley Pidgeon's translation of 'Joni Wesele'

---

101 Ibid.

102 Fiji District correspondence — some regarding constitution, MOM 386, ML; 1943 Synod meeting minutes, PMB 1138.

103 'Explanatory notes on the proposed constitution for a separate Indian District in Fiji', June 1943, F/3/1945–59D, NAF.

104 R Deoki to W Green, circa August 1943, F/1/1943, NAF.

105 C Germon to H Bock, 22 November 1944, F/1/1944, NAF.

(John Wesley), a biography of the father of Methodism.[106] In 1944, Tuilovoni commenced his probation with the Reverend Wesley Pidgeon at Tavua, where they worked together to respond to the call to indigenise church structures.[107] Pidgeon wrote to Green that year:

> We have not established our 'Lotu Wesele' on a Fijian basis. Rather, we have adapted our Church organisation to the needs of the Fijian people and thus we have kept them in definite fellowship of the 'mother' church and through her with World Methodism and the World Church.[108]

Pidgeon and Tuilovoni established Fijian youth groups, grounded in Fijian culture. They translated the constitution, hymns, and what we can presume was Handel's version of the hallelujah chorus, and created Fijian dramas.[109]

As acculturation work occupied minds at Tavua, the Indo-Fijian branch continued to flounder with limited numbers and its minority status within the mission. Deoki believed that the Indo-Fijian branch would remain a mission and would not become a fully fledged church 'for a good many years', effectively remaining in the shadow of the Fijian church that was far closer to independence.[110] With so few members, Deoki recognised that the Indo-Fijian Methodist community would struggle to be financially self-sustaining. Even so, he requested that he be awarded 'missionary status in regard to salaries and allowances'.[111] He believed that this would not only 'end a lot of heart-burnings', but it would 'make room for the appointment of more Catechists and Workers'.[112] Green informed Burton of Deoki's request. In a lengthy response, Burton listed a raft of justifications for the mission's refusal to raise Deoki's wage and status. He echoed the concerns earlier outlined by Wright, that raising Deoki's wage would significantly slow progress towards an independent Indo-Fijian church, and added that it would also 'create difficulties with our Fijian Ministers and with our Indian Ministers in India'.[113] The limited number of Indo-Fijian converts crippled the ideal of self-governance and financial self-support, stalling devolution. This had significant political consequences.[114]

---

106 H Bock to Cyril Germon 17 November 1944, F/1/1944, NAF; J W Bready, *England: Before and After Wesley: The Evangelical Revival and Social Reform*, New York, Harper, 1938.
107 T Baleiwaqa, 'Setareki Akeai Tuilovoni', p. 1.
108 W Pidgeon to W Green, n.d., OS4 1946-63, NAF, pp. 4–5; also cited in T Baleiwaqa, 'Setareki Akeai Tuilovoni', p. 14.
109 T Baleiwaqa, 'Setareki Akeai Tuilovoni and the Young People's Department of the Methodist Church in Fiji (1951–1957)', Bachelor of Divinity thesis, Pacific Theological College, 1987, p. 21.
110 R Deoki to W Green, 11 July 1944, F/1/1944, NAF.
111 Ibid.
112 Ibid.
113 Minutes, cited in J W Burton to R Deoki, 30 November 1944, F/1/1944, NAF.
114 Ibid.

The difficulties of implementing self-support meant that Deoki's demands were left unmet. Burton wrote directly to Deoki: 'like your brethren in India, and your Ministerial brethren in Fiji, you are a Minister of an Indigenous church which ultimately we hope will be self-governing, self-propagating and self-supporting'.[115] Burton argued that the 'Board has no such sentiments as race, but feels it must maintain the policy which, in its judgement, is the only one to ensure a permanent Christian Church in Fiji'.[116] Burton reminded Deoki that he had been appointed as superintendent of an independent circuit, 'with the same rights and privileges as any other Minister, and so far as material support is concerned, you have been given salary and allowances and accommodation such as not been given to any other Minister of an Indigenous church'.[117] Burton stated that there had been no limit placed on Deoki's salary, but if he wanted a higher salary he would have to do so by dipping into funds allocated to the Indo-Fijian branch of the mission: 'It must be remembered that the Board's contribution is not a subsidy to any individual worker, but a general grant to the Indian church as a whole to assist it until such time as it can be entirely self-supporting.'[118] Burton thus placed Deoki in the difficult position of having to decide what was more important: a pay rise, or the transition to self-governance for the Indo-Fijian mission.

European missionaries were well aware of the growing support around Fiji for self-governance within the mission. The Toko farmers had requested an independent Fijian church, and there was more than ample evidence of disaffection within the Indo-Fijian branch. Something had to be done to address racialism in the mission's structure and day-to-day practice. Burton tried to show that he was against the racialist character of the mission by training what he called a 'new type of missionary' for work in the islands, and demanded the dissolution of the European synod. However, the mission still bore the marks of the earlier evolutionist ideologies, as evidenced by the continuation of the racialised wage system. Burton struggled to reverse this. He saw it was necessary to try to address the anti-colonial sentiment, but he could still see the distinctions between European, Indo-Fijian and Fijian that had been made firmly a part of the mission's structure. The matter was further complicated by the low numbers of Indo-Fijian converts, which limited the Indo-Fijian branch's progress towards self-support. Missionaries in the field also continued to grapple with two divergent ideals of minimising racialisation within the mission, and creating a church that was culturally relevant. Old mission methods, particularly translation of Methodist texts, remained a part of mission work,

---

115 Ibid.
116 Ibid.; B Stanley, 'The Church of the Three Selves: A Perspective from the World Missionary Conference, Edinburgh, 1910', *Journal of Imperial and Commonwealth History*, vol. 36, no. 3, 2008.
117 Minutes, cited in J W Burton to R Deoki, 30 November 1944, F/1/1944, NAF.
118 Ibid.

despite undermining efforts at inclusiveness. European missionaries continued to struggle to reconcile the demands of indigenous congregations and ministers with their methods of establishing self-supporting, self-propagating and self-governing churches.

CHAPTER SEVEN
Defining the Path to Independence

Missionaries realised that the post-war period provided opportunities to break down racial barriers within the mission, but culture, which was used to shape the mission's identity and organise its membership, remained a preoccupation. Both Fijian and Indo-Fijian 'cultures' had been co-opted into the mission, albeit in idealised and essentialised ways, and this process of acculturating Christianity had accentuated the differences between the colony's ethnic communities. At the end of World War II, there was mounting discontent among Fiji's Methodists, and a sense of impending conflict in the mission.[1] Missionaries increased their efforts to diffuse hostilities between the Fijians and Indo-Fijians and promote reconciliation. These efforts were often hampered by missionaries' concurrent interest in protecting Fijian rights, as the Indo-Fijian population officially became the colony's majority. By the late 1940s, European missionaries tended to support Fijian paramountcy in the mission, due to the need to maintain a friendly alliance with Fijians and to protect the majority of their membership.

Members of both the colonial administration and the Methodist mission seemed to feel the need to 'repair' Fijian society in the wake of World War II, and the rationale was racial. There was considerable tension in the west of Viti Levu, especially as Indo-Fijian farmers had been displaced. Indo-Fijians were derided because only small numbers had enlisted to fight in the war, despite the fact that this would have led to many losing their farms.[2] The 1946 census showed

---

1   J A Bennett, 'War, Emergency and the Environment: Fiji, 1939–1946', *Environment and History*, vol. 7, no. 3, 2001, p. 264; A Ravuvu, *The Façade of Democracy: Fijian Struggles for Political Control, 1830–1987*, Suva, Fiji, Reader Publishing House, 1991, pp. 62–63.
2   B V Lal, *Broken Waves: A History of the Fiji Islands in the Twentieth Century*, Honolulu, University of Hawai'i Press, 1992, p. 123; B V Lal, 'For King and Country: A Talk on the Pacific War in Fiji', in G M White (ed.), *Remembering the Pacific War*, occasional paper series 36, Honolulu, Hawai'i, Center for Pacific Islands Studies, School of Hawaiian, Asian and Pacific Studies, University of Hawai'i at Mānoa, 1991, p. 20.

that the Indo-Fijian community numbered 120,414 people, outnumbering the 118,070 of the Fijian community.[3] In that same year, there were 102,567 Fijians who regularly attended the Methodist church, and 102 *talatala* overseen by eight European missionaries.[4] Missionaries and colonial administrators alike were concerned about which community would constitute Fiji's majority in the future. Many wondered what implications a growing Indo-Fijian population might have for protecting Fijian rights. They also wondered how the colony's new majority should be represented in governance systems.[5] Aware that these political issues needed to be dealt with, and with the strain of the war now over, the colonial administration turned its attention to 'reconstruction' in the colony.[6] The Reverend Wesley Pidgeon, who had returned to Australia on deputation work in 1946, described the mission's concurrent 'rehabilitation' work, in response to the perception that increased contact between cultures during the war had been detrimental for the Fijian community. He believed that Fijians had been through a drastic period of change. They had taken up their gardening tools, but 'then the army came along and taught them to beat their pruning hooks not into spears, but into tommy guns, and sent them out to fight'.[7] To Pidgeon, the military had promoted an advanced method of warfare that pushed Fijian culture to move rapidly through stages of social transition that he felt it was not yet ready for.

More than the exposure to new technologies, though, Pidgeon was concerned about the four years of close association between Fijian and European soldiers. Fijian troops had 'lived in officers' messes, enjoyed all the privileges of white people, and learned their vices. It is going to be hard to rehabilitate them'.[8] Pidgeon seemed to believe that a type of cultural reversal was possible, that Fijian soldiers could be reconditioned for village life after they had been exposed to a style of life that he believed was reserved for Europeans. Pidgeon had possibly been influenced by Elkin's instructions to missionaries, published in 1934, in which he spoke of culture contact, but these offered little clarity on the approach missionaries should take when working in a complex nexus of multiple races and cultures.[9] Gillian Cowlishaw has argued that Elkin's

---

3   Fiji Bureau of Statistics — Key Statistics: June 2012, Population, 1.2A, Census Population by Ethnicity.

4   A Thornley, 'Custom, Change and Conflict: Fijian Wesleyan Ministers, 1835–1945', in R J May and H Nelson (eds), *Melanesia: Beyond Diversity*, Canberra, Research School of Pacific Studies, The Australian National University, 1982, p. 124.

5   M Kaplan and J Kelly, *Represented Communities: Fiji and World Decolonization*, Chicago, University of Chicago Press, 2001, pp. 109–10.

6   C Newbury, '*Bose Vakaturaga*: Great Council of Chiefs, 1875–2000', Pacific Studies, vol. 29, nos. 1 and 2, 2006, p. 100; A P Elkin, 'Reconstruction and the Native Peoples of the South-West Pacific', *Mankind*, vol. 3, no. 5, 1943, pp. 133–35.

7   'Natives of Pacific Islands Present Problem of Rehabilitation', *The Recorder*, Port Pirie, South Australia, 6 May 1946, p. 1.

8   Ibid.

9   A P Elkin, *Missionary Policy for Primitive Peoples*, Morpeth, NSW, St Johns College Press, 1934.

theories provided a confused sense of the connection between race and culture, which stemmed from the temptation to see indigenous cultures as being in a static state.[10] Missionaries who had been under Elkin's instruction struggled to comprehend this post-war environment and changes to colonial society, adopting a protectionist position.

As in previous decades, missionaries were applying theories of functional anthropology in order to understand concepts of culture, considering this process essential to stemming the tide of nationalism.[11] In 1946, the Reverend Cyril Cato, now principal of the Davuilevu theological school, told a congregation in Tasmania that Fijian nationalism was on the rise. He encouraged mission workers in Fiji to have 'some conception of the native tradition and outlook'.[12] If they did so, they would realise that they were 'dealing with a people emerging from child-like trust in, and obedience to, certain classes of Europeans into a sensitive and doubting adolescence'.[13] His paternalism was palpable. Like Pidgeon, Cato commented on the close association between Fijians and American and New Zealand forces during the war: 'Tens of thousands of soldiers were in Fiji, sometimes presenting aspects of behaviour and familiarity of approach which were new to the Fijians.'[14] Contrary to Pidgeon's theorising, however, Cato used the process of individual human development to describe what he believed was occurring in Fiji: progress that could not be reversed but was constantly moving forward. Cato's vision for the post-war period would not involve a reversal of the war's changes but rather an effort to embrace and promote 'progress', even when this did not 'enhance white prestige'.[15] Missionaries such as Doug Telfer continued to engage in the same ceremonies and protocols in Fiji's villages as they had done before the war, all the while contemplating broader issues of change and development.

By this time, Cato was engaging with ideas about the indigenisation of Christianity. In 1947, he published an article in the anthropological journal *Oceania* about the Fijian attempts to merge Christianity with 'animistic' and 'ancestral' belief systems.[16] While he pointed to the need to prepare missionaries for working in 'primitive societies', he also noted the problems in the government's approach to persecuting traditional medicine men, suggesting that this would not diminish their power but force the traditional practices 'underground'. Cato was engaging

---

10   G Cowlishaw, 'Colour, Culture and the Aboriginalists', *Man*, vol. 22, no. 2, 1987, p. 230.
11   D Wetherell, *Charles Abel and the Kwato Mission of Papua New Guinea 1891–1975*, Melbourne, Melbourne University Press, 1996, p. xvi.
12   'Fiji Faces New Problems', *The Examiner*, Launceston, Tasmania, 16 May 1946, p. 3.
13   Ibid.
14   Ibid.
15   Ibid.
16   A C Cato, 'A New Religious Cult in Fiji', *Oceania*, vol. 18, no. 2, 1947, p. 147.

with anthropological ideas to think through the complexities he witnessed while working in the islands, and was contributing to anthropological discussions about the Pacific in the process.[17]

As anthropological theories incorporated ideas about cultural transmission and integration, missionaries were able to creatively engage with ideas about how culture might be incorporated into mission programs. Pidgeon alluded to several staff who hoped to establish a 'distinctly Fijian society based on some Fijian tradition or custom'.[18] However, he admitted to having no 'clear vision of a possible basis or form', for how the Fijian church might develop.[19] He was concerned that the mission had not been established on a 'Fijian basis':[20]

> Rather, we have adapted our Church organisation to the needs of the Fijian people, and thus we have kept them in definite fellowship with the 'Mother' church and through her with world Methodism and the World Church. The organisation of a distinctly Fijian society may tend toward nationalism within the Church.[21]

Pidgeon tapped into the International Missionary Council debates, hoping to 'give to our youth the "World Church" vision'.[22] But the process of drawing a Fijian church into the world church would be difficult if they were not able to use the literature produced by the ecumenical community, as he felt a Fijian church would have to create its own body of literature: 'We would not be able to draw on the experience of other places, or use their literature to any great extent, if we launched something purely Fijian.'[23] He was also apprehensive about launching a project in the post-war period. He asked: 'Can we afford to experiment at this stage of transition in Fiji?'[24] Pidgeon felt the responsibility of guiding the society through what he viewed as a crucial transitional phase.

Potential for the mission to transition to self-governance remained high on the agenda within the Fijian branch. Cato took Sukuna's appointment as Director of Native Affairs as a sign that 'positions previously occupied only by white men would be held by native ministers'.[25] Cato recommended revisions to the mission's constitution that would allow *talatala* into roles previously held by European ministers.[26] That year, the Reverend Apisai Bavadra replaced the Reverend

---

17   Ibid., p. 153.
18   'On youth work', W Pidgeon to W Green, OS4 1946–63, pp. 4–5.
19   Ibid.
20   Ibid.
21   Ibid.
22   Ibid.
23   Ibid.
24   Ibid.
25   'Fijians Rely Less on whites', *The Mercury*, Tasmania, 16 May 1946, p. 6.
26   'Fiji Faces New Problems', *The Examiner*, Tasmania, 16 May 1946, p. 3.

Henry Bock as Ra District Superintendent, the first *talatala* to superintend that circuit.[27] It had taken 26 years after Robarobalevu's appointment at Bua for indigenous superintendency to be normalised within the mission.

Overall, in the post-war period there was a growing sense that changes were necessary. In the colonial administration, A A Ragg stated, as part of the Legislative Council's deliberations about the potential needs to change the 'Deed of Cession' to accommodate Indo-Fijians in 1946, that it was necessary for Fijians to move outside of the communal system to cease their becoming 'a placid race of mental and moral invertebrates'.[28] Even those not entirely convinced by A A Ragg's efforts to denounce all Fijian customary practices were willing to abide by the need for Fijians to find 'salvation' in the 'gospel of work', through 'thrift, industry and enterprise'.[29] While Fijians such as Ratu George Toganivalu requested continued allegiance with Europeans through deferential requests, leading Indo-Fijian politicians A D Patel and Vishnu Deo denounced the administration's rhetoric. It was, they contended, evident that the whole debate about the Deed of Cession was a slight against Indo-Fijians, deployed to stir antagonism, and it was a problem that the British had conjured through the introduction of Indian labourers anyway. Indo-Fijians were having to defend their ongoing presence in the colony at the highest possible places of government.[30]

Amidst the debate about social change, the missionaries' leadership also changed with a new general secretary, the Reverend A R Gardner, replacing Burton in 1946. W Rex Steadman, still chairman of the Indo-Fijian branch, saw Burton's departure as an opportunity to promote Deoki's status within the mission. By 1946, Deoki had worked as a superintendent in Suva, but there were lingering reservations about appointing him to work independently in the west of Viti Levu, where he would be more isolated and less easily supervised. He was 40 years old, efficient and experienced. Steadman argued that 'Methodist precedent' dictated that Deoki should be appointed superintendent, 'unless racial discrimination be observed'.[31] He appealed to Gardner for support in giving Deoki greater responsibility, pointing to the work that both Deoki and his wife had carried out within the mission, spending 'generously of their own money to get young people together and awaken their interest in the things for

---

27   Ministerial Index, accessed at Uniting Church Archives, Elsternwick.
28   CSO CF 166/13, cited in B V Lal, *Broken Waves: A History of the Fiji Islands in the Twentieth Century*, Honolulu, University of Hawai'i Press, 1992, p. 141.
29   Ibid.
30   Ibid., p. 142.
31   To A Gardner, 10 January 1946, HO/1946, NAF.

which our church stands'.[32] Steadman hoped the mission would demonstrate its commitment to self-governance in the Indo-Fijian church by giving Deoki greater autonomy as the institution embarked in a new direction.

Gardner had limited opportunity to act on Steadman's request. After three years as general secretary, he left and the Reverend Cecil Gribble filled the position in 1948. Gribble remained in the job for 23 years.[33] He was not entirely dissimilar from Burton — both had been influenced by the League of Nations between the world wars, and were attuned to debates within the ecumenical movement relating to indigenous churches.[34] Originally from a middle-class family in Ballarat, he had completed his honours year in history in Melbourne under the supervision of Professor Ernest Scott.[35] After completing his Master of Arts in 1928 at the University of Melbourne, he toured Australia's remote communities as a singing evangelist and witnessed the results of settler colonialism first-hand.[36] He travelled from Alice Springs to Katherine, Darwin, Camooweal, Cloncurry, and finally to Charters Towers.[37] He visited a Methodist mission in Arnhem Land and said that the community had 'been unspoiled by contact with the white civilisation'.[38] There was no doubting the impact of this trip on his opinions regarding indigenous governance and mission strategy. Probably the greatest factor in the decline of the native race', he argued in 1936, was 'that killing sense of inferiority and hopelessness which comes over a primitive

32   Ibid.

33   C F Gribble, 'Cecil Frank Gribble Interviewed by D Ritch [sound recording]', 1990–1991, TRC 2731, tape 4, side 2.

34   'League of Nations: Delegate to Union Congress', *The Mercury*, Hobart, 21 July 1936, p. 4; F Paisley, 'Citizens of their World: Australian Feminism and Indigenous Rights in the International Context, 1920s and 1930s', *Feminist Review*, no. 58, 1998, pp. 72–73; 'Burnie', *Advocate*, Tasmania, 12 October 1936, p. 6.

35   C F Gribble, 'Cecil Frank Gribble Interviewed by D Ritch [sound recording]', 1990–1991, TRC 2731: cassette 1 of 19, side 1; E Scott, 'Foreword', in J Lyng, *Non-Britishers in Australia: Influence on Population and Progress*, Melbourne, Macmillan and Co. with University of Melbourne Press, 1927. Lyng's commentary on Pacific Islanders was derogatory, referring to their 'low standard of civilisation', for example (p. 192); C F Gribble, 'Cecil Frank Gribble Interviewed by D Ritch [sound recording]', 1990–1991, TRC 2731: cassette 1 of 19, side 1.

36   'In the Churches: Devonport Methodist', *The Advocate*, Tasmania, 19 June 1937, p. 9; C F Gribble came from a long line of Methodist missionaries who had worked in Australia. See C Halse, 'Halse, C, 'The Reverend Ernest Gribble: Successful Missionary?', *Lectures in North Queensland History*, vol. 5, 1996, pp. 218–47; R Moran, *Sex, Maiming and Murder: Seven Case Studies into the Reliability of Reverend E R B Gribble, Superintendent, Forrest River Mission 1913–1928, as a Witness of the Truth*, Bassendean, WA, Access Press, 2002; 'A singing evangelist', *Northern Standard*, Northern Territory, 5 July 1929, p. 2; 'Orchestral Concert', *The Horsham Times*, 4 December 1923, p. 5; 'Preacher and Singer', *The Advertiser*, South Australia, 17 September 1930, p. 16; 'Katherine Notes', *Northern Territory Times*, 5 July 1929, p. 3; 'Methodist', *Brisbane Courier*, 30 March 1929, p. 10; C F Gribble, 'Cecil Frank Gribble Interviewed by D Ritch [sound recording]', 1990–1991, TRC 2731: cassette 1 of 19, side 1.

37   'Methodist', *The Brisbane Courier*, 22 June 1929, p. 7.

38   C F Gribble, 'Methodist Missionary's Work in North Australia', *The Advocate*, Tasmania, 15 October 1936, p. 8.

people when it comes into contact with a great civilisation. It is all something too big for it to understand, and it dies under its spell.'[39] He described the Aboriginal men and women as:

> a strong, virile race, many of them being almost perfect physique, and the Christian message is leading them to a life of industry and honesty which has surprised those who have regarded the natives as incapable of showing any traits of character.[40]

Gribble admired Theodor Webb's efforts to encourage Aboriginal Australians at the Arnhem Land mission into agricultural industry, suggesting that taking up farming work had brought out the best in Aboriginal farmers.[41] Racial and cultural evolutionism loomed large in Gribble's consciousness. He spoke easily of introducing indigenous communities to industry, taking it for granted that this would encourage an inevitable and essential step in human progress.[42] Gribble did not necessarily equate industry with western civilisation, but rather as a natural progression in social evolution.[43]

Gribble endorsed the protectionist approach adopted by Theodor Webb in Arnhem Land as chairman of the Methodist North Australian District, believing that the mission's physical separation from the European community provided space to maintain indigenous culture.[44] In 1937, he wrote:

> Scientists and missionaries alike believe that the only possible way to save this primitive race, once the possessors of the continent, is to grant them large areas of land and to allow them there to live their own native life and to develop their own tribal social organisation. Here they can be free from the disintegrating influences of the white civilisation, with its vices, its diseases, and its generally demoralising effect upon the more primitive culture.[45]

39   Ibid.

40   Ibid.

41   T Webb, *Spears to Spades*, Sydney, Department of Overseas Mission, 1938.

42   B Stanley, *The Bible and the Flag: Protestant Missions and British Imperialism in the Nineteenth and Twentieth Centuries*, Leicester, England, Apollos, 1990, p. 160.

43   S Suchet, '"Totally Wild"?: Colonising Discourses, Indigenous Knowledges and Managing Wildlife', *Australian Geographer*, vol. 33, no. 2, 2002, pp. 141–57, 146; Gribble's perspectives were similar to A P Elkin. See R McGregor, 'Wards, Words and Citizens: A P Elkin and Paul Hasluck on Assimilation', *Oceania*, vol. 69, no 4, 1999, pp. 246, 249.

44   T Webb, 'Tribal Organisation in Eastern Arnhem Land', *Oceania*, vol 3, no 4, 1933, p. 406; E Wells, *Reward and Punishment in Arnhem Land, 1962–1963*, Canberra, Australian Institute of Aboriginal Studies, 1982, pp. 31–32; C F Gribble, 'Methodist missionary's work in North Australia', *The Advocate*, Tasmania, 15 October 1936, p. 8; See H Morphy, 'Mutual Conversion?: The Methodist Church and the Yolnu, with particular reference to Yirrkala', *Humanities Research*, vol. 12, no. 1, 2005, epress.anu.edu.au/wp-content/uploads/2011/02/hrj-ch06.pdf, accessed 13 May 2013, p. 45.

45   'Natives in the North: Report of Abduction: Government Criticised', *Examiner*, Tasmania, 17 April 1937, p. 5.

Gribble's ideas were similar to Burton's and Elkin's.[46] Gribble was nominated to work in the Tongan Methodist mission, where he remained from 1939 until 1945 as Principal of Tupou College and then Director of Education for Tonga's government.[47] Gribble had straddled the divide between mission and colonial government in the Pacific, and had long considered questions of race and culture.

When Gribble moved in to the position as General Secretary for Methodist Overseas Missions, protectionist policies that had been used to justify the isolation of Aboriginal communities from the broader Australian public were being abandoned in favour of assimilation. In 1948, Gribble met with Elkin and representatives from other denominations at a conference to discuss the future mission policies for indigenous peoples. This conference advocated a change from protectionist to assimilationist policies.[48] Gribble and his colleagues were not entirely convinced by Elkin's arguments for assimilation, as they believed that the Methodist mission's long history of segregation had allowed culture to be sustained rather than diluted or diminished, through encouraging early education in indigenous vernacular, for example.[49]

Gribble was concerned that increased interaction between indigenous and non-indigenous communities would disturb the ability to evangelise effectively. His own approach in the mission field had been to leave 'culture' alone. Sione Havea, a Tongan minister, remembered Gribble's time in Tonga: 'he was always closely attached to the people ... but he was detached from our culture.'[50] Gribble reflected later: 'I've always pointed out to missionaries that when they go out to these places overseas, they must not interfere with the culture and custom of the people.'[51] The meeting's outcomes echoed the colonial debates regarding the indigenous community in Fiji and the influence of European

---

46   A P Elkin, *Missionary Policy for Primitive Peoples*, Morpeth, NSW, St Johns College Press, 1934.

47   A H Wood, *Overseas Missions of the Australian Methodist Church: Tonga and Samoa*, vol. 1, Melbourne, Aldersgate Press, 1975, p. 242.

48   T Wise, *A P Elkin: The Self-made Anthropologist*, Sydney, George Allen and Unwin, 1985, p. 159. While assimilation was adopted at various times in different Australian states, this was a full five years before Paul Hasluck officially introduced an assimilation policy in the Northern Territory. R McGregor, 'Wards, Words and Citizens: A P Elkin and Paul Hasluck on Assimilation', *Oceania*, vol. 69, no 4, 1999, p. 243.

49   H Richardson, 'Coming to Grips with our Native Problem', *Courier Mail*, 18 September 1948, p. 7; C F Gribble, 'Cecil Frank Gribble Interviewed by D Ritch [sound recording]', 1990–1991, TRC 2731, tape 4, side 2; Gribble admitted in his 1990 interview that they had made mistakes in the way the Methodist mission had organised Croker Island mission. See C F Gribble, 'Cecil Frank Gribble Interviewed by D Ritch [sound recording]', 1990–1991, TRC 2731, tape 5 side 1; N Riseman, 'Disrupting Assimilation: Soldiers, Missionaries and Aboriginal People in Arnhem Land During World War II', in A Barry, J Cruickshank, A Brown-May and P Grimshaw (eds), *Evangelists of Empire?: Missionaries in Colonial History*, www.msp.unimelb.edu.au/missions/index.php/missions/article/viewFile/20/22, accessed 13 May 2013, pp. 246–47.

50   C F Gribble, 'Cecil Frank Gribble Interviewed by D Ritch [sound recording]', 1990–1991, TRC 2731, tape 4, side 2.

51   Ibid.

culture during the war. Elkin's strategies were applicable to several mission fields — it was up to Gribble to determine whether it would be appropriate to continue encouraging a segregated model in Fiji or to move toward assimilation.

Though Gribble by now held the reins of the mission, Burton continued to be involved and publish his opinions on mission strategy. He had been in discussion with anthropologists throughout the 1940s, presenting a discussion paper in 1945 titled 'Culture Contact in the Pacific'.[52] In his 1949 publication, *Modern Missions in the South Pacific,* it was evident that Burton was grappling with the same questions about social change as his colleagues. He believed Fijians needed to move from the 'old native order' to the new 'complex' form of society.[53] Burton repeated his reference to the Robert Browning poem that he had included it in his 1917 layman's missionary lecture: 'Man is hurled/From change to change unceasingly.'[54] Burton's use of Browning's phrase showed the prolonged relevance it held for him. It engaged with the passage of time, and an innate belief that individuals were thrown almost violently, certainly without much control, through periods of alteration. Burton overtly applied this concept to his perceptions of race and culture, and his discussions about indigenous churches and industry.

Despite his apprehension about cultural contact and convolution, Gribble felt more sure about the devolution of the Fijian church and promoted self-governance. With the financial security of the Fijian branch assumed, Gribble turned his attention to making sure that non-European leaders were well-equipped for greater responsibility and leadership. Many of his colleagues had looked to the Tongan church as an exemplar of indigenous church governance but, in Gribble's opinion, Tongan church independence was 'more in name than in fact. For the past forty years a European has been the President of the Tonga church, and if there had not been sound European leadership, the Church might well have disintegrated.'[55] Gribble suggested that full independence was not secured while European missionaries remained at the head, although he still argued that continuing European missionary presence had strengthened the church. Many indigenous leaders from around the world stated that they did not intend to evict European missionaries, and sought their continued involvement.

52   J W Burton, 'Culture Contact in the Pacific', Australian Institute of International Affairs, cited in G Gray, 'H Ian Hogbin: "Official adviser on native affairs"', in G Gray, D Munro and C Winter (eds), *Scholars at War: Australasian Social Scientists, 1939–1945,* Canberra, ANU E Press, 2012, p. 84.

53   N Thomas, *Out of Time: History and Evolution in Anthropological Discourse,* Michigan, University of Michigan Press, 1989, pp. 88, 106–7.

54   J Phelan, 'Robert Browning and Colonialism', *Journal of Victorian Literature,* vol. 8, no. 1, 2003, pp. 81, 104; J W Burton, *Modern Missions in the South Pacific,* Great Britain, Wm Carling and Co Ltd, 1949, p. 11.

55   C Gribble to M Wilmshurst, 19 September 1949, MOM Correspondence papers, File 1949, ML.

Gribble believed that Fiji could become self-supporting under an indigenous president, as this would indicate true independence, and European missionaries would still be employed in the young church.[56]

Gribble was in step with the ecumenical mission movement, where similar arguments were put forward about continuing European missionary presence past the point of independence. Gribble's involvement in the National Missionary Council in Australia ensured his continued focus on international debates relating to indigenous rights, decolonisation and devolution.[57] One of Gribble's first overseas trips as general secretary was in 1950, to newly independent India. Here he witnessed the work of the United Church of Southern India led by the Reverend Lesslie Newbigin.[58] Any anxiety he had about anti-colonialism was allayed by his positive experience with Prime Minister Nehru, who 'gave the impression that [Indians] were proud to belong to the British Commonwealth'.[59] After their meeting, Gribble wrote that 'the country was now in the mood to welcome missionaries'.[60] He was also encouraged when he met eight ordained Indian ministers at the Methodist mission in Azamgarh, arguing that they 'could hold their own with any minister in Australia'.[61] Gribble held the church union in India as a model for the rest of the world; but it was not church union that inspired him most during his trip, it was the belief that anti-colonialism could be overcome with the promise of independence.[62]

The continuation of European missionary presence was a precarious point; it needed to be managed carefully to avoid accusations of oppressive colonial intent. Missionaries argued that 'younger' churches needed ongoing support from their 'mother' churches. Elkin had maintained that a continued European presence was required in the Pacific missions during the post-war period. He assumed that the European missionaries would be anthropologically trained and equipped to assist 'primitive' cultures towards civilisation.[63] The conceptualisation of culture offered by anthropologists offered a way for missionaries to reconcile the indigenous church ideal with understandings of racial and cultural difference. In his 1949 publication, Burton wrote:

---

56   Ibid; C Forman, 'Tonga's Tortured Venture in Church Unity', *Journal of Pacific History*, vol. 13, no. 1, 1978, p. 4; C F Gribble to M Wilmshurst, 19 September 1949, MOM Correspondence papers, File 1949, ML.
57   'Pacific Conference', *Examiner*, Launceston, Tasmania, 19 April 1950, p. 17.
58   'The Churches: Methodists Plan Missions in N G', *The Sydney Morning Herald*, 12 August 1950, p. 7; 'Points from the pulpit: Indian church gives lead to the world', *Examiner*, Tasmania, 19 May 1952, p. 3; G Wainwright, *Lesslie Newbigin: A Theological Life*, Cary, NC, USA, Oxford University Press, 2000.
59   'Prestige in India: Britain's Name Held in High Regard', *The West Australian*, Perth, 22 November 1950, p. 17.
60   Ibid.
61   Ibid.
62   'Points from the Pulpit: Indian Church Gives Lead to the World', *Examiner*, Tasmania, 19 May 1952, p. 3.
63   A P Elkin, 'Civilised Aborigines and Native Culture', *Oceania*, vol. 6, no. 2, 1935, p. 119.

In the Christian Church, which is now in many areas part of the indigenous culture, there will be demands for more power and for wider leadership. Already much has been done to make the churches in the South Pacific self-governing, self-supporting and self-propagating, but there are still positions held by the European missionary which might be entrusted to indigenous clergy.[64]

Calls persisted for the transition of authority from European to indigenous hands. This had significant ramifications for the Fijian mission where, despite Burton's earlier efforts to dismantle European power by removing the European synod, the mission's constitution in Fiji had kept the European missionaries at the mission's apex. The united synod had only limited indigenous input, as it was still run by European missionaries. Gribble took up Burton's recommendations to dissolve the European synod in Fiji. The Fijian and Indo-Fijian synods each had their own European chairman, and Gribble set his sights on filling these particular positions with Fijian and Indo-Fijian ministers.

In 1950, Gribble and Burton met with Fijian members of the mission to gauge the desire for an independent Fijian church, and devise a strategy for devolution, determined to ensure a Fijian ministry would assume control of the church in Fiji.[65] Those who attended the meeting — including Ratu Edward Cakobau, Jekope Ravoka, Inosi Vatucicila, Paula Seru, Apolosi Bavadra, Asaele Mata and Peni Tirikula — became the architects of Fiji's independent Methodist church. They defined the shape of the future church and the speed at which it would be constructed. From the outset, all agreed that the mission's devolution should continue at a slow pace.[66] The mission board was curious about whether the 'rank and file of Fiji' supported the idea of a Fijian conference. Jekope Ravoka replied that the majority of the Methodists in Fiji knew very little about the idea of church independence, suggesting that it was not in the mind of the membership but rather just of synod.

The mission needed to ensure chiefly support for devolution. Ratu Edward Cakobau was present at this meeting and had been a leader in the colony for many years, helping to bring resolution to the 1943 strikes held in the sugar industry, for example.[67] Historian Brij V Lal has suggested that he was 'perhaps the most

---

64   J W Burton, *Modern Missions in the South Pacific*, Great Britain, Wm Carling and Co Ltd, 1949, p. 68.

65   Gribble had been in Suva to observe the South Pacific Conference Meeting. C F Gribble, 'A New Voice for the South Pacific', *International Review of Missions*, vol. 39, no. 156, 1950, pp. 431–38; 'Methodists in Fiji', *The West Australian*, 15 April 1950, p. 10. J W Burton attended the same conference as the Australian delegate. See G Fry, 'The South Pacific "experiment": Reflections on the Origins of Regional Identity', *Journal of Pacific History*, vol. 32, no. 2, 1997, p. 182.

66   'Report of the discussions between the Board representatives and the Leaders of the Church in Fiji', May 1950, File: Towards an independent conference, MOM Fiji 1950, ML.

67   B V Lal, *Broken Waves: A History of the Fiji Islands in the Twentieth Century*, Honolulu, University of Hawai'i Press, 1992, p. 133; 'Ratu Sir Edward Cakobau', in S Firth and D Tarte (eds), *20th Century Fiji: People who Shaped this Nation*, Suva, USP solutions, University of the South Pacific, 2001, p. 111.

widely loved Fijian chief in this century'.[68] It had been nearly 10 years since the Toko farmers' request for independence, which had received widespread chiefly support, but members of this meeting said that the chiefs had not requested the church's independence; perhaps they meant they had not requested it in the form that they now were ready to pursue.[69] Burton believed the community needed to be better informed about what independence would mean. Paula Seru and Ratu Edward Cakobau suggested that chiefs be informed first, and then the annual meetings, quarterly meetings and superintendents of the circuits, before the circuit sections.[70] The Reverend Inosi Vatucicila, superintendent at Bau, suggested that they work according to the existing mission 'custom' of consulting with the chiefs as part of the preparation for quarterly meetings. This was their usual method of 'circulating information and obtaining opinion'.[71]

While the *talatala* at the meeting in 1950 suggested to Gribble and Burton that the chiefs knew little of the idea of self-support, Gribble later wrote to retired missionary A I Buxton that the 'most forceful elements of the community' were in favour of it. He continued: 'I think it will be a matter of assuring the Church again of our desire ... and of taking some actions which will indicate our sincerity even though these may be very small steps.'[72] Gribble wanted Fijian ministers to receive greater autonomy and responsibility with self-governance, and knew that the process they were putting in motion would allow *talatala* to appoint their own ministers.[73] While there was a need for the mission leaders to clarify what responsibilities *talatala* would assume, he relied on the ambition of the local ministry to drive the church towards independence.

At this meeting in 1950, Inosi Vatucicila anticipated that European missionaries would offer comment on indigenous custom at this point of transition, particularly regarding the role of chiefs. He encouraged their direction, requesting that 'anything concerning Fijian custom or affairs must be stated clearly', so that

---

68   B V Lal, *Broken Waves: A History of the Fiji Islands in the Twentieth Century*, Honolulu, University of Hawai'i Press, 1992, p. 205.

69   Ibid., p. 1.

70   Ibid.; A Thornley, 'Fijian Methodism: 1874–1945: The Emergence of a National Church', PhD thesis, The Australian National University, 1979, p. 285; Norton has suggested that in 1963, Edward Cakobau was amongst those open to introducing more inclusive policies for an independent Fiji. R Norton, 'Accommodating Indigenous Privilege: Britain's Dilemma in Decolonising Fiji', *Journal of Pacific History*, vol. 37, no. 2, 2002, p. 142.

71   'Report of the discussions between the Board representatives and the Leaders of the Church in Fiji', May 1950, File: Towards an independent conference, MOM Fiji 1950, ML, p. 1.

72   Gribble to A I Buxton, 26 April 1950, p. 4, 'Report of the discussions between the Board representatives and the Leaders of the Church in Fiji', May 1950, File: Towards an independent conference, MOM Fiji 1950, ML.

73   'Report of the discussions between the Board representatives and the Leaders of the Church in Fiji', May 1950, File: Towards an independent conference, MOM Fiji 1950, ML, p. 4; The chairman remained responsible for ministerial appointments. S Andrews to C F Gribble, 15 June 1951, HO/1/1952, pp. 1–2.

changes to be made within the church be made explicit.[74] This allowed European missionaries to take part in advising the process in which changes might be implemented. Despite the presence of Ratu Edward Cakobau, Paula Seru asked Apolosi Bavadra if it was right that the method for obtaining church independence was determined before putting it to the chiefs? Bavadra thought not. According to Jekope Ravoka, there were 'two ways of doing things', indicating that they were following the 'church way' by going first to annual meetings. This did not discount the opinion of chiefs, as Cakobau was present at the meeting, and Ravoka believed that they would 'hear what the chiefs in all areas think when the resolutions come back to Synod'.[75] Asaele Mata agreed with this, acknowledging that many chiefs attended the mission's annual meetings and would find out about it then.[76] Chiefs were not excluded from discussions about independence, but they were not integral to the decision-making process either. *Talatala* and European missionaries took control of determining continuity or change in church structure, not the chiefs.[77] All agreed, however, that the planning for self-support would be useless without the backing of the mission's general membership, which would not be secured unless the idea was presented carefully.[78] 'The point at issue', Tippett later suggested, 'is whether we are to ask the Annual Meetings if they want a Conference, or whether we assume we do and put up a plan'.[79] Either way they went about it, these approaches secured the prime position of the *talatala* over the process of devolution, even if it was in collaboration with Europeans. At this meeting, the *talatala* had defined their own leadership in the movement towards self-support within the church, albeit in the presence of one of the islands' leading chiefs.

Racial integration was recommended by *talatala*, not members of the mission board or locally based European missionaries. The Reverend Apisai Bavadra asked the next big question: 'What about the Indians?'[80] As superintendent at Nailaga, Ba, in an area with a high Indo-Fijian population, this was a question of great importance for Bavadra's ministry. It also pointed to Deoki's absence from

---

74   'Report of the discussions between the Board representatives and the Leaders of the Church in Fiji', May 1950, File: Towards an independent conference, MOM Fiji 1950, ML, p. 5.

75   Ibid.

76   Ibid. For more information on Mata please see A H Wood, *Overseas Missions of the Australian Methodist Church: Fiji*, vol. 2, Melbourne, Aldersgate Press, 1978, p. 382.

77   The mission's new position was contrary to the colonial administration which continued formal consultation with chiefs through the Great Council of Chiefs. R Norton, 'Accommodating Indigenous Privilege: Britain's Dilemma in Decolonising Fiji', *Journal of Pacific History*, vol. 37, no. 2, 2002, p. 137. While Garrett has pointed to Tuilovoni's appreciation of chiefs within the church, he was absent from this important meeting. J Garrett, *Where Nets Were Cast: Christianity in Oceania since World War Two*, Suva, Institute of Pacific Studies, University of the South Pacific in association with the World Council of Churches, 1997, p. 393.

78   'Report of the discussions between the Board representatives and the Leaders of the Church in Fiji', May 1950, File: Towards an independent conference, MOM Fiji 1950, ML, p. 2.

79   Ibid.

80   Ibid., p. 4. It is likely that Apisai Bavadra is related to the later Fijian Prime Minister, Timoci Bavadra. The Bavadra family is from Vuda in western Viti Levu.

the meeting. The Reverend Peni Tirikula, then superintendent in Suva, declared: 'Our ultimate aim is complete union — with Indians and part-Europeans also.'[81] While he advocated union, Tippett, who was also present at the meeting, suggested they continue with separate synods, as this was similar to the model used in Victoria, Australia, where the Chinese mission was kept distinct from the rest of the state's Methodist congregations. Again, mission strategies used in Australia were applied in the Pacific.[82] However, Jekope Ravoka pushed for an inclusive single church conference.

In 1950, 20 *talatala* were allowed to sit in the united synod, with 13 representatives of the Indo-Fijian ministry.[83] This produced a ratio of three *talatala* to two Indo-Fijian ministers in synod.[84] Bavadra said that there was no intention of asking a Fijian church to carry the other races, but wondered if there would be potential for an interchange of Fijian and Indo-Fijian ministers in the new conference. When posed with this question, Gribble referred to other examples of Indian ministers working in the Pacific, as the South India Church had recently sent an Indian minister to Papua. The Reverend Stanley Andrews said that the question of Fijians ministering to the Indo-Fijian community had never been discussed. He thought that this might not occur for 40 or 50 years.[85] There was no reference made to Deoki's ministry and how he might diversify and minister to Fijian congregations. The missionaries struggled to imagine how the two branches of the mission might merge. The system of segregation persisted with the belief that the two cultures were irreconcilably different.

The attitudes of Burton and Gribble were important in the post-war era. Burton had promoted improvements to European missionary training as a means of moving the missions towards devolution, and Gribble extended this by turning his attention to the training of non-European ministers. His aim was to train them to a high standard so that missionaries would happily hand over responsibility to their non-European colleagues. Yet there were anxieties about the rising number of Indo-Fijians in Fiji, and the power they might gain in the near future. Burton accompanied Gribble to Western Australia in 1951 where he was quoted by the press in an article provocatively titled 'Indians "beginning to oust whites in Fiji"'. He reportedly said that the 'Indians were now playing a game of Nemesis': Indo-Fijians were the enemy.[86] Within the Methodist mission, the great majority of the membership remained Fijian. Missionaries catered

81   Ibid., p. 2.
82   'Report of the discussions between the Board representatives and the Leaders of the Church in Fiji', May 1950, File: Towards an independent conference, MOM Fiji 1950, ML, p. 4.
83   S Cowled to C F Gribble, 20 September 1951, HO/1/1952, NAF.
84   S Andrews to C F Gribble, 20 September 1951, HO/1/1952, NAF, p. 2.
85   'Report of the discussions between the Board representatives and the Leaders of the Church in Fiji', May 1950, File: Towards an independent conference, MOM Fiji 1950, ML, p. 5.
86   'Indians "Beginning to oust whites in Fiji"', *The West Australian*, Perth, 10 May 1951, p. 9.

to the bulk of their membership, and tended to place Fijian interests above the needs of the Indo-Fijian community. The suggestion that the Fijian and Indo-Fijian branches of the mission might work together in a new conference was not gaining traction with European missionaries, but it was being discussed seriously at the local village level amongst *talatala*.[87]

Culture remained the predominant paradigm used by missionaries in Fiji to understand social change and it was used in the post-war period to assess the effects of the war on Fiji's society. Some felt that, with rehabilitation, the changes wrought by the wartime interaction between European, Indo-Fijian and Fijian peoples could be reversed. World War II had upset the neat lines of segregation and the cultures that had been previously considered protected were now altering at a faster pace than observers liked, forcing missionaries to consider abandoning the segregated mission structure for a more integrated model.

However, even though there was a realisation that the colony had changed, culture remained the main excuse for keeping the two branches of the mission apart. This separation was informed not only by European missionaries but also by the ideas of Indo-Fijian and Fijian mission leaders. Within the Indo-Fijian community at large there were fears that, while Indo-Fijians constituted the majority of the colony's population, the colonial administration's primary aim was to safeguard Fijian interests. Fijian paramountcy was still extended into the mission, with Indo-Fijians remaining the minority of the membership, and being well behind the Fijian mission in progressing towards self-support.[88] The mission's structure was revised, with greater consultation with the Fijian than the Indo-Fijian branch. Deoki was resigned to the fact that the Indo-Fijian Methodists would be marginalised. The mission walked a tenuous line between cultural sensitivity and racial discrimination, and its workers in the field often struggled to reconcile this. With renewed support for the ecumenical movement's calls for devolution, missionary attention turned more critically to the question of how to adapt the self-support concept to Fiji's plural society.

---

87 Meeting called by Reverend Deoki to 'discuss the findings of the constitution committee in the circular of 23 March 1950'. The meeting was chaired by Deoki and attended by A C Cato, Ram Narayan, Williami, I Lapthorne, G Davies and F Caleb, Thursday 30 March 1950, F/3/1948–1960B, NAF.
88 R Deoki to M Wilmshurst, 1 April 1950, F/3/1948–1960B, NAF.

CHAPTER EIGHT
Devolution in a Divided Mission

During the 1950s, European missionaries struggled to reconcile the segregation of the mission with a growing international movement for self-government and independence, blowing on the 'wind of change'.[1] This chapter revolves around the politics of race in discussions about independence within the church, debated most consistently around the mission's bases at Davuilevu at Nausori, and in Suva. Self-representation in synod became an important focus for Indo-Fijian Methodists as the mission neared independence and they attempted to assert their identity within this overwhelmingly Fijian institution. The 'three selves' church policy continued to shape the work of European missionaries and their support for training both Fijian and Indo-Fijian ministers, but devolution was occurring at a different pace in each mission branch. This chapter traces European anxieties about Fiji's demographics, and investigates how these ideas influenced mission policy for self-support, self-governance and self-propagation.

During the 1950s, European missionaries, with Fijian and Indo-Fijian ministers, deliberated problems arising from racial segregation within the mission and considered whether the two Methodist communities could be amalgamated. Gribble and Burton had deliberated the mission's transition to independence with leaders from the Fijian branch in 1950. Ramsey Deoki attended another meeting on 30 March 1950 to discuss the findings of the constitution committee. The committee sought a constitution that would 'provide for all Methodists in Fiji and hold us as one church'.[2] However, plans for a united Fijian church were superficial, as the strategies discussed did not entirely eradicate racial boundaries.

---

1   R Ovendale, 'Macmillan and the Wind of Change in Africa, 1957–1960', *The Historical Journal*, vol. 38, no. 2, 1995, p. 456.
2   Meeting called by R Deoki to 'discuss the findings of the constitution committee in the circular of 23 March 1950', 30 March 1950, F/3/1948–1960B, NAF.

The conciliatory rhetoric of 'one church' conflicted with the entrenched segregation of the two major ethnic spheres of the Methodist community. The committee believed that unity and diversity could both be achieved if the powers of this united synod were limited; the district synods would have great authority.[3] The committee discussed how they might achieve these outcomes, and believed that they needed open lines of communication between district superintendents and the mission board, and the ability to bypass the existing united synod. The united synod had previously stifled the initiatives of the Indo-Fijian branch, so if the committee members could circumvent it, they could more easily take advantage of the historic support offered by the mission board for 'younger' churches.[4] The consensus of the meeting was to not diminish the mission's Fijian identity, but rather to secure a strong Methodist church run by Fijian and Indo-Fijians. The desire to continue the racial division demonstrates a variation on the trend that anthropologist John Kelly has noticed from this period. Kelly has argued that Indo-Fijians were now the 'racial majority', which caused anxiety about Fijian futures, Indo-Fijian leaders sometimes aspiring to a 'minority status' to try and mute their presence, so as to minimise the potential for conflict. However, in the Methodist community, where Indo-Fijians were the minority, Indo-Fijians had to assert their rights to ensure that their own positions were not diminished, which they decided could be best achieved by requesting the continuation of segregation.[5]

The mission had remained a primarily Fijian institution, despite the growing numbers of Indo-Fijian Methodist ministers and members (there were 236 Indo-Fijian members in the Methodist church in 1947).[6] Creating a Methodist church that was both 'indigenised' and met the needs of both existing mission districts was going to be difficult. The Reverend T C Carne, who had worked in the Methodist mission to India before relocating to the Pacific to work with the Indo-Fijian community, wrote to Gribble in 1951 to discuss who might become chairman of the united synod. Carne said he would rather not, feeling it essential that the chairman of the united synod be from the Fijian district and know Fijian language and culture:

---

3   Ibid.

4   Ibid.

5   J Kelly, 'Aspiring to Minority and Other Tactics against Violence', in D Gladney (ed.), *Making Majorities: Constituting the Nation in Japan, Korea, China, Malaysia, Fiji, Turkey, and the United States*, California, Stanford University Press, 1998.

6   A H Wood, *Overseas Missions of the Australian Methodist Church: Fiji-Indian and Rotuma*, vol. 3, Aldersgate Press, Melbourne, 1978 *Overseas Missions of the Australian Methodist Church: Fiji-Indian and Rotuma*, p. 80.

I feel very deeply that the Fijian Church needs the Head of our Church in Fiji to be one of themselves. Maybe many of my views about the future of this colony are wrong, I hope they are, but I want the Fijian community to have every bit of honour and every chance of leadership.[7]

Encouraging Fijian leadership in the mission fostered an alliance between European missionaries and *talatala*, to the exclusion of the Indo-Fijian community. Despite having worked with the Indo-Fijian community, Carne believed that a *talatala* should take the lead. Carne resisted blurring the lines between the mission's two districts, despite recent discussions indicating that *talatala* were interested in having greater movement across the mission's internal boundaries.

Deoki continued to push for increasing ministers' wages, still resenting European missionaries' control of pays and accounts.[8] In December 1951, Carne supported this, recommending that Indo-Fijian ministers have their pay raised.[9] Gribble, however, suggested that there would be 'difficulties' if the *talatala* found out that the Indo-Fijian ministers started on a higher rate than themselves. He admitted that there were 'different standards of living and the ability of the Fijian to receive much more help from his people than the Indian, but it bristles with difficulties'.[10] Maintaining the racially codified pay system had been justified through the practical needs of the ministers in each district, on the basis of cultural difference, because missionaries had believed that *talatala* would be sustained within the communal system with contributions from villages towards their food and housing. However, by the 1950s, urban drift and industrialisation had made it increasingly difficult for villages to provide for ministers. Deoki's pointed remarks highlighted the racial base of this system and outweighed the claims that the system catered to the cultural needs of any staff member. The essentialised notions of Fijian culture that led Europeans to assume that *talatala* would receive hospitality in the villages could no longer be depended on in post-war, industrialising Fiji.

The colony's racial demographics were also central to European missionaries' responses to Fiji's involvement in the Malayan conflict. Fijian commandos were enlisted for service, under Britain's direction, to fight against what was

---

7   T C Carne to C Gribble, 27 December 1951, MLMSS Meth Ch OM (MOM) 527, ML.
8   Missionaries also controlled the private accounts of indigenous ministers. C G Dundon, 'Raicakacaka: "Walking the road" From Colonial to Post-colonial Mission: The Life, Work and Thought of the Reverend Dr Alan Richard Tippett, Methodist Missionary in Fiji, Anthropologist and Missiologist, 1911–1988', PhD thesis, Australian Defence Force Academy, UNSW, 2000, p. 45.
9   T C Carne to C F Gribble, 7 December 1951, MOM 527, ML; C F Gribble to T C Carne, 15 April 1952, MOM 527, ML.
10   C F Gribble to T C Carne, 14 May 1952, MOM 527, ML.

considered to be a communist insurgency.[11] The deployment of 850 soldiers from Fiji stirred heated discussion within the mission, particularly because 800 of these troops were Fijian.[12] The Reverend Stanley Cowled, the mission's new chairman in 1951, had worked in both Papua and Fiji, and had served alongside Fijian troops in the Solomon Islands during World War II. He served on the Fijian Legislative Assembly during his time as chairman. He was a highly mobile chairman, and the Reverend Stanley Andrews repeatedly had to stand in for him. He went to visit the troops in Malaya after their deployment. In Cowled's absence, Andrews wrote to Gribble outlining a critique of the lack of Indo-Fijian involvement. He had read correspondence printed in Fiji's newspapers that revealed concerns that the Fijian battalion might use their jungle warfare tactics against non-Fijian peoples when they returned to Fiji.[13]

Andrews had spoken to *talatala* about the battalion being sent to Malaya, and he found that no one supported the war but, due to an agreement between Ratu Sir Lala Sukuna and the British military, and the longstanding alliance with Britain, they felt that the troops must go. The chiefs were encouraging people to enlist by quoting the Bible. He had heard some say: 'Without the shedding of blood, there is no progress for our people.'[14] Some *talatala* had asked Andrews whether they could enlist, but he had refused their requests, concerned for their moral wellbeing. Ratu Edward Cakobau, who had been involved in recent discussions about church independence, was no doubt playing a role in rallying troops as one of the battalion's leaders.[15] This was evident from Gribble's comments in March 1952 that there was a racial undercurrent to European missionaries' concerns. Addressing church colleagues in Australia, Gribble said:[16]

> … Fiji was fighting for its racial existence as the Indians had increased to 127,000, thus exceeding the Fijians in population by 7,000. The action of sending 1,000 young Fijians between the ages of 18 and 26 to Malaya would alter its racial balance.[17]

11   B V Lal, *Broken Waves: A History of the Fiji Islands in the Twentieth Century*, Honolulu, University of Hawai'i Press, 1992, p. 149.

12   Ibid.; S Andrews to C F Gribble, 21 November 1951, HO/1/1952, NAF. For more information on Fijian involvement in the Malayan conflict please see T R Nawadra, *Ai Matai – Malaya: 1st battalion, Fiji Infantry Regiment, Far East Land Forces, 1952–1956*, Suva, History and archives unit, Republic of Fiji Military Forces, 1995; D Munro, 'The Making of Ai Matai: A Cautionary Tale in Fijian historiography and Publishing', *Pacific Studies*, vol. 20, no. 3, 1997, pp. 61–79. Peceli Ratawa, a young Fijian Methodist at the time, recorded the enthusiasm around Nakama about enlisting for Malaya. P Ratawa, *When the Spirit Says Move: An Autobiography*, Geelong, Printshop, 1996, p. 11.

13   S Andrews to C F Gribble, 21 November 1951, HO/1/1951, NAF, p. 1.

14   Ibid.

15   See 'Ratu Sir Edward Cakobau', in S Firth and D Tarte, *20th Century Fiji: People Who Shaped this Nation*, Suva, USP Solutions, University of the South Pacific, 2001, p. 111.

16   S Emde, 'Feared Rumours and Rumours of Fear: The Politicisation of Ethnicity During the Fiji Coup in 2000', *Oceania: Relations in Multicultural Fiji: Transformations, Positionings and Articulations*, vol. 75, no. 4, 2005, p. 387.

17   'Methodist Crusade to Continue', *Northern Star*, Lismore, NSW, 6 March 1952, p. 8.

Gribble appealed to the secretary of state for Britain's colonies, Oliver Lyttleton, to allow Fijian troops to remain at home in Fiji:

> One cannot see the growing strength of the Indian community in Fiji without realising that the Fijian is involved in a struggle for his very existence. It seems to us that to take a large community of their chosen young men at this time is to do Fiji an injustice.[18]

Gribble's concerns about racial demographics perpetuated the sense that the *vanua* was under threat. Despite there being no outright conflict between the two communities in Fiji, there was a sense of competition over which race would be the majority in the islands.[19] Gribble was wary of Fiji becoming a 'little India in the Pacific', and had taken to monitoring changes in this Pacific population.[20] Far from being an irrelevant, isolated view issued from Australia, Gribble's comments travelled into the Fijian mission field through Tuilovoni, who acted as conduit between the mission board and field. Tuilovoni translated the correspondence into Fijian and reported Gribble's opinion to his colleagues at a district meeting in February 1952.[21] Australian anxieties about race in Fiji were therefore moving from Sydney's mission board into the mission districts, and was no doubt discussed by ministers as they travelled back to their villages.

Gribble sent out a questionnaire to gauge the sentiments of missionaries and local ministers regarding the mission's education committee, and many took this as an opportunity to comment on a variety of issues. Gribble's survey was distributed at a time when public criticism of missions was on the rise throughout the Pacific. At the government–missions conference at Port Moresby in 1952, an unnamed government officer had claimed that:

> Christian missions of long experience handle native customs unsympathetically or attempt to destroy or interfere with native practices except where human life and health are involved, or where, in partly civilised communities, standards of decency are ignored.[22]

---

18 C F Gribble to Lyttleton, n.d., MOM 527, ML.
19 A Ravuvu, *The Façade of Democracy: Fijian Struggles for Political Control, 1830–1987*, Suva, Fiji, Reader Publishing House, 1991, p. 63; G H L Pitt Rivers, *The Clash of Culture and the Contact of Races*, New York, Negro Universities Press, 1927, p. 1; S Emde, 'Feared Rumours and Rumours of Fear: The Politicisation of Ethnicity During the Fiji Coup in 2000', *Oceania: Relations in Multicultural Fiji: Transformations, Positionings and Articulations*, vol. 75, no. 4, 2005, p. 387.
20 The imagining of Fiji as a 'little India in the Pacific' had been reiterated ten years before in J W Coulter, *Fiji: Little India in the Pacific*, Illinois, Chicago, University of Chicago Press, 1942.
21 Fiji Mission District meeting minutes, 4 February 1952, box 97, 1952 correspondence, MOM 527, ML; Fiji Mission District Meeting minutes 16 November 1951, MOM 527, ML; B V Lal, *Broken Waves: A History of the Fiji Islands in the Twentieth Century*, Honolulu, University of Hawai'i Press, 1992, pp. 149–50.
22 C F Gribble, 'Mission Work in New Guinea', *Sydney Morning Herald*, 15 November 1952, p. 2.

Gribble argued that the missionaries' training in anthropology had helped to eliminate colonial tendencies in mission. The course that Elkin and Burton had endorsed during the 1930s remained in place, and the anthropological training supplied to missionaries became part of their defence when accused of destroying indigenous cultures. Several denominations now sent their missionaries to do the anthropology course at the University of Sydney as a standard part of preparation for the field, 'in order that the life and culture of the people may be approached with understanding and appreciation, and some of the past mistakes of both Government and missions avoided'.[23]

One anonymous mission worker's response to Gribble's questionnaire seemed to display the qualities that anthropological training would provide, arguing it was imperative that Fijian language be used in synod, lest the 'contribution' of the *talatala* be 'lost'.[24] Discussing mission business in the vernacular was considered crucial to building the confidence of the indigenous leadership. Another unidentified respondent suggested that the 'Fijian and Indian churches are at very different stages in their respective evolutions; nor can it be said that they are evolving in the same form'.[25] It was evident that missionaries were still thinking in terms of cultures progressing through stages of development, and while the cultures in the two mission branches were not being described as incompatible, they were still seen as markedly different. Missionaries dared not divert from grounding the church in culture and indigenisation. They believed that segregation would preserve the 'individual rights of the Fijian synod', and create a viable 'young church'.[26]

Another respondent was concerned that 'the present social and political situation in Fiji indicates a grave danger in any attempt to short-circuit Fijian rights',[27] which might give rise to nationalist, anti-colonial movements amongst Fijian congregations. The reification of indigenous culture still seemed to be the way in which to demonstrate support for their rights in the face of the growing Indo-Fijian population. The concerns that missionaries had aired in the past were evidently still provoking a protectionist discourse, devised in response to the seemingly ever-growing Indo-Fijian community.

For all of their anthropological training, missionaries maintained a distance from Fijian and Indo-Fijian communities through the style of ministry, which involved a lack of personal interaction. In the Indo-Fijian branch, the mission's strategy of evangelisation through institutions such as orphanages, schools

23   Ibid.
24   'Function of the Education Committee', unnamed, n.d., box 97, 1952 correspondence, MOM 527, p. 2.
25   Ibid., p. 3.
26   Ibid.
27   Ibid.

and hospitals had led to a sort of indirect evangelisation.[28] Methodist members begrudged the lack of personal interaction with missionaries, taking it as a personal affront.[29] The Reverend John Robson, an Australian missionary who arrived in Fiji in 1952, commented on how much he enjoyed being among his Australian colleagues in the Davuilevu grounds.[30] Giving some perspective of the larger ramifications of missionary seclusion, Gribble warned that there was a 'danger' in socialising only with expatriates, and also warned that Robson would not develop his Fijian language skills 'as quickly or as easily as if you were out close to the village life'.[31] More diplomatic than some of his predecessors, Gribble identified the propensity of the European missionaries to exude an air of superiority. He attempted to facilitate change through mentoring.

Missionaries recognised the importance of training non-European ministers to fill their positions, but in 1952 Gribble still felt it essential to keep the European staff in Fiji.[32] Even the most progressive missionaries, such as Alan Tippett, who had worked hard to improve the theological curriculum and break down barriers between Fijian and Indo-Fijian students at Davuilevu during the previous decade, struggled to abandon a critical perspective of non-European ministers. Tippett admitted that the time had come to increase the number of Fijians working in administrative positions but that 'such leaders are certainly very hard to find this year'.[33] More training was deemed necessary before indigenous people would be able to take over the mission. Potential leaders were trained both locally and overseas, assisted by American scholarship programs which sponsored theological education for Pacific ministers. The Reverend Setareki Tuilovoni, the mission's rising star, had received the American 'Crusade for Christ' scholarship in 1947 and encouraged other *talatala* to apply, having since returned to Fiji to lead the Youth Department. As Tippett said in 1952: 'He is doing a European's job. He is the first-fruit of the scholarship system and the Fijian Church is very proud of him.'[34]

28　H Bock to J W Burton, 13 October 1941, response to questionnaires regarding state of Indian work in 1941, CY3465, MOM 238, ML.

29　C F Gribble wrote to D T Niles, 11 March 1952, 1953 correspondence, MOM 527, ML; 'Findings and comments on "Memorandum concerning our church schools in Fiji", meeting 16 May 1950, minutes. Meeting held in Lautoka, chaired by Deoki.' File: towards and independent conference Fiji 1950, ML.

30　J Garrett, *Where Nets Were Cast: Christianity in Oceania since World War Two*, Suva, Institute of Pacific Studies, University of the South Pacific in association with the World Council of Churches, 1997, p. 393; J Robson to C Gribble 18 May 1953, 1953 correspondence, MOM 527, ML.

31　C F Gribble to J Robson, 15 June 1953, 1953 correspondence, MOM 527, ML.

32　C F Gribble to Telfer, 12 June 1952, 1952 correspondence, MLMSS MOM 527, box 97, ML.

33　A R Tippett to C F Gribble, 4 January 1952, 1952 correspondence, MLMSS MOM 527, box 97, ML.

34　A R Tippett to C F Gribble, 29 May 1952, 1952 correspondence, MLMSS MOM 527, box 97, p. 2, ML.

Theological ideas, particularly the 'three selves' church concept, continued to guide missionary approaches to church development. In 1953, Tippett methodically listed the ways in which Fiji's mission was already self-supporting.[35] The mission's broadcast programs in Fijian and English on station ZJZ, making use of new technology as radios became increasingly available for Fijians during the 1940s and 1950s.[36] Tippett said that those listening to the program would be witness to the mission's autonomy, describing it as 'an organism living its own life, developing, struggling in its own environment, facing its own problems, making its own decisions, financing its own enterprises'.[37] Tippett adopted a paternalistic discourse to describe the Fijian mission's relationship with Australia, suggesting that 'special gifts show the mother love of the Home Church for her children, and the children appreciate it'.[38] Despite the paternalism, he believed in the potential of indigenous Christians to be capable of a full and rich religious life.[39] He believed that Methodism was not something simply transplanted and forced upon indigenous society, but had evidently become self-propagating.

Gribble reflected on the mission's role in colonialism in his speech to the annual mission board meeting in 1954. Here he stated his concern that the church had been accused of 'identification with Western influence, with colonialism, and economic exploitation'.[40] These perceptions had challenged the mission to ensure that it was truly a 'church of God'. Mission policy was changing to incorporate this analysis, 'with emphasis on the fact that the Christian community is above nationalism and race'.[41] Gribble considered Fiji to be particularly problematic case study, because of tensions between the Indo-Fijian and Fijian communities. He said: 'We have a great hope that these two members of the human family will learn to make a home together in Fiji.'[42] As the shift to independence progressed steadily throughout the 1950s, the mission still sought to increase its Indo-Fijian membership. Gribble believed that the biggest of the mission's challenges in the post-war years was the evangelisation of the Indo-Fijian community and

35   B Stanley, 'The Church of the Three Selves: A Perspective from the World Missionary Conference, Edinburgh, 1910', *Journal of Imperial and Commonwealth History*, vol. 36, no. 3, 2008; Tippett kept copies of 1949 Ecumenical Review, for example, which was produced by the WCC. See Tippett collection, St Marks National Theological Centre, Tip 69/43/1.

36   A R Tippett, 'The Methodist Church in Fiji', *The Spectator*, 3 June 1953, p. 338; B V Lal, *A Time Bomb Lies Buried: Fiji's Road to Independence, 1960–1970*, Canberra, ANU E Press, 2008, p. 16.

37   A R Tippett, 'The Methodist Church in Fiji', *The Spectator*, 3 June 1953, p. 338

38   Ibid.

39   B Stanley, *The Bible and the Flag: Protestant Missions and British Imperialism in the Nineteenth and Twentieth Centuries*, Leicester, England, Apollos, 1990, p. 172.

40   'Missions Have World Problem', *Courier Mail*, Brisbane, 22 May 1954, p. 6.

41   Ibid.

42   Ibid.; 'The New Challenge in Fiji', *The Spectator*, 17 March 1954, p. 10.

encouraging their 'reconciliation' with Fijians.[43] European missionaries and *talatala* seemed united by the challenge of Indo-Fijian evangelisation, with the Indo-Fijian community depicted as a problem that the other two shared.

While speaking of reconciliation, the acculturation of faith remained paramount. Gribble, Germon and Tippett continued to try to enhance indigenous theological training. Tippett believed that teaching should be culturally appropriate in order to induce greater individual engagement with the Bible and elicit new indigenous theological perspectives. Ministers were trained in biblical translation, and increasingly believed that western cultural perspectives of Christianity had inhibited indigenous theologies.[44] In 1954, Tippett boasted that the mission was publishing translated Christian literature, including a series of articles written by mission chairman Stanley Cowled and a brochure on the centenary of Cakobau's conversion.[45] Tippett had been personally preparing a prayer book for use by Methodist class leaders: 'fifty-two studies of Scripture passages showing the use and nature of prayer, and each is followed by suggestions for a prayer: a study for a year of Sunday mornings.'[46] While translating material into Bauan dialect — now the standardised Fijian language — tended to reinforce the cultural divisions in the mission, Tippett argued, as his predecessors had, that Christianity embedded in culture reflected a truer engagement with the Word of God. There were, by this time, Fijian theological students who understood Hindi and were able to transcend some of these linguistic boundaries if they chose to.[47]

Acculturation was also under way in the Indo-Fijian district. Working in the Indo-Fijian district, the Reverend Alan Loy had noticed a 'resurgence of India's historic faiths'.[48] Loy held missionaries responsible for the resurgence in culture amongst Indo-Fijians, as they had made recent efforts to 'retain and built up Hindu custom, culture and belief. Hindu and Muslim festivals, Indian religious films, and singers from India all are used as a media to build up a living religious culture.'[49] Promoting culture was only just starting to gain momentum in the Indo-Fijian branch of the mission. The cultural revival Loy noticed was probably also due to the growing surge in diaspora identity creation in the Indo-Fijian

43   'Progress in Work of Missions', *The Advertiser*, Adelaide, 4 March 1953, p. 3.

44   C G Dundon, 'Raicakacaka: "Walking the road" From Colonial to Post-colonial Mission: The Life, Work and Thought of the Reverend Dr Alan Richard Tippett, Methodist Missionary in Fiji, Anthropologist and Missiologist, 1911–1988', PhD thesis, Australian Defence Force Academy, UNSW, 2000; C W Forman, 'Finding Our Own Voice: The Reinterpreting of Christianity by Oceanian Theologians', *International Bulletin of Missionary Research*, vol. 29, no. 3, 2005, p. 115.

45   S Cowled, *Na Veisiko ki Maleya, Suva, Sa tabaki main na Vale ni Taba I vola ni Lotu Wesele*, 1954.

46   A R Tippett, 'A Book is Being Printed', *The Spectator*, 27 October 1954, p. 7.

47   P Ratawa, *When the Spirit Says Move: An Autobiography*, Geelong, Printshop, 1996, p. 17.

48   A W Loy, 'Overseas Missions: The Church in Fiji-India', *The Spectator*, 28 March 1956, p. 13.

49   Ibid.

community. Missionary efforts to embed Hindu and Islamic customs within Christian — particularly Methodist — practice were thus combined with efforts within the broader community to celebrate Indo-Fijian culture.[50]

In 1955, 15 European ministers and nine sisters remained in the mission, charged with supervising 145 *talatala* and the Reverend Ramsey Deoki, still the lone Indo-Fijian minister. There were 32,677 recorded Fijian Methodist church members (with approximately 100,000 more adherents). Indo-Fijian membership had grown, with 469 members that year.[51] However, Indo-Fijian students had ceased to apply to Navuso Agricultural School.[52] European missionaries were mindful of the protests occurring amongst sugar and oil workers by the mid-1950s and hoped to prevent the industrial agitation flowing into the mission, as equal wages continued to be a point of tension.[53] Loy observed:

> Racial feeling is not obvious but is deep-going. This presents a challenge which our Church is not only well aware of but by combined services, through a United Synod and plans for co-racial Youth Club seeks to bring nearer the day when all racial groups will be gathered into one living fellowship.[54]

Loy advocated unity and 'creating living centres of true community'.[55] However, most of the missions programs continued to be segregated, with youth groups coordinated for each community. A group was founded specifically for Indo-Fijian youth called the Dudley Youth Group. It was directed by T C Carne and named after Hannah Dudley, one of the first missionaries to the Indo-Fijian community. Activities included lectures, music, debates, games and singing hymns. The Dudley Youth Group occasionally engaged with its Fijian equivalent in order to 'foster inter-racial friendship'. Carne told the youth involved, 'we were all first Christians and then Indians and Fijians'.[56] Carne reiterated that churches were the perfect places to form friendships, as it was 'where the things that join are uppermost. Such Youth Clubs and joint meetings will strengthen our Methodist witness in Fiji.' He said, 'this is essential to our existence'.[57] Tuilovoni also had great faith in the youth groups. By 1956, he reported that

---

50   C Voigt-Graf, 'Transnationalism and the Indo-Fijian Diaspora: The Relationship of Indo-Fijians to India and its People', *Journal of Intercultural Studies*, vol. 29, no. 1, 2008, p. 88.

51   S Cowled to public relations officer, 9 August 1955, F/2/Vol 6 Fiji-Fijian, NAF.

52   Director of Agriculture to Cowled, 28 March 1955, O 10/21B, F/2/v7 1946–63, NAF; D Walkden Brown, DVD 5–8.

53   J Leckie, 'Workers in Colonial Fiji: 1870–1970', in C Moore, J Leckie and D Munro, (eds), *Labour in the South Pacific*, Townsville, James Cook University, 1990, pp. 58–59; J Heartfield, '"The dark races against the light?" Official Reaction to the 1959 Fiji Riots', *Journal of Pacific History*, vol. 37, no. 1, 2002, p. 75. See also A Mausio, 'The "Fijian dilemma": The Revolving Door Syndrome in Ethnic Fijian Rural Development, *Fijian Studies*, vol. 5, no. 1, 2007, p. 48.

54   A W Loy, 'Overseas Missions: The Church in Fiji-India', *The Spectator*, 28 March 1956, p. 13.

55   Ibid.

56   T C Carne, 'Dudley Youth Club', *The Spectator*, 26 October 1955, p. 4.

57   Ibid.

they had established an 'inter-racial' Christian Youth Group, which he hoped would bring the 'two peoples together'.[58] Observers commented that culturally specific institutions in Fiji should be abolished, and in this instance the mission was keeping up with public opinion.[59]

The World Council of Churches and International Missionary Council encouraged Australia to take a leading role in training Pacific church leaders, partly at the insistence of Tuilovoni and the Reverend Sione Havea, a Tongan minister.[60] Gribble continued to foster local mission leaders as part of what he called a 'post-war experiment'. Ministers from Tonga, Fiji and India studied at various colleges across Australia, with Tongans at Leigh College in Sydney, Fijians at King's College in Brisbane, and Indians and Indo-Fijians at Wesley College in Adelaide. Gribble believed that this training would build strong foundations for the 'national leadership in the church',[61] and that there could be no greater support offered to the 'younger churches' than to help them to 'develop their own Christian leaders'.[62]

The President of the Victorian and Tasmanian General Methodist Conference, the Reverend A Harold Wood, who had worked in Tonga from 1924 to 1937, attended the 1956 World Methodist Conference at Lake Junaluska, North Carolina.[63] The anti-colonial attitudes held by conference delegates brought him to question the pace of devolution in Fiji, and to see if the process could be hastened. He looked for ways in which to indicate the progress made so far towards the 'three selves' church principle. European missionaries in Fiji demonstrated that the mission was self-propagating by sending ministers overseas for training and ministerial work.[64] The Reverend Kolinio Saukuru was one of these indigenous missionaries. He was from a chiefly family in Kadavu, and the Reverend Charles O Lelean had identified his talent while he was still at school. Saukuru had since worked for 15 years as a missionary in Australia's Arnhem Land before returning to Lautoka in Fiji's Ra circuit.[65]

---

58 'Overseas Missions: The Voice of the Younger Church', *The Spectator*, 16 May 1956, p. 13.
59 A Ravuvu, *The Façade of Democracy: Fijian Struggles for Political Control, 1830–1987*, Suva, Fiji, Reader Publishing House, 1991, p. 51.
60 'Overseas Missions: The Voice of the Younger Church', *The Spectator*, 16 May 1956, p. 13.
61 C F Gribble, '"No Greater Thing"', *The Spectator*, 10 August 1955, p. 1.
62 Ibid.; 'Fijian Slant on the Appeal', *The Spectator*, 10 August 1955, p. 1.
63 I Breward, 'Wood, Alfred Harold (1896–1989)', *Australian Dictionary of Biography*, National Centre of Biography, The Australian National University, adb.anu.edu.au/biography/wood-alfred-harold-15624/text26824, accessed 4 May 2013.
64 A H Wood, 'Issues of Race and Peace at Lake Junaluska', *The Spectator*, 17 October 1956.
65 'Missionary', *The Mercury*, Hobart, 10 September 1949, p. 7; 'Fijian Minister Ill', *The West Australian*, Perth, 9 January 1950, p. 10; A R Tippett, 'The Methodist Church in Fiji', *The Spectator*, 3 June 1953, p. 338; A Thornley, 'Custom, Change and Conflict: Fijian Wesleyan Ministers, 1835–1945', in R J May and H Nelson (eds), *Melanesia: Beyond Diversity*, Canberra, Research School of Pacific Studies, The Australian National University, 1982, pp. 126–27.

Similarly, the Reverend Sakenasa Rokotunidau, known to the Australian media as Sakenasa Roko, visited Australia in 1950 to attend the Methodist Theological College in Brisbane before returning to minister around Fiji's goldfields.[66]

The mission also ensured that Indo-Fijians had opportunities to undertake ministerial training overseas. Two new Indo-Fijian leaders commenced probation in 1953. One of the new leaders was Daniel Mustapha, the son of one of Hannah Dudley's converts, who was born in 1930. He was a strong scholar, but had left his studies to work for Morris Hedstrom in Suva. The other was Edward Caleb from Namosau, six years senior to Mustapha. Caleb had been teaching in Rakiraki and Wailailai. At the time of his nomination for probation he was a superintendent of the Toorak Sunday School in Suva.[67] Ordaining these young men would ease Deoki's workload, increasing Indo-Fijian self-governance. By 1955, Caleb and Mustapha were training in Australia at Wesley Theological College in Adelaide with other delegates from India. They stayed with the Reverend Arthur Blacket, who had worked in the Indo-Fijian branch of the mission and represented it at the International Missionary Conference in India nearly 20 years before. He reported that both men had positive opinions about overseas missions.[68] They were part of a new generation who were benefiting from Deoki's hard-fought efforts.

The cultural implications of training ministers overseas concerned observers. Some feared that international experience would dilute Fijian cultural understanding and practice. The Reverend Anare Raiwalui, who attended the 1952 World Council of Churches Youth Conference in Travancore, India, spoke at an event in Suva in 1955, reiterating a point that he had heard made by a 'distinguished High Church dignitary': 'No Church can be said to belong to the land unless the clergy as well as the laity belong to the place in which they are operating.'[69] A writer for the Australian Methodist publication *The Spectator* interpreted this as a show of support for training 'men and women in the mission districts'.[70] However, this remark also related to Fijian bids to assert and preserve connections between the *vanua* (land), *lotu* (church) and the *iTaukei* (people).[71] *Talatala* had to maintain connection to *vanua* by practicing *vakaturaga* (respect for chiefs). However, despite the aforementioned efforts of Germon, Bock and Tippett to enhance the theological curriculum at Davuilevu, more work was required to achieve independence. They argued that drastic changes in theological education were still needed to improve the standards

---

66 'Fijian Preacher', *Sunday Mail*, Brisbane, Queensland, 11 June 1950, p. 3.
67 T C Carne to C F Gribble, box 527, 1953 correspondence, MOM 527, sheet 1121, ML.
68 A W Loy, 'Overseas Missions: The Church in Fiji-India', *The Spectator*, 28 March 1956, p. 13; A James, 'Overseas Missions Centenary Fund Appeal', *The Spectator*, 31 August 1955, p. 17.
69 A K Raiwalui, 'Fijian Slant on the Appeal', *The Spectator*, 10 August 1955, p. 1.
70 Ibid.
71 Ibid.

of the ministry and 'meet the fast growing demands of a fast growing mixed-population'.[72] Non-European ministers pushed for overseas training for their elite candidates while concurrently working to improve domestic theological training. Opening opportunities for better quality theological training at home would mean that there was less threat of severing the tie between the ministry and the *vanua*.[73]

A Wesley Amos continued to aid self-support since finishing his missionary service in 1923. He agreed that improvements in ministerial training were integral for increasing local autonomy.[74] In 1955 he wrote: 'The European missionary must be prepared to hand over authority to the island leaders just as soon as they are found capable and worthy.'[75] Since Amos's time in the mission field, the number of ordained European missionaries had dropped from 15 to nine. He echoed Raiwalui's warning about the implications of foreign education, arguing that the bulk of the ministry should be trained in Fiji, as 'those who come to Australia will merely copy our general mode of life, which is far beyond the needs and capacity of their island fields to provide'.[76] Such arguments reflected the desire to maintain the existing social order in Fiji, and efforts were still being made to limit indigenous ministers seeking what was considered to be a 'European' lifestyle, which Amos believed was not sustainable in Fiji.[77]

Despite training more local ministers, the mission continued to receive criticism about the pace of devolution. In 1955, the Reverend Austin James from Victoria, Gribble's brother-in-law, who had worked in the mission at Azamgarh, India,[78] declared: 'A Church must not always go on being led and ruled by foreigners. It will remain weak and "foreign", and never win for our Lord the final loyalty of the people.'[79] The missionaries of this period generally conceded that their time in the field was temporary, and most did not expect the life-long career in the mission that earlier generations had enjoyed. Austin James argued that it was now time for missionaries to leave the colonies.

---

72   Ibid.

73   A R Tippett, *The Christian (Fiji 1835–67)*, Auckland, Institute Printing and Publishing Society, 1954, p. 14; M Tomlinson, 'Sacred Soil in Kadavu, Fiji', *Oceania*, vol. 72, no. 4, 2002, p. 244.

74   A H Wood, *Overseas Missions of the Australian Methodist Church: Fiji*, vol. 2, Melbourne, Aldersgate Press, 1978, p. 390.

75   A W Amos, '1855–1955', *The Spectator*, 10 August 1955, p. 4.

76   Ibid.

77   A D Ravuvu, *The Fijian Ethos*, Suva, Institute of Pacific Studies, University of the South Pacific, 1987, pp. 18–19; M Mamdani, 'Historicising Power and Responses to Power: Indirect Rule and its Reform', *Social Reform*, vol. 66, no. 3, 1999, p. 865; S Chand, 'Ethnic Conflict, Income Inequality and Growth in Independent Fiji', State, Society and Governance in Melanesia discussion paper, vol. 97, no. 6, 1997, digitalcollections.anu. edu.au/bitstream/1885/40388/3/ssgm97-6.pdf, accessed 9 December 2013, p. 3.

78   'For Overseas Mission: Party at Home of President' *The Examiner*, 18 November 1938, p. 7; 'Improvements in India: New Constitution', *The Examiner*, Tasmania, 7 January 1938, p. 6.

79   A James, 'Overseas Missions Centenary Fund Appeal', *The Spectator*, 31 August 1955, p. 13.

> As the spirit of nationalism and independence spreads throughout the world
> it will touch the life of Pacific Churches. If we have not prepared for this
> then there will be discontent and relations between people and missionaries,
> between mother Church and daughter Church will tend to be embittered … It is
> opportunity and training and equal fellowship that exorcises the last traces of
> the inferiority complex.[80]

James argued, as others had done, that Australia should assume a primary role
in preparing indigenous ministers, and added that church members needed to
do more. He noted:

> Many are the signs all through the world that the period of white domination is
> at an end. The Church can in its own work bring this period to an end in such
> a way as to ensure fruitful relations of co-operation in the future. By providing
> the proper leadership for the Churches of the Pacific we shall so strengthen their
> inner life that they will be strong to resist the many forces of evil in the world.[81]

Austin James's criticisms rang in the ears of many missionaries. In March
1957, Stanley Cowled wrote to Gribble to refute the mission board's claim that
they were moving too slowly towards independence. He wanted to hand the
chairmanship to Setareki Tuilovoni, but Tuilovoni had rebuffed this suggestion,
because indigenous ministers were still working under Europeans in China
and India, where they had access to higher quality of education through their
universities.[82] Cowled also said that Tuilovoni had mentioned 'that Indian and
Chinese culture and intellect are of a higher standard than the Fijian'.[83] It is
fair to say, though, while the earlier statements suggest that there had been
greater opportunities for indigenous education in other British colonies, that
the final line of Tuilovoni's comment reflected the continuing influence of
evolutionist ideas in the mission. The perception that Fijians lagged behind
other races in terms of intellect continued to be a stumbling block. Cowled
knew that the eyes of the world were upon them. He insisted that they were
'anxious to hand over responsibility. We Europeans on the staff have said again
and again to the Fijians, "give us the young men of ability, and we will do the
rest".'[84] A Harold Wood toured the Pacific missions as President General of the
Australian Methodist Church that year. His main aim was to assess progress

---

80 Ibid.
81 Ibid.
82 One of the reasons given by missionaries for the infrequent promotion of Fijians within the mission was
the lack of educational opportunities in Fiji. This suggested that if Fijians had access to better education, they
would be able to move into the positions held by European missionaries. Yet, in colonies where education
was considered to be better quality — such as China and India — non-European ministers were still often
excluded from leadership positions, or, when they were not excluded, European missionaries remained in the
mission field.
83 S Cowled to C F Gribble, 8 March 1957, File 1956–7, MOM, ML.
84 Ibid.

towards the goal of self-support. His report pointed to the decreasing number of Australian missionaries working in Pacific mission fields as evidence that European missionaries were encouraging self-governance:

> Whatever is happening in regard to self-government is through the vote of the young churches themselves. If progress is thought to be somewhat slow this is because of the wish of these young churches. In Fiji, the Australian missionaries are stationed by the Synod, that is, by their Fijian brethren who are in a great majority.[85]

Wood and Gribble had enough experience with the Pacific to understand that cultural protocols and expectations were being navigated and took time. Both European missionaries and local ministers were trying to define their position in relation to the broader community and effectively train people to manage social change. The ministry in particular, with its new experiences and training opportunities, was shoring up its new position in Fiji's society.

Tippett took his role as guide to social transition and indigenisation seriously during this time. He recalled that at the 1957 District Synod, Tuilovoni described the 'native' ministry as *lewe ni kabakaba* (inhabitants of the ladder):

> In spite of sin and separation the ladder was there, and there was contact between heaven and earth, and the angels symbolised the restoring of the broken fellowship. You are responsible, like those angels, for going up and down in between the holy God and the sinful world, taking up the cries of needy men and women, bringing them the blessing from above. This is your ministry as mediators.[86]

Tippett likened the minister's role to that of the *mata-ni-vanua*, who were responsible for negotiations between chiefs and commoners. This was a demonstrated attempt to define the ministry not as chiefs or as a replacement for chiefs, but rather as a variation on the role of the *mata-ni-vanua*.[87] Typical of Tippett, he tried to recognise the ways in which Christianity was fitting into the Fijian context.

In 1958, the number of European missionaries in Fiji had dropped to 10, Fijian ministers numbered 156, and there were three Indo-Fijian ministers — Deoki, Caleb and Mustapha. Fijian and Rotuman adherents totalled 134,574, members 38,000, and Indo-Fijian adherents had swelled to 2,000, with members at 773.[88] Gribble consoled Cowled, who had suggested that the political and

---

85   W E Bennett papers, 'Report of Board of Missions on Visit to Fiji, Tonga and Samoa, June/July 1957', FF/32; A H Wood, report, 17 July 1957, FF/32.
86   A R Tippett, *Oral Tradition and Ethno-history: The Transmission of Information and Social Values in Early Christian Fiji, 1835–1905*, Canberra, St Marks Library, 1980, p. 57.
87   Ibid.
88   S Cowled to G Rawnsley Esq., 19 September 1958, F/2/vol 6 Fiji-Fijian, NAF.

racial situation in Fiji had slowed indigenous autonomy. Gribble wrote that 'sometimes I think that a certain amount of pressure is to be put on the people to accept greater responsibility'.[89] The frank nature of their discussions reflected the different dynamic that had emerged between the mission board and the field under Gribble's leadership. Independence was considered inevitable and to be within reach.

However, discontent in the Indo-Fijian community was not so much from the continued presence of European missionaries but the continuation of the hierarchical aspects of the racialised system of governance, applied to wages for example. Cowled wrote to Wood in 1959 that even the most radical anti-colonialists amongst the Indo-Fijian 'have repeatedly said that we need more, not fewer, European missionaries'.[90] Cowled replied: 'Some of these say they will "fight to the death until the inequality of salaries is dead and buried".'[91] Regardless of Gribble's efforts to ease the relationship with Indo-Fijian ministers, much of the broader Indo-Fijian community continued to associate the mission with colonialism. Cowled reiterated what he had heard from missionary the Reverend Doug Fullerton regarding Indo-Fijian perceptions of the mission: 'Indians generally, and rural Indians in particular, identify the missionaries with the CSR Co. This Indian said, the Indians think the missionary is a supporter of the status quo and therefore are on the side of the CSR.'[92] This was perilous. The close affiliation between the CSR and the mission in the past still lingered. Strikes throughout the previous decades had aired the frustrations felt by Fijian and Indo-Fijian farmers with their working conditions.[93] Until the mission was able to sufficiently differentiate itself from the CSR, known for the appalling conditions forced upon indentured Indian workers, it would have only limited success. Deoki, the most vocal opponent to the racialised nature of the church, had commenced calls for unity but was rarely heard over the din of missionary preoccupation with the Fijian branch. Cowled seemed conflicted as to how to have European missionaries continue working in Fiji while addressing the criticisms of colonialism.

Tippett wrote a letter to Gribble in 1959 that summarised the confusion surrounding the perceived need for unity as the mission neared independence. He described the 'fear of losing identity' that had emerged in both branches of the mission. He was pleased that the revisions to the constitution, adopted

---

89 C F Gribble to S Cowled 22 March 1957, File 1956–7, MOM.

90 C F Gribble to R Deoki 6 March 1952, Gribble to Telfer, 12 June 1952, box 97, 1952 correspondence, MOM 527, ML.

91 S Cowled to A H Wood, 9 April 1959, F/1/1946–63 (e), NAF.

92 Ibid.

93 B V Lal, *Broken Waves: A History of the Fiji Islands in the Twentieth Century*, Honolulu, University of Hawai'i Press, 1992, p. 131.

in 1946, had dissolved the European synod.[94] It had been replaced with the united synod, where Fijians and Indo-Fijians could come together, yet Tippett believed that the responsibilities of the united synod were too few. The bulk of mission work was done by the Fijian and Indo-Fijian synods, independent of one another. He did not think that these two synods should merge, as he hoped to preserve culture in each community. Unity was being pushed, he thought, in a 'western' fashion, and to continue to force it would be fatal for worship in both districts. Tippett had recommended the mission move to independent church conference status with the existing structure of the United, Fijian and Indo-Fijian synods. He felt that it was both the natural path for the mission and would allow both Fijians and Indo-Fijians to continue to worship in their 'respective culture patterns', and would not necessarily stop 'integration' from occurring, 'which we must achieve or perish'.[95] Always considerate of culture, Tippett was concerned that most of his European colleagues in the synod 'think in Australian and not in Fiji', and had very different opinions to his own in terms of theology and anthropology. He was not sure whether he was outdated or 'haywire', and worried that the mission was taking the wrong course.[96]

Chiefs dismissed the suggestion for the continuation of separate synods. Tippett, by then a member of the teaching staff at Davuilevu, was 'horrified' when some recommended that a 'purely Fijian' church conference be established instead. Tippett had taken issue with the influence of chiefs in the church in the 1940s, and he was again critical of their ability to sway the opinion of ministers in the synod. Tippett believed that the chiefs' main concern about integration was the feared loss of identity, which he felt was 'not without some justification'.[97] He had, however, already commenced efforts towards integrating the church, with some of his students from Davuilevu ministering at monthly joint services held at Dilkusha, and evangelising at the Nausori market.[98] In 1960, Hindi would be taught at Davuilevu for the first time. Some of the students could already speak some Hindi, and one Hindi-speaking Fijian student had already offered to work in the Indo-Fijian branch.[99]

There were significant hurdles that had to be crossed in order for the mission to become independent. Ministerial training, both international and domestic, was an important issue that received a great deal of attention throughout the 1950s. While Pacific ministers had greater opportunities for training overseas in Australia or the United States of America, European missionaries in the field

---

94 D Telfer, *Of Love and Privilege*, Fullarton, South Australia, Colin Telfer, 2009, p. 51.

95 A R Tippett to C F Gribble, 26 September 1959, TIP 70/38/6.

96 Ibid., pp. 9–10.

97 Ibid., p. 5.

98 P Ratawa, *When the Spirit Says Move: An Autobiography*, Geelong, Printshop, 1996, p. 17.

99 Ibid., p. 6.

worked to improve the standards of theological education at the Davuilevu theological school. Enhancing ministerial training would, it was hoped, increase European confidence in local ministers and encourage them to hand responsibility to the 'young' church.

The colony's complex racial divisions formed another hurdle. Local ministers did not necessarily want to expel European missionaries from the islands, but they certainly wanted autonomy. The most difficult challenge was not anti-colonial sentiment, though that was a source of anxiety, but the question of whether segregation could be dissolved to create a unified Fijian church. While early discussions suggested that unity could be achieved through the creation of one church, there were still many who sought a church divided, with synods and circuits split according to race, if not entirely separate churches for Fijians and Indo-Fijians. There was a tension between the calls for unity from the international ecumenical movement and the concepts and politics around culture and race. Anthropologists and ecumenical leaders discussed the methods and impact of achieving integration and assimilation; there was resistance or lack of confidence about pursuing this path in Fiji's Methodist communities. As the mission drew closer to independence, the mission's leadership was perplexed about how to draw the Fijian and Indo-Fijian communities together into one church.

CHAPTER NINE

Disunity: Failed Efforts at Integration

In the 1960s, some local ministers pushed for racial unity and integration in Fijian Methodism with new vigour, while others were content with the existing system that segregated the mission. European missionaries were shifting from protectionist policies, designed to limit the influence of Europeans on indigenous peoples, to consider policies of integration that increased cross-cultural engagement. One of the most crucial issues facing the mission leadership was concurrently being deliberated by the Fijian government: whether it would be possible to change the existing system of separation and better integrate the Fijian and Indo-Fijian communities. This chapter guides us through the debates that emerged during the creation of a constitution for the independent Methodist church.

By 1960, there was no doubt that the mission was destined for independence. An elite leadership was already in training, with hopes pinned on the Reverend Setareki Tuilovoni to assume the role of chairman (or an equivalent position) in the autonomous church. Baleiwaqa, a Fijian historian who wrote about Tuilovoni's work with the Methodist Youth Department, described Tuilovoni as not being 'the native messiah against the whites, but the product of the struggle of both Fijian and Australian ministers to develop local leadership'.[1] The mission had capitalised on the 'world church' network to ensure that the mission's elite had access to high quality education programs. Tuilovoni studied at Drew University's theological school in New Jersey in the 1950s. In April 1961, chairman Stanley Cowled appealed to the board of missions of the Methodist Church in New York for financial support to assist Tuilovoni

---

1   T Baleiwaqa, 'Setareki Akeai Tuilovoni and the Young People's Department of the Methodist Church in Fiji (1951–1957)', Bachelor of Divinity thesis, Pacific Theological College, 1987, p. 7.

to complete a Master of Sacred Theology.[2] These discussions culminated in Tuilovoni's candidature at Union Theological Seminary in New York, which he began later that year. Tuilovoni wrote his thesis on the topic of church unity in the Pacific, having seen first-hand the challenges confronting missions in Fiji and across the globe. He had been attending international ecumenical events for years, including the 1957 International Missionary Council Conference in newly independent Ghana.[3] His thesis, titled 'Church and Unity in the South Pacific', synthesised his diverse experiences overseas and in the Pacific, looking at the global and local aspects of the church. As he wrote his thesis, he delivered sharp messages to the mission's leaders at home in the hope of influencing the shape of the post-colonial Fijian Methodist Church.

In 1960, Alan Tippett, by then principal at Davuilevu, asked *talatala* in training what they perceived to be Fiji's 'modern problems'.[4] Students offered various responses, which Tippett selectively reproduced in the Australian Methodist publication *The Spectator*. The students wrote about 'progress', and the 'breakdown of custom and the swing to the European way of life'.[5] Tippett used these student responses to argue that 'the present students do not belong to the past':[6]

> When they do worry about the breakdown of custom, it is because of the problems caused by *rapid* breakdown, not the change itself. On the other hand a good deal of their thinking on religion is culturally conditioned — more than they themselves realise. They are truly young men of two worlds.[7]

Tippett encouraged his students to consider the Fijian cultural paradigm, and how this might be used to understand and respond to social change. Change was accepted as inevitable, but the pace at which it occurred was problematic, just as the pace of the devolution of the church had become an issue in the late 1950s. So much about social transformation was linked to temporal notions of progress. The *talatala* described the rapid alterations occurring within the colony, but some things remained the same. Tippett argued that religion was 'culturally conditioned', and that Fijian Methodism in many ways housed

---

2   *Time Magazine*, 19 April 1954, www.time.com/time/covers/0,16641,19540419,00.html, accessed 27 September 2012; E Smith to S Cowled, 14 April 1961, PMB 1072, reel 2.

3   World Council of Churches Archives Inventory, archives.oikoumene.org/Query/detail.aspx?ID=68117, accessed 27 September 2012.

4   A R Tippett, 'What the Theological Student in Fiji Thinks', *The Spectator*, 13 January 1960, p. 14; J Garrett, *Where Nets Were Cast: Christianity in Oceania since World War Two*, Suva, Institute of Pacific Studies, University of the South Pacific in association with the World Council of Churches, 1997, p. 238.

5   Ibid.

6   Ibid.

7   Ibid.

a custom-bound past, built around chiefly power. Tippett felt uneasy about the power still enjoyed by chiefs, and their influence in the mission, which was counter-productive to efforts to establish a democratically fashioned mission.

Complicating matters further, European missionaries were not entirely disengaged from chiefly culture. Lesslie Newbigin, a pivotal figure in the international ecumenical movement, visited Fiji in 1960. He observed that 'missionaries, in the main, are put by the people into a chiefly category and I suppose it is very easy for we human mortals to behave in a chiefly fashion if we get the chance'.[8] There was continued inequity between European and non-European staff, at a time when European missionaries desperately needed to walk beside, rather than ahead of, local ministers. Even so, the same delineations and allegiances that had emerged within the colonial administration, where indigenous Fijians and Europeans were perceived as oppositional to Indo-Fijians, were operating within the mission.[9]

In 1960, Gribble, still the General Secretary of Methodist Overseas Missions, attempted to maintain a rhetoric of unity. He held the mission up as a beacon of hope while Fiji faced economic and political instability: 'it is wholesome to find the Church ready to give an example of racial unity and acceptance of responsibility to it.'[10] Both the Fijian and Indo-Fijian synods made, in Gribble's words, a 'historic decision to work towards autonomy and to submit a constitution for a Fijian conference'.[11] Gribble congratulated the European missionaries for standing alongside 'Indian and Fijian churchmen determined to overcome caution, suspicion and fear'.[12] Tuilovoni identified fear as the major obstacle to progress towards reconciliation and unification. The legacies of long-term segregation marred the mission's administration, evangelisation and worship, and finances. The Indo-Fijian branch was still significantly smaller in membership than the Fijian branch (there were 559 Indo-Fijian members of the Methodist mission in 1955).[13] The mission's workers struggled to fathom how the independent church would financially sustain programs in the Indo-Fijian community. Considering the mission's finances, Tuilovoni wrote: 'The Conference will succeed if the Methodist people put aside their racial prejudice and enter into this venture by faith, and not by fear.'[14] Gribble recalled, 30 years later, that they had:

8   L Newbigin to C Gribble, 29 April 1960, 1952–65 Fiji-Fijian 1960–1, MOM Fiji Papers, ML.
9   R Norton, 'Accommodating Indigenous Privilege: Britain's Dilemma in Decolonising Fiji', *Journal of Pacific History*, vol. 37, no 2, 2002, p. 134.
10   Ibid.
11   C F Gribble, 'The Older Pacific Churches', statement at the board of missions now in session in Sydney, *The Spectator*, 31 August 1960, p. 14.
12   Ibid.
13   A H Wood, *Overseas Missions of the Australian Methodist Church: Fiji-Indian and Rotuma*, vol. 3, Aldersgate Press, Melbourne, 1978, p. 80.
14   S Tuilovoni to J Robson, 9 April 1962, F/7/J, NAF, p. 3.

A MISSION DIVIDED

to go cap-in-hand to the Indian Synod because they didn't want the Fijian conference, they were afraid. They were afraid that they wouldn't get the helpers for their schools, they were afraid that they wouldn't get the money, the financial support that came from the Board of Missions ... they were afraid of being left alone.[15]

Tuilovoni had similar recollections. The Reverend Setareki Rika had eventually stood up at the 1963 United Synod and said, pointedly, that there was 'strong racial antagonism in the minds of a number of Fijian laymen'.[16] His colleagues had lost sight of the fact that they all belonged to one family, living in 'God's household'.[17]

European missionaries not only struggled to see how the two branches could be brought together, but also with how to manage anti-colonialism. Missionary Cyril Germon read Lesslie Newbigin's *A Faith for this One World?*, in which Newbigin depicted 'western cultural and political penetration' as a bilateral struggle between white races and colonised peoples.[18] Newbigin argued that western culture no longer had 'the right and power to dominate and replace the cultures of Asia and Africa'.[19] While in earlier decades European missionaries had been more conscious of widespread rejection of Christianity by the Indo-Fijian community, Tippett now admitted that some Fijians had become hostile to Christianity because of its association with 'western culture and power'.[20] He believed that the faith 'taught some good ethics, but has not demonstrated the love she preaches'.[21] Despite efforts to acculturate Christianity, the practice of exclusion through maintaining race and class divides had been contrary to Christian values.

With anti-colonialism on the rise, mission leaders were surprised to still hear local leaders convey their hope that European missionaries would stay in the islands. *Talatala* who attended a youth camp in Fiji 1961 told C J Wright, a leader of the Australian Methodist youth movement, that 'Fijians are not objective enough, not impartial enough' to run the church.[22] However, Wright adopted Gribble's position, that despite their reluctance, *talatala* — who he deemed quite capable

15   C F Gribble, 'Cecil Frank Gribble Interviewed by Diana Ritch [sound recording]', 1990–1991, TRC 2731, tape 5, side 2.
16   Ibid.
17   S Tuilovoni to S Andrews, 5 January 1972, PMB 1072.
18   L Newbigin, *A Faith for this One World?*, London, SCM Press, 1961, p. 107.
19   Ibid., pp. 108–9.
20   'Our Missionary Perspective', part two, *The Spectator*, 1 November 1961, p. 14.
21   Ibid.
22   C J Wright, 'South Pacific Encounter', *The Spectator*, 29 November 1961, p. 13.

— should be encouraged to take 'fuller responsibility'.[23] He felt sure that when Tuilovoni returned to Fiji from the United States, he would be 'in a position to foster this legitimate urge towards independence'.[24]

With his extensive experience overseas, Tuilovoni had adopted the highly idealistic rhetoric of the International Missionary Council, but Deoki stood beside him to push for unity in their burgeoning church.[25] Tuilovoni tried to translate his conceptualisations of unity from his thesis to the Pacific context. Like Newbigin, Tuilovoni remained hopeful that the church would be able to overcome colonial boundaries.[26] Newbigin had argued that equal partnership could exist between 'older' and 'younger' churches where they were able to adopt a 'supra-national character', 'so that men may be able to recognise in the missionary operation, not the coming of a particular human cultural or political influence but the mission of him who belongs equally to all races and nations, and being the Saviour of all'.[27] Newbigin's plan was good in principle, but was undermined by the everyday reality of mission operations that had been designed and developed during the heyday of Empire and mirrored the divisions imposed by colonial administrations. Despite his own experience of this, Tuilovoni wrote in a similar vein:

> This is the marvellous thing about the Church. When she is in her rightful place she does transcend racial and other barriers. The political situation in which islands of the Pacific are involved could make church unity difficult yet not impossible. On the other hand the political dependence of native peoples may be an important factor in executing church unity in the South Pacific.[28]

Tuilovoni considered the potential for true social cohesion in the Pacific to be dampened by the continued presence of colonial powers. In a decolonised Pacific, amalgamation would be more readily achieved, with Pacific Islanders central to local church administration, rather than manipulated by 'dependency' on colonial ties.

---

23   Ibid.

24   Ibid.

25   This was one way in which the international discourse of indigenous rights travelled to Fiji. E W Larson and R Aminzade, 'Nation-states Confront the Global: Discourses of Indigenous Rights in Fiji and Tanzania', *The Sociological Quarterly*, vol. 48, no. 4, 2007, p. 804.

26   The research conducted by historians are far more critical of the role of missionaries in colonisation include J Comaroff and J Comaroff, *Of Revelation and Revolution*, vols 1 and 2, Chicago, University of Chicago Press, 1991; B Stanley, *The Bible and the Flag: Protestant Missions and British Imperialism in the Nineteenth and Twentieth Centuries*, Leicester, England, Apollos, 1990; L Sanneh, *Translating the Message: The Missionary Impact on Culture*, Maryknoll, NY, Orbis Books, 2009; A Porter, *Religion Versus Empire? British Protestant Missionaries and Overseas Expansion, 1700–1914*, Manchester, Manchester University Press, 2004.

27   L Newbigin, *A Faith for this One World?*, London, SCM Press, 1961, pp. 115–17.

28   S Tuilovoni, 'The Church Unity in the South Pacific', PMB 1072.

A constitution committee was appointed to discuss the parameters of the independent church, meeting for the first time in August 1961. The committee planned to submit a draft constitution for approval to the general conference in Adelaide in 1963, so they had two years to deliberate questions of integration within the church.[29] A meeting on 15 September 1961 at Dudley House School in Suva included representatives from all districts of the mission, including European missionaries.[30] The Reverend L D Fullerton, then chairman of the Indo-Fijian district, reiterated his hopes for a 'ministry of reconciliation'.[31] With this ideal in mind, the committee formulated three proposed structures for the conference. Proposal A continued the existing structure of racial segregation.[32] Proposal B had one conference for all, with a Fijian synod that would incorporate six districts: Rewa, Bau-Ra, Lau, Lomaiviti, Ba-Nadroga, and Vanua Levu Rotuma. The Indo-Fijian synod would remain separate but be answerable to the conference.[33] Proposal C was described as follows:

> That there be a Conference, a Conference Committee of Details, and six Annual Meetings (comparable to the Fijian Annual Meetings in geographical distribution), and that there be an Indian Advisory Committee to meet before the Annual Meeting and submit recommendations to the Annual Meetings on matters concerned with the work of the Church among the Indian people. Indian and Fijian representatives would meet together in the Annual Meetings. The Indian Advisory Committee would be roughly equivalent in personnel to the Indian Synod.[34]

Proposal C was the most integrated of the models. Most of the meeting's attendees decided that adopting this model would be a 'premature development'.[35] They were able to discuss these proposed models at quarterly meetings with Methodists in each circuit and report on their preferences at the next meeting.

29   'Report from Fiji', *The Spectator*, 23 August 1961, p. 14.
30   Those present included L D Fullerton, R R Deoki, C H T Germon, M T Dreu, J B Wilton, S Rika, S A Tuilovoni, P K Davis, M N Tora, P Campbell, M Prasad and D J Rogerson, H Charan, R Buiniqio, G N Bamford and J S Bhagwan.
31   L D Fullerton, 'Pacific Missionaries', *The Spectator*, 1 June 1960, p. 7; Fullerton went on to write a thesis in 1969 at Drew University titled 'From Christendom to Pluralism in the South Seas: Church–State Relations in the Twentieth Century', where he argued that 'folk churches' had become predominant in the Pacific, where a 'church is broadly accepted within a particular culture and reinforces the cultural values and the political status quo.' See J E Bush, 'Claiming a Christian State Where None Exists: Church and State in the Republic of Fiji', *Pacifica*, vol. 12, no. 1, 1999, p. 63.
32   Conference constitution committee meeting, day 2, 16 September 1961, minutes, F/J/7, p. 3.
33   Ibid., p. 1.
34   Ibid., p. 2.
35   Ibid.

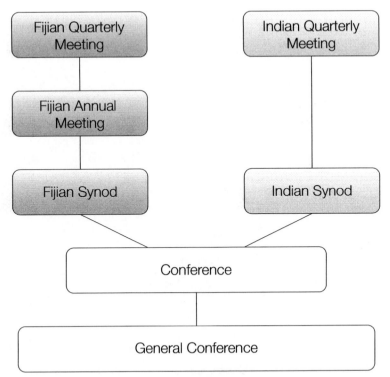

Figure 11: Proposed church structures.
Source: Author's research.

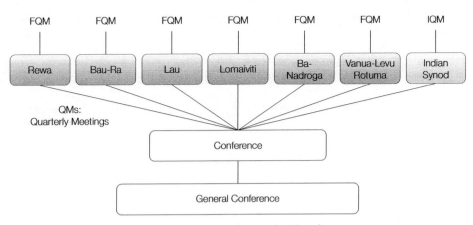

Figure 12: Fijian quarterly meetings in each circuit.
Source: Author's research.

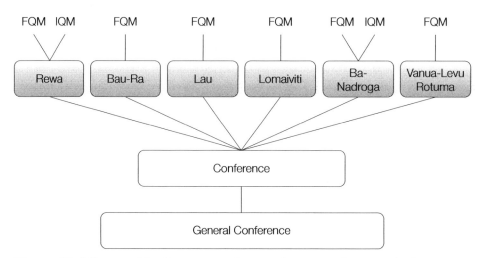

Figure 13: Fijian and Indian quarterly meetings sending resolutions to integrated annual meetings.
Source: Author's research.

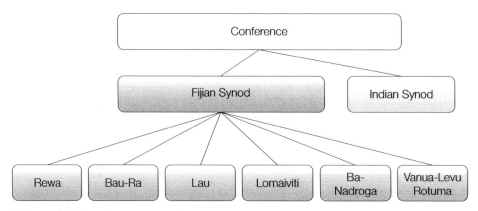

Figure 14: Conference and synod structure.
Source: Author's research.

While ministers sought feedback on these proposed models at the village level, Gribble kept abreast of anthropological debates, seeking inspiration on how racial barriers might be bridged. He was aware of the criticisms coming from Australian anthropologist Catherine Berndt about the concept of the 'native church'. Berndt was Elkin's protégé, but was not as sympathetic to missions as he had been.[36] She too explored questions of 'integration', 'segregation', and the

---

36   G Gray, '"You are … my anthropological children": A P Elkin, Ronald Berndt and Catherine Berndt, 1940–1956', *Aboriginal History*, vol. 29, 2005, pp. 80, 85.

native church policy in an article published in 1961. Focusing specifically on Methodist efforts in Arnhem Land, she spoke about the accommodation or tolerance of Aboriginal culture. She described the acceptance of the idea of a 'native church' within Methodist circles, which Methodists did not view as being segregated or producing social or political inequality, even though it had established an inequitable racial system. She believed that despite its claims of accommodating Aboriginal culture, the policy had required 'the Europeanising ideal to predominate. What appeared to be a permissive or positive approach to Aboriginal culture for example the use of a local language, can only be a matter of temporary expediency, a more skilful way of achieving that end.'[37] While Berndt observed the Methodist mission's application of the 'three selves' church policy in the Australian context, the same approach to culture and building a 'native church' had been used in the Pacific. She rightly observed that the ideals of equity and the acculturation of Christianity never quite overcame the issue of race. The mission's application of the 'three selves' church policy — to establish self-governing, self-supporting and self-propagating indigenous churches — had hardened racial boundaries in both the Australian and Pacific contexts.

The 1962 draft constitution declared that the Fijian church would have complete autonomy over 'doctrine, discipline, organisation, land and property — in the group of islands and Rotuma', but that it would still 'be subject to the jurisdiction and control of the General Conference of the Methodist Church of Australasia'.[38] The racial division of the Methodist community remained a source of heated debate. Tuilovoni was frustrated with the persistence of the racialised wage system. He explained that implementing an equitable pay scheme would institute a sense of 'oneness' and 'belonging', and allow Fijian and Indo-Fijian ministers to work in either district of the church without complications.[39] He asked that members of the constitution committee 'put aside personal involvement in the ministerial salary' and bring Methodists in Fiji together 'irrespective of their race, colour, or social status'.[40] There was one person in particular whose recommendations caught Tuilovoni's ire. This was the mission's accountant, J E Nix.[41] Nix had recommended that the conference should continue its existing method of pay: European ministers would be paid £1,000 per annum, Indo-Fijian ministers £700 per annum, and Fijian

37   C Berndt, 'The Quest for Identity: The Case of the Australian Aborigines', *Oceania*, vol. 32, no. 1, 1961, pp. 21–22.

38   'Jurisdiction', 'Constitution for submission to Conference Constitution Committee 15/6/62', Part V, F/7/J, NAF, p. 5.

39   S A Tuilovoni, 'Financing the Ministry', n.d., F/7/J, NAF, p. 2.

40   Ibid., p. 3.

41   A H Wood, *Overseas Missions of the Australian Methodist Church: Fiji*, vol. 2, Melbourne, Aldersgate Press, 1978, p. 377.

and Rotuman ministers a mere £120 per annum.[42] Tuilovoni condemned this suggestion, submitting his opinion to acting chairmen of the Fijian district, the Reverend C A Hatcher.[43] Tuilovoni felt that it would work against 'the unity that has been established in the conference':[44]

> The scheme of salaries proposed by Mr Nix on the basis of three separate racial groups will result in the very thing that has come to many other countries and which they are beginning to accept. If it be true that Fijian, Indian and Rotuman ministers are soldiers in one army, there should be one system of salaries and not many different scales as proposed by Mr Nix.[45]

Tuilovoni continued:

> Mr Nix's scheme is less Christian than the Government, where there is one salary for all, and they are not divided on the basis of race or any other group. As they work for one Government, there is one source only from which they are paid, which is not divided on the basis of what each separate group respectively gives to the Government.[46]

Tuilovoni suggested that the money for wages come from one pool, as the Indo-Fijian congregations would not be able to afford to pay their ministers the sum of £700 per annum as required.[47] He suggested that the wages be made the same for all:

> … if this could be done, we will be able to say: (1) that we stand together in one level of mutual love in Christ's church, (2) there will be nothing in which you missionaries are distinct from the rest of us; at present we do not think of you and us on the same level together. Your spiritual work will have greater effect among men when they know that you have given yourselves for them.[48]

Tuilovoni did not demand that European missionaries exit the mission at the point of independence, but if they were to stay in Fiji, they had to work on an equal basis with non-European ministers. The long-standing system of racially codified wage distribution had to end if there was going to be any legitimacy to claims of Christian brotherhood in the Methodist church in Fiji. Tuilovoni understood that while European missionaries might require a different rate of pay associated with living away from their homeland, 'Fijian and Indian

---

42 S Tuilovoni to J Robson, 9 April 1962, F/7/J, NAF, p. 5.
43 A H Wood, *Overseas Missions of the Australian Methodist Church: Fiji*, vol. 2, Melbourne, Aldersgate Press, 1978, p. 372.
44 S Tuilovoni to J Robson, 9 April 1962, F/7/J, NAF, p. 3.
45 Ibid.
46 Ibid.
47 Ibid.
48 S Tuilovoni to C A Hatcher, Acting Chairman, 27 January 1962, F/7/J, NAF.

ministers truly belong to the Church, and there should not be two distinct rates of salary. Where possible let all people of the Church share together in supporting ministers.'[49] For this he recommended:

It should be the responsibility of the whole church, when it is inter-racial, to provide for minister's salaries according to a scale which will make it possible for a leader to fulfil his duties well, and for all ministers to be able to do their work adequately … Within the fold of Christ there is no Indian or Fijian, European or Rotuman, Chinese or Part-European. They are members of one family and partners together in those things that build up the whole household.[50]

At the April 1962 Conference Constitution Committee Meeting, when revising the existing three-tier system of pay, the committee adopted Tuilovoni's position, and the minutes stated that when it came to ministerial stipends there would 'be no difference (Fijian and Indian) as we are united in one Conference'.[51] Tuilovoni believed that the foundations of the church, developed in the previous century, had allowed discrimination to proliferate within the mission.[52] The mission's organisation had to be redeveloped if there was to be any reconciliation. 'There will be many things to unite', he said, 'such as land, the funds of the Church and other things that were previously divided'.[53] As Maelin Pickering-Bhagwan has illustrated in her essay on these debates, Tuilovoni advocated the integration of congregations, for Fijians to be able to minister to Indo-Fijian congregations and vice versa, and for anyone to be able to enter any Methodist church in Fiji, regardless of race, and be welcomed as part of the community.[54] He believed that sharing worship would 'build up the mutual knowledge and fellowship of those of different races in one village or preaching place'.[55]

Tuilovoni made a final comment about the rhetoric used to discuss work in the mission and which fostered a sense of exclusion. He wrote that many acknowledged that evangelising the Indo-Fijian community was important, but that the mission could not continue to single out Indo-Fijians.[56] He felt that people had spoken of the need for evangelistic work with the Indo-Fijian community incessantly, which was unnecessarily stating the obvious, to the point where it was purposefully overstated in order to exacerbate difference.[57]

---

49   S Tuilovoni to J Robson, 9 April 1962, F/7/J, NAF, p. 3.
50   Ibid., p. 5.
51   Meeting, Conference constitution committee, Dudley House School, 27 April 1962, F/7/J, NAF.
52   S Tuilovoni to J Robson, 9 April 1962, F/7/J, p. 3.
53   Ibid.
54   Ibid.; M Pickering-Bhagwan, 'A Historical Examination of the Indian Synod's Amalgamation into the Conference of the Methodist Church of Fiji and Rotuma', thejournalofaspiritualwonderer.blogspot.com.au/2013/05/a-historical-examination-of-indian.html.
55   S Tuilovoni to J Robson, 9 April 1962, F/7/J, p. 3.
56   Ibid.
57   Ibid., p. 2.

Tuilovoni pushed the mission to embrace its full membership rather than discussing only the colonies' two dominant races, expanding the mission's vision to other Pacific Islanders.

Symbolic of efforts to enhance the inclusion of Indo-Fijian membership, the meetings for the Conference Constitution Committee continued to be held at the Dudley House School in Suva, initially built solely for the Indo-Fijian branch. By this time it was a school for both Indo-Fijian and Fijian children.[58] When the committee met again in June 1962, amalgamation was again discussed, particularly the wage system. Delegates agreed to revisit the constitution every three years 'to determine whether the Church is ready to take the next step in integration or not'.[59] Complete integration was not yet possible, despite the international pressure to move towards an integrated model.

At the June 1962 Constitution Committee Meeting, members considered ways in which the mission's spheres could be brought together. They particularly advocated integration at a congregational level, recommending that steps towards this end to be taken immediately.[60] Despite this, in 1962 the mission board heard that the united synod had decided to move ahead with proposal B, which was similar to the existing system of governance. An Indo-Fijian annual meeting would replace the Indo-Fijian annual synod — a largely superficial change.[61] The system of segregation between the two cultures would remain embedded in the independent church structure.

It was evident that Tuilovoni's ideas were incredibly influential in these meetings. In a significant step towards self-governance, Tuilovoni assumed the role of President of the United Fiji Synod in 1962.[62] This meant that the period of transition to independence was now underway and, for the first time, Fijian leadership was fully recognised.

There was still considerable work to be done to prepare the mission for complete autonomy. Discussions about equal wages continued at the constitution committee's meetings throughout 1963, with ministers requesting parity in pay. Nix's wage scheme had been abandoned, and John Robson, who was

---

58   J Garrett, *Footsteps in the Sea: Christianity in Oceania to World War Two*, Suva, University of the South Pacific in conjunction with the World Council of Churches, 1992, pp. 396–97.

59   Those present included Fullerton, Davis, Tabulutu, Vatucicila, Salway, Drou, Robson, Wilton, Deoki, Waqairawai, Buiniqio, Bhagwan, Campbell and Rogerson. Meeting re: conference constitution committee held at Dudley house school, Suva, 29 June 1962, F/7/J, NAF.

60   Conference Constitution Committee meeting, Dudley House School, 29 June 1962, F/7/J, NAF.

61   'Acting Chairman's Report to the Annual Meeting of the Board of Missions, 1962, on proposals for a Fiji Conference, Methodist Church in Fiji United Synod, F/J/7, NAF.

62   F/7/J, NAF; J Garrett, *Where Nets Were Cast: Christianity in Oceania since World War Two*, Suva, Institute of Pacific Studies, University of the South Pacific in association with the World Council of Churches, 1997, p. 393.

now chairman, felt that they had 'accepted the principle of integration', and 'equalisation', but that they could not make the scheme progress. The Reverend Doug Fullerton, who had continued to work on church committees in Australia through his engagement with the National Missionary Council in the 1960s while he worked as a missionary in Fiji, described the new 'integrated' system they created as a 'two level ministry with different functions and different salary'.[63] The committee reasoned that it would cost £150 per minister per year, 'if all monies for salaries were pooled'.[64] The salaries would be too low for ministers to live on, and they needed to be increased, but no resolution came about at this meeting.[65]

At the Conference Constitution Committee Meeting on 8 February 1963, the push for integration was stalled again.[66] Racial representation was discussed, as Indo-Fijian ministers were evidently concerned that they were to be outvoted if they merged with the Fijian district. John B Wilton, who would become principal at Davuilevu in 1964, suggested the concerns that a majority/minority dynamic may be managed by capping the number of *talatala* who could work at any one time.[67] However, Robson said that this would not be appropriate; he diverted the discussions away from merging, and suggested that it would be better to have two separate churches, or form a church that would be primarily Fijian.[68] Those who were shaping Fiji's independent church were preoccupied with demographics.[69] There was no other alternative offered. To ensure its needs were heard, the Indo-Fijian synod supported the new conference model with seven annual meetings, six of which would discuss Fijian matters, and a seventh that would discuss the Indo-Fijian work. The Fijian synod wanted a more blended model, however, suggesting that 'there should be only six integrated Annual Meetings, which would be attended by representatives of both the Fijian and Indian Churches'.[70] A report regarding the proposed conference read:

---

63 General Secretary to Hickin, 25 September 1959, L D Fullerton to attend Conference of Australian Churches in Melbourne, Australia, February 1960, National Missionary Council minutes, MOM 448–449, ML; Conference Constitution Committee meeting, Dudley House School, 8 February 1963, F/7/J, NAF, p. 2.

64 Ibid.

65 Ibid.

66 This meeting was attended by Tuilovoni, Fullerton, Robson, Wilton, Germon, Deoki, Dreu, Mastapha, Ratu Rusiate Buiniqio, Ali, Singh, Bhagwan, Campbell, and Rogerson.

67 A H Wood, *Overseas Missions of the Australian Methodist Church: Fiji*, vol. 2, Melbourne, Aldersgate Press, 1978, p. 335.

68 Conference Constitution Committee meeting, Dudley House School, 8 February 1963, F/7/J, NAF, p. 2; A Thornley, 'Fijian Methodism: 1874–1945: The Emergence of a National Church', PhD thesis, The Australian National University, 1979, pp. 284, 286.

69 J Kelly, 'Aspiring to Minority and Other Tactics against Violence', in D Gladney (ed.), *Making Majorities: Constituting the Nation in Japan, Korea, China, Malaysia, Fiji, Turkey, and the United States*, California, Stanford University Press, 1998, p. 190; M Kaplan, 'When 8.870 - 850 = 1: Discourses Against Democracy in Fiji, Past and Present', in D Gladney (ed.), *Making Majorities: Constituting the Nation in Japan, Korea, China, Malaysia, Fiji, Turkey, and the United States*, California, Stanford University Press, 1998, pp. 198–99.

70 'Acting Chairman's Report to the Annual Meeting of the Board of Missions, 1962, on proposals for a Fiji Conference', F/7/J, NAF, p. 2

The Fijian Synod showed an understanding of the hesitation and fears of a minority church, such as the Indian Church. The whole question was approached in an atmosphere of Christian love, and it seems that the strong minority vote in the Fijian Synod in favour of seven Annual Meetings (which was not passed) was recognition that this was the wish of the Indian Church. The Fijian Synod further resolved by an almost unanimous vote that the Fijian Church would accept happily whatever decision the United Synod felt was right for the Church as a whole.[71]

These meetings revealed aspirations for solidarity between Fijians and Indo-Fijians, but also the arguments put forward for continued separation. Ultimately, the ministry left the united synod to decide the fate of the mission. Seen by many as a Fijian institution, Indo-Fijian ministers felt compelled to assert their ethnic difference in a bid to ensure representation and minimise their marginalisation within the mission as it decolonised.[72] The minutes demonstrated that there was care taken in these meetings to hear and appreciate the contribution of Indo-Fijian ministers in the process of devolution, an effort at inclusion in the midst of continued exclusion.

The opinions of ministers in the field were shaped by international discussions in the global era of decolonisation and by Australian anthropologists. Monitoring events in Fiji, Gribble had been influenced by Catherine Berndt's earlier criticism of Methodist missions and their efforts to preserve and engage with indigenous culture. Berndt had worked in both Australia and Papua New Guinea and was, as a result, familiar with some of the challenges in the Pacific context. Gribble also corresponded with Ronald Berndt, Catherine Berndt's husband, who advised him to continue to support the retention of indigenous culture, as it would remain relevant to the 'here and now'.[73] Gribble sought Berndt's advice on assimilation, integration and protectionism.[74] From Gribble in the General Secretary's Office in Sydney to those in the field, missionaries had been confounded by the dilemma of reconciling their interest in safeguarding culture and working towards a systematic program of social integration, though the process of acculturation could now potentially continue in the independent

---

71 Ibid.
72 J Kelly depicts the indigenous Fijian concept of love as being the main Christian (Methodist) Fijian concept for love. Kelly's description in this way further amplifies the paramountcy of an indigenous 'version' of Methodism in Fiji. Doing so further distinguishes the difference between Hindu and what it is to be Methodist in Fiji, and in doing so polarised Indo-Fijian and indigenous Fijian Methodists, despite his best efforts not to homogenise the Indo-Fijian community (p. 186). J Kelly, 'Aspiring to Minority and Other Tactics against Violence', in D Gladney (ed.), *Making Majorities: Constituting the Nation in Japan, Korea, China, Malaysia, Fiji, Turkey, and the United States*, California, Stanford University Press, 1998, pp. 183–84; R Norton, 'Culture and Identity in the South Pacific', *Man*, vol. 28, 1993, p. 744.
73 R M Berndt to C F Gribble 29 April 1963, National Missionary Council minutes, MOM 448–449, ML, p. 3.
74 Ibid.

church if it was to remain segregated.[75] In April 1963 Gribble consulted with an Arthur Elemore, who told Gribble that he preferred the term 'integration' to 'assimilation', as he felt it carried more respect for 'ethnic entity and difference, as well as standing in contrast to "segregation" which is the policy now rejected'.[76] This discussion directly reflected the decisions made regarding Fiji's conference constitution.

Ministers were clearly influenced by international debates about racial equality as the Fijian church moved towards independence. The messages emerging from the International Missionary Council, particularly Newbigin's publications, remained influential, but did not offer a clear guide for reconciliation in a multicultural context. While people within the church had hoped for unity between the Fijian and Indo-Fijian districts of the mission, the church remained divided through to the independent era. This division remained in order to ensure that the voices of Indo-Fijian Methodists were not drowned out amidst a Fijian majority of the ministry and membership. Negotiations over the church's new constitution in the early 1960s did not break down the racial divisions that had existed within the mission throughout the twentieth century. The responses of European missionaries and local ministers to the issues raised in the lead up to independence demonstrate the legacy of racialist ideas. Even during this era, wages were arranged according to an arbitrary racial and cultural hierarchy. Missionaries were guided as much by anthropology as ecumenism throughout this period of decolonisation, and had a better sense of the impact of colonialism on colonised people, but the racial categorisation which had been so much a part of the colonial Fiji could not be easily dismantled.

---

75   D A Chappell, 'The Crisis of Bipolar Ethnicity on the Great Frontier: Nativist "Democracy" in Fiji, Malaysia, and New Caledonia', *Journal of World History*, 1990, p. 185.
76   A Elemore to C F Gribble, 24 April 1963, National Missionary Council minutes, MOM 448–449, ML.

Conclusion

On 10 October 1964, 20,000 people spilled onto the streets of Suva and into Albert Park to mark the birth of Fiji's Methodist Church. The Reverend Setareki Tuilovoni was inducted as its president by the President General of the Australasian Methodist Church, the Reverend Frank Hambly, and by the Reverend Cecil Gribble, General Secretary of the Methodist Church of Australia's Department of Overseas Missions.[1] 'In the still swelling sea of faces around us', wrote one retired missionary who attended the event, it was visibly 'time for Independence!'[2] This ceremony marked the symbolic end of Australasian colonisation of Fijian Methodism.

The mission was part of the transnational imperial network. Typical of colonial institutions, the Methodist mission created boundaries that went beyond the practical limits of language difference. Methodists in Fiji were categorised according to class, race and culture. It was along these lines that processes of inclusion and exclusion were defined. The mission's connections to the International Missionary Council and the World Conference of Churches, the Methodist Overseas Missions of Australasia, and Australian anthropologists informed the way that missionaries approached their work. These networks sometimes affirmed the divisions that missionaries had established in Fiji, however, they also sometimes encouraged missionaries to question their methods. The 'three selves' policy, drawn from the international ecumenical movement, brought missionaries to reflect on their own position within the colonial power dynamic. The debates that emerged around the implementation of self-support, self-governance and self-propagation in Fiji illuminated many of the complexities of governing the colony, and how Europeans, Indo-Fijians and Fijians engaged with each other.

---

1   A H Wood, *Overseas Missions of the Australian Methodist Church: Fiji*, vol. 2, Melbourne, Aldersgate Press, 1978, p. 347; R H Green, *My Story: A Record of the Life and Work of Robert H Green*, Melbourne, 1978, p. 359.

2   R H Green, *My Story: A Record of the Life and Work of Robert H Green*, Melbourne, 1978, p. 360.

Missionary approaches to the 'three selves' church policy contributed to the decision to divide the mission according to race in 1901. Essentialised perceptions of Fijian and Indo-Fijian cultures that depicted the two peoples as irreconcilably different were incorporated into the mission's structure. The 'three selves' church concept required the establishment of 'native churches' that reflected the national character, and with two distinct communities, missionaries believed this required two separate missions in Fiji. The creation of separate spaces for religious practice contributed to strengthening the expression of different cultural identities.[3] Missionaries developed these ideas about governance in the same circles and were exposed to the same ideas as colonial administrators. Both were often engaging in the latest debates about race and culture occurring in anthropology. How they responded to these arguments and applied them to their own working lives depended on each person's character and the limitations placed on them by their institution or conditions in the locality where they worked.

In both the 'Fijian' and 'Indo-Fijian' parts of the mission, non-European peoples were excluded from positions of status. Ideas about race and culture were fused with ideas about class. In Fiji, customary hierarchies could be translated into the colonial context. Chiefly status gave Fijians some leverage into certain spheres of the colony's upper classes throughout the early twentieth century. Similarly, those who had attained certain levels of education could ascend the class system. However, as education was often only available to people of certain races, and quality education afforded only to a few, there were limits on class mobility. European missionaries controlled access to education, attendance at synods, and ministerial appointments to roles such as circuit superintendent and district chairman. The boundaries became more fluid over time, and this book has followed the ways in which Fijians became gradually more socially mobile. *Talatala* were admitted into synods and financial sessions in the first decade of the twentieth century. Theological education was enhanced, which paved the way to self-governance. From 1930 onwards, *talatala* were employed as circuit superintendents, and in 1962 the mission instated its first Fijian president. The Indo-Fijian branch of the mission lagged behind the Fijian branch. Indo-Fijians were not able to enter theological education in Fiji until 1927, and were not circuit superintendents until 1939.

While the Indo-Fijian branch trailed behind the Fijian branch in fulfilling the 'three selves' church policy, missionaries often considered the Indian 'race' and 'cultures' to be stronger and more sophisticated than their Fijian counterparts. The mission constructed a racial hierarchy that mirrored the colonial system

---

3   R Norton, 'Ethno-nationalism and the Constitutive Power of Cultural Politics: A Comparative Study of Sri Lanka and Fiji', *Journal of Asian and African Studies*, vol. 28, nos 3–4, 1993, p. 181.

of categorisation. A wage scale was created according to the assumed needs of their workers, based on essentialist understandings of each culture. European missionaries were paid a wage that was usually double the amount paid to Indo-Fijian ministers, and more still than indigenous ministers. The European wage was set to support a 'European' lifestyle; Indo-Fijian workers were paid a wage deemed adequate to support an 'Indian' lifestyle, which equated with that paid to Indo-Fijian mission workers in India; and Fijian mission workers were paid an amount that was assumed to be subsidised by the communal system of reciprocity. The mission instituted a racial system of pay that remained in place throughout the 64 years covered in this book. Knowing that race and culture fed the decisions to allocate wages in this way, non-European ministers — especially Ramsey Deoki — made wages the focus of their contests against colonial power. This was because the wage scale was one of the most tangible, visible emblems of inequity in the mission. Whether it was exclusion from financial meetings, or being denied equal rates of pay, non-European ministers were frustrated by the limitations placed on their equal involvement in the mission's economies.

John Kelly suggested that there was precedence placed on protecting Fijian rights and that race became the key organising factor in Fiji, rather than class.[4] This promoted a non-transformative or protective mode of colonialism. There were several points at which the colonial administration's desires to implement a non-transformative style of governance directly contributed to the shape of the mission. One of the best examples of this was the separate labour ordinance created for Fijians in 1912, as discussed in Chapter Four. This ordinance set Fijians apart from the Indo-Fijian workers in Fiji at the same time as it attempted to diminish the impact of colonialism on the communal social system. The mission's policies tended to mirror the colonial administration's system of separation and cultural acclimatisation. Robert Norton has noted that this system gave rise to Fijian paramountcy, a process that was exemplified by the history of Fiji's Methodist mission.[5] With the overwhelming majority of the mission's membership being Fijian, Fijian culture and custom became central to the mission's identity. This occurred despite lingering concerns about the possibility of indigenous extinction in the first three decades of the twentieth century, an idea informed by demographic trends. It seemed to most that Fiji was destined to become an Indian state over the following decades. While there were efforts to encourage more modern relationships between Fijian and the *vanua*, there was always an effort made to sustain certain parts of indigenous culture, and this fed an indigenous paramountcy that was mirrored and promoted by the colonial administration.

---

4   J Kelly, 'Fear of Culture: British Regulation of Indian Marriage in Post-indenture Fiji', *Ethnohistory*, vol. 36, no. 4, 1989, p. 383.
5   R Norton, 'Chiefs for the Nation: Containing Ethnonationalism and Bridging the Ethnic Divide in Fiji', *Pacific Studies*, vol. 22, no. 1, 1999, pp. 21–50.

Allusions to land, or the *vanua*, in mission discussions also often revealed attempts to ensure — at least emblematically — Fijian ascendency. This was demonstrated most clearly in the mission's efforts to ensure Fijian access to land through aiding Fijians to demonstrate that they could work in ways that would make it profitable in a western sense. The conceptualisation of the *vanua* and the Fijians' birthright emerged several times: in 1912, Henry Worrall likened the relationship between Fijians and Indo-Fijians to the Biblical story of Esau and Jacob; and in the 1920s, Benjamin Meek, Principal of the Methodist Navuso Agricultural School, described the land as the Fijians' birthright. This discourse was also prevalent in discussions in 1930s Melbourne, as Arthur Lelean negotiated support from businessmen for the independent farming schemes that he believed would help to secure financial self-support for the mission. While Lelean endorsed a more transformative mode of colonialism with greater indigenous engagement in capitalist economies, the same hallmarks of dialogics operated around land, labour and belonging that marginalised Indo-Fijians. European missionaries at times exacerbated the resulting tensions. Anxieties about maintaining Fijians' connection to *vanua*, a phenomena that anthropologists such as Matthew Tomlinson have observed over the past three decades, have their roots in Fiji's most devoted Methodist villages, such as Toko.

As discussed in the final chapter, some of the Indo-Fijian Methodists who represented the mission's racial minority met independence with trepidation. This is similar to Maelin Pickering Bhagwan's conclusions about the debates around amalgamation in the mission.[6] Beyond the issues of land, racism, finances, and autonomy, there was also a sense that amalgamation would lead to a loss of identity. Indo-Fijians would have to be submissive to Fijians to ensure that their programs were financed and that they would maintain some significant role in the governance of the independent church. The pre-eminence given to Fijian culture was evident in Tippett's booklet, created for the independence celebrations in 1964:

> There were now three loyalties that every Fijian had to consider — the Land (Vanua), to the Church (Lotu) and the Government (Matanitu). This triple loyalty pattern makes the Fijian situation different from that of the other races in the Colony, but the Fijian acceptance of this reality is manifest in speeches and prayers on all public occasions. It raises problems which the new Conference will have to face.[7]

---

6   M Pickering-Bhagwan, 'A Historical Examination of the Indian Synod's Amalgamation into the Conference of the Methodist Church of Fiji and Rotuma', thejournalofaspiritualwonderer.blogspot.com.au/2013/05/a-historical-examination-of-indian.html.

7   C Germon's personal archives, A Tippett, 'Fiji Methodist Conference, July 1964', Independence commemorative booklet, p. 25.

Tippett directed this specifically to a Fijian audience, to the exclusion of the small yet significant Indo-Fijian Methodist community. As Norton and others have argued, Christianity became central to the Fijian 'cultural complex'.[8] Christianity was rarely considered a part of Indo-Fijian community identity — Methodist Indo-Fijians inhabited a marginalised status in both their own and the Methodist community.

Indo-Fijian Methodists were sidelined in the mission, despite missionaries' efforts to defend their liberties. One of the most important transnational connections for Indo-Fijian Methodists was with Christian leaders, such as Charles Freer Andrews, in India. The mission recruited Indian and European catechists and missionaries, supporting the mobility of men and women from India to Fiji and vice versa, trying to find workers who would respect and accommodate Indo-Fijian cultures. Through travel and correspondence, the mission's workers remained abreast of developments in anti-colonial movements and methods for managing colonialism and decolonisation in India. However, this was always counteracted by the flow of anti-colonial politics from the broader social scene into the mission, such as the demands for self-governance influenced by Gandhi's Home Rule campaign in Fiji during the 1920s, and crusades against unequal labour conditions. Concepts of culture informed the creation of a system that so closely aligned with racial segregation that they were resisted throughout the colonial period.

While European missionaries pledged their dedication to the concept of establishing native churches, their commitment was often strangled by theories of racial or cultural difference. This book has highlighted the various ways in which European missionaries used ideas from mission councils and anthropology to respond to the presence of two distinct racial and cultural groups in Fiji. The discourse of unity and integration that proliferated during the 1950s and 1960s was incongruent with the reality of Fiji's divided society. This study of the Methodist mission offers an understanding of the legacies of the racial and cultural boundaries that existed within Fiji's colonial society. At the time it separated from Australia, the Methodist Church of Fiji was still segregated according to race and culture, and it will be worth the reader's consideration as to how this paralleled with the independence of Fiji as a nation state.

---

8   R Norton, 'Culture and Identity in the South Pacific', *Man*, vol. 28, 1993, p. 747; C Toren, 'Making the Present, Revealing the Past: The Mutability and Continuity of Tradition as Process', *Man*, New Series, vol. 23, no. 4, 1988; M Jolly, 'Epilogue: Multicultural relations in Fiji — between despair and hope', *Oceania: Relations in Multi-Cultural Fiji: Transformations, positionings and articulations*, vol. 75, no. 4, 2005, pp. 418–30, 419; J Kelly, 'Fear of culture: British regulation of Indian marriage in post-indenture Fiji', *Ethnohistory*, vol. 36, no. 4, 1989, pp. 372–91, 383; J Ryle, 'Burying the Past – Healing the Land: Ritualising Reconciliation in Fiji', in Y Fer (ed.), special issue, *Archives des Sciences Sociales des Religions: Changing Christianity in Oceania*, Janvier–Mars 2012, no. 157, pp. 89–111; J Ryle, *My God, My Land: Interwoven Paths of Christianity and Tradition in Fiji*, Farnham, Surrey, Ashgate, 2010, p. xxx; M Tomlinson, *In God's Image: The Metaculture of Fijian Christianity*, Berkeley, University of California Press, 2009, p. 6.

It is also important to consider ways in which these historical fractures are reflected in commemorations for the mission's history. The Methodist Church of Fiji had its golden jubilee in September 2014, at which the Toko farmers were incorporated into celebrations with special visits from church dignitaries. There are important shifts occurring in today's church, thanks in part to the efforts of leader James Bhagwan. While at times there are signs of the same old ethnicised divisions operating, as with Methodist ministers' comments around the time of the 2014 national elections,[9] leaders such as Bhagwan represent a new phase for the church that eschews division and works towards greater unity. Hopes are alive for a more multicultural church. One of the greatest signs of the church's efforts to attend to this divided past was the reconciliation ceremony held for the Reverend Josateki Koroi in 2014. Koroi — a moderate leader — had been ousted forcefully from the Methodist offices and ejected from his position as president by ethno-nationalists within the Methodist church in 1987.[10] When speaking to Koroi about this in 2010, it was evident that the events still caused considerable consternation. This reconciliation process — even if it is only a symbolic gesture — will make a considerable difference for individuals, as well as shifting the public perception of the Methodist church as a site where racial antagonism is incited.

Despite the intensely detailed research I have included in this book, it remains rather a general history. Having spanned such a sweeping historical period, there is potential for finer, more comprehensive research on people, places and events that have been referred to only briefly. These could include studies into some of the individuals who worked in the mission, such as Setareki Tuilovoni, Charles Lelean, Arthur J Small, and Richard L Burton. The mission's female workers also demand much closer attention, though I have included them wherever possible. Morven Sidal's work on Hannah Dudley has been fairly comprehensive, but figures such as Dr Dorothy Delbridge, who worked at the Ba hospital, need to have their work recognised and properly added to the historical record.[11] Other aspects of the mission's history, such as the use of mission houses as

---

9   Two weeks before the 2014 election, Reverend Iliesa Naivalu, a minister from the Methodist church, circulated a letter in which he advised Fijians to vote 'wisely' to ensure that Fiji becomes a Christian state. In doing this, he was encouraging people to vote for SODELPA, a party that promotes indigenous Fijian ascendancy. Naivalu's letter adopted exclusivist language that had been the hallmark of Fiji's ethno-nationalist politics: 'Christianity was being engraved in the lives of the *iTaukei* people.' He accused the state of trying to 'downgrade the God Almighty, his Son Jesus Christ and the Holy Spirit to be equal with idols that are being worshipped in Fiji today', and suggested that the Methodist church wanted to aid 'good relations and interaction of the different ethnic groups in Fiji', but stated that peace would only exist if indigenous hegemony was maintained. See K Close-Barry, 'What's so Anti-Christian about Equality?', *Republika*, October 2014, pp. 30–32, issuu.com/republikamag/docs/october_2014.

10   Losalini Rasoqosoqo, 'Reverend Koroi Praises Reconciliation', *Fiji Sun*, 28 August 2014, fijisun.com. fj/2013/08/28/reverend-koroi-praises-reconciliation/; D Tarte, *Fiji: A Place to Call Home*, ANU Press, 2014, ch. 17.

11   M Sidal, *Hannah Dudley: Hamari Maa: Honoured Mother, Educator, and Missioner to the Indentured Indians in Fiji, 1864–1931*, Suva, Fiji, Pacific Theological College Press, 1997.

markers of status, could be elaborated on by conducting oral histories in the areas where mission houses were located. Such studies would further enhance our understanding of displays of status and the maintenance of boundaries during the colonial period. As others have noted of Fiji, two ethnicised nationalisms emerged throughout the colonial period.

That missionaries attempted to establish a 'national church', but could not reconcile their ideas of race, suggests that the Methodist mission played a role in consolidating the ethnic divisions that have continued into the post-colonial period. Although this is an historical study, it can inform the way we understand the Methodist church, and Fijian nationalism as it exists today.

Glossary

buli	Local administrator.
galala	Independent; used in this book to refer to independent farming.
iTokatoka	The next division after the *mataqali*. Each *mataqali* may have several *iTokatoka*.
kerekere	A request.
lali	Drum.
lewe ni kabakaba	Inhabitants of the ladder.
lotu	Church.
mataqali	Nayacakalou has described the *mataqali* as a 'patrilineal social group'.[1] Each village may have two or more *mataqali*.[2] The *mataqali* is generally considered the primary division in the village. Tomlinson has described the *mataqali* as the subclan to the *yavusa*.[3]
roko	District governor.
sirdar	Title commonly given to Indian foremen on sugar plantations.
solevu	Ceremonial exchange.

1   R Nayacakalou, *Leadership in Fiji*, Oxford, University of the South Pacific in association with Oxford University Press, 1975, p. 3.
2   Ibid., p. 14.
3   M Tomlinson, *In God's Image: The Metaculture of Fijian Christianity*, Berkeley, University of California Press, 2009, p. 35.

tabua	Whale teeth, presented with a *magimagi* (cord made of coconut fibre) for ceremonies and presentations.
talanoa	Discussion, conversation.
talatala	Fijian ordained minister/s.
tikina	Indigenous Fijian administration is based on the *koro,* or village, headed by a *Turaga ni Koro* elected or appointed by the villagers. Several *koros* combine to form a *tikina,* two or more of which comprise a province.
vanua	In the most simplistic sense, *vanua* means 'land', but the term invokes a much broader reference to Fijian spiritual connections to land. The land is considered a source of *mana*, of power.[4] Nayacakalou also describes the *vanua* as the largest political unit in Fiji.[5]
vakamisioneri	A payment system whereby villages would present payment to go towards mission activities and programs.
vakaturaga	According to chiefly protocols, with respect to chiefs.
vaka viti	In the 'Fijian way'.[6]
yavusa	Anthropologist Matthew Tomlinson has described the term *yavusa* as similar to the term 'clan'. A *yavusa* is made up of a conglomeration of kinship groups.[7]

---

4   I S Tuwere, *Vanua: Towards a Fijian Theology of Place*, Suva, Fiji, Institute of Pacific Studies, University of the South Pacific, 2002, pp. 10–11.

5   R Nayacakalou, *Leadership in Fiji*, Oxford, University of the South Pacific in association with Oxford University Press, 1975, p. 36.

6   R Nayacakalou, *Leadership in Fiji*, Oxford, University of the South Pacific in association with Oxford University Press, 1975, p. 15.

7   J Ryle, personal communication, 11 August 2014.

Bibliography

Reports and online resources

'Commission re: Native Church: Information Collected for the Consideration of the Commission', Melbourne, The Methodist Society of Australasia, Spectator Publishing Company, 1923.

Fiji Bureau of Statistics – Key Statistics: June 2012, Population, 1.2A Census Population of Fiji by Ethnicity, www.statsfiji.gov.fj/Key%20Stats/Population/1.2%20pop%20by%20ethnicity.pdf, accessed 22 March 2013.

Fiji Methodist Centenary Souvenir, 1835–1935, Suva, Methodist Missionary Society of Australasia, 1935.

Ministerial Index, accessed at Uniting Church Archive, Eslternwick.

Report of Commission III: Education in Relation to the Christianisation of National Life, with supplement: presentation and discussion of the report in the Conference on 17th June 1910 together with the discussion on Christian literature, Edinburgh and London, Oliphant, Anderson and Ferrier, 1910.

Time Magazine, 19 April 1954, www.time.com/time/covers/0,16641, 19540419,00.html, accessed 27 September 2012.

World Council of Churches Archives Inventory, archives.oikoumene.org/Query/detail.aspx?ID=68117, accessed 27 September 2012.

Mitchell Library (ML)

Arthur James Small Diaries, 1885–1925, MLMSS 3267.

John Wear Burton Further Papers, 1900–1970, MLMSS 2899 Add on 990.

Methodist Church of Australasia. Department of Overseas Missions – Archives, 1855–1939, CY 2671, CY 2706.

Methodist Church of Australasia. Department of Overseas Missions, Further Records, 1844–1971, 1976, 1978, 1980, MOM 386, 448, 449, 524, 527, 627, 628.

Methodist Church of Australasia. Department of Overseas Missions Records, 1855–1953, MOM 106, 204, 232, 233, 238.

Methodist Church of Australasia. Department of Overseas Missions – Records, 1830–1969, Meth. Ch. (O.M.) 317, 319.

Methodist Church Overseas Mission. Mission District Minutes, MOM 184, CY 3027, 3038, 3040, 3310.

National Archives of Fiji (NAF)

Australia, Great Britain, NS, USA, F/1/1946–63 (e).

Ba Circuit Correspondence: F/3/1948–1960B.

Conference Constitution, 1960–3, F/7/J.

Fiji District Papers, 1869–1947. Each is listed as 'F/1/1900', for example, the last four digits marking the year that the correspondence was produced or the file that it is found in the archive. I have cited 1901–1904, 1921, 1923, 1928–1934, 1939, 1943–1944.

Fiji-Fijian District Government Correspondence, F/2/Vol 6, F/2/v7 1946–63.

Miscellaneous Papers, Correspondence and Papers of Rev. C O Lelean, 1905–1937.

Movement for Independent Conference in Fiji, MOM Correspondence and Papers, Fiji 1905–1953, File 1949.

Ra Circuit Correspondence: F/3/1947–8m, F/3/1945–59D.

Macuata Circuit Correspondence: F/6/1926/31.

Head Office Correspondence: HO/1946, HO/1/1951, HO/1/1952.

OS4 1946–63.

Tippett Collection, St Marks Library

Ecumenical Review, World Council of Churches, 1949, TIP 69/43/1.

Letters and Papers from Fiji, TIP 70/38/6.

Letters and Personal Journals from Fiji, TIP 70/39/1/3.

Pacific Manuscripts Bureau

'Annual Synod Minutes and Journals, 1854–1945, together with Miscellaneous Correspondence, 1869–1899, Methodist Church of Fiji', PMB 1138.

'Fiji, Reports and Photographs from the Methodist Mission in Fiji, 1929–1930', PMB 1325.

'Hilda Mary Steadman — Papers, 1913–1975', PMB 1074.

'L Barnard, "Experiences by land and sea", 30 Aug 1929–11 Feb 1930, Nabouwalu'.

'Memories of Winifred McHugh', PMB 156.

'Setareki Tuilovoni, 1916–1983, Papers', PMB 1072.

Newspapers articles, mostly sourced from Trove, National Library of Australia (arranged by date)

'Wesleyan General Conference: Sitting in Brisbane', *The Chronicle*, Adelaide, 25 May 1901, p. 15.

'A Visitor from Fiji: The Rev J S [sic] Small: Progress of Mission Work: Coolie Labour and the Sugar Industry', *The Brisbane Courier*, Brisbane, 27 May 1901, p. 9.

'Methodist General Conference: The Fiji Missions', *The Advertiser*, 4 June 1904, p. 9.

'New South Wales. Hindoos in Fiji: A Missionary's Story', *Morning Post*, Cairns, 6 March 1907, p. 5.

'Orientalisation of the Pacific', *Clarence and Richmond Examiner*, Grafton, 9 March 1907, p. 15.

'Church Notes', *The Advertiser*, Adelaide, 28 November 1908, p. 14.

'Methodism and Indian Missions', *The Spectator*, 5 March 1909, p. 381.

'The Annual Conference 1909 Ministerial Session', Victoria/Tasmanian Conference, *The Spectator*, 5 March 1909, p. 373.

'Rev J W Burton in Wesley Church', *The Spectator*, 12 March 1909, p. 423.

'Race Disappearance: The Case of the Fijians', *Northern Star*, Lismore, 17 January 1913, p. 3.

'Race Disappearance: A Vanishing Population: The Fijians Dying Out: And the Reason Why.' *The Daily News*, Perth, 1 February 1913, p. 12.

'Doomed Islanders: Decay of the Race: Ravages of Consumption', *The Sydney Morning Herald*, 24 May 1913, p. 19.

'The Call of the Pacific', *The Spectator*, 20 February 1914, p. 307.

'Welcome to Rev J W Burton', *The Spectator*, 1 May 1914, p. 719.

'Foreign Mission Demonstration', *The Spectator*, 2 April 1915, p. 287–88.

'Church News', *Advertiser*, Melbourne, 13 May 1916, p. 2.

'Indians in Fiji: Indenture System: Address by Visiting Missioner', *The West Australian*, 17 April 1917, p. 4.

Jervis, S, 'Methodist Missionary Working in Fiji', cited in 'Notes from the Churches', *Chronicle*, South Australia, 30 August 1919, p. 50.

'Indian Strike Riots in Fiji: Report by the Governor', *The Mercury*, Tasmania, 20 February 1920, p. 5.

'India in Fiji', *The Spectator*, 9 June 1920, p. 422.

'Missionary Enterprise: Stimulating the Work: Interview with J W Burton', *The Register*, Adelaide, 9 October 1922, p. 8.

'Orchestral Concert', *The Horsham Times*, 4 December 1923, p. 5.

Burton, J W, 'Fiji: Labour and the Future', *The Sydney Morning Herald*, 27 September 1924, p. 11.

'Missionary Conference: Native Church Problems: Address by Dr J R Mott', *The Argus*, Melbourne, 13 April 1926, p. 13.

'Fiji', *Townsville Daily Bulletin*, 23 September 1926, p. 3.

'Shipping', *Examiner*, Launceston, 1 January 1927, p. 1.

'The Great Ba Circuit', *The Spectator*, 20 April 1927.

'Returning to Fiji: Rev D N Deller Farewelled', *The Brisbane Courier*, 26 May 1927, p. 9.

'Australia's Responsibility in the Pacific', *Northern Standard*, Darwin, 8 July 1927, p. 2.

Meek, B, 'Agricultural Education in Fiji', *The Missionary Review*, 5 March 1928, p. 12.

'Courageous Meeting: International Missionary Council', *The Brisbane Courier*, 10 April 1928, p. 11.

'Missionary Societies. Conference in Melbourne', *Examiner*, Tasmania, 14 April 1928, p. 14.

'Methodist', *The Brisbane Courier*, 30 March 1929, p. 10

'Methodist', *The Brisbane Courier*, 22 June 1929, p. 7.

'Katherine Notes', *Northern Territory Times*, 5 July 1929, p. 3

'Mission Work Exemplified', *Frankston and Somerville Standard*, Victoria, 6 July 1929, p. 4.

'A Singing Evangelist', *Northern Standard*, Northern Territory, 5 July 1929, p. 2.

'The Churches', *Albury Banner and Wodonga Express*, 20 December 1929, p. 14.

'The Innocents Abroad: "Sorry to stow away": Some Sidelights on Suva', *Western Mail*, Perth, 14 August 1930, p. 16.

'Preacher and Singer', *The Advertiser*, South Australia, 17 September 1930, p. 16.

'Across Viti Levu: Rebuilding Towns: Successful Fijian Farmers', *The Spectator*, 30 September 1931.

G H Findlay, 'A Missionary Problem in Fiji', *The Spectator*, 13 January 1932, p. 33.

'Liquor Laws and Mixed Races: Fijian System Aggravates Racial Feeling', *The Advertiser*, Adelaide, 6 May 1932, p. 16.

Green, R H, 'Fiji Synod 1933', *The Spectator*, 11 April 1934, p. 301.

'Missionary Difficulties: J W Burton's Analysis', *The Advertiser*, 25 May 1934, p. 15.

'Missionary Work', *The West Australian*, Perth, 9 June 1934, p. 14.

'Native Races: Problems of the Pacific. Rev J W Burton's Address', *The Sydney Morning Herald*, 19 February 1935, p. 8.

Amos, A W 'Fiji Revisted', continued from 20 November 1935, *The Spectator*, 27 November 1935, p. 975.

Amos, A W, 'The New Fiji', *The Spectator*, 29 January 1936.

'League of Nations: Delegate to Union Congress', *The Mercury*, Hobart, 21 July 1936, p. 4.

'Burnie', *Advocate*, Tasmania, 12 October 1936, p. 6.

'Natives in the North: Report of Abduction: Government Criticised', *Examiner*, Tasmania, 17 April 1937, p. 5.

'In the Churches: Devonport Methodist', *Advocate*, Tasmania, 19 June 1937, p. 9.

'Improvements in India: New Constitution', *Examiner*, Tasmania, 7 January 1938, p. 6.

'Mission Conference, World Meeting at Madras', *The West Australian*, Perth, 29 November 1938, p. 3.

'For Overseas Mission: Party at Home of President', *The Examiner*, 18 November 1938, p. 7.

'Confirms Unity of the Church: Madras Conference Opens Today', *The Advertiser*, South Australia, 12 December 1938, p. 22

'Indian Education', *Fiji Times and Herald*, 15 July 1941, p. 8.

'Methodist Mission 104th Annual Synod', *Fiji Times and Herald*, 15 October 1941, p. 5.

'Message of the Church: "Strategy in missions"', *Advocate*, Tasmania, 10 June 1943, p. 4.

'Task for Church After War: New Methodist President's Concern', *The Argus*, 1 March 1945, p. 2.

'Natives of Pacific Islands Present Problem of Rehabilitation', *Recorder*, Port Pirie, 6 May 1946, p. 1.

'Fiji Faces New Problems', *The Examiner*, Launceston, 16 May 1946, p. 3.

'Fijians Rely Less on Whites', *The Mercury*, Tasmania, 16 May 1946, p. 6.

H Richardson, 'Coming to Grips with Our Native Problem', *Courier Mail*, 18 September 1948, p. 7.

'Personal', *The Argus*, Melbourne, 6 August 1949, p. 12.

'Missionary', *The Mercury*, Hobart, 10 September 1949, p. 7.

'Fijian Minister Ill', *The West Australian*, Perth, 9 January 1950, p. 10.

'Pacific Conference', *Examiner*, Launceston, 19 April 1950, p. 17.

'Fijian Preacher', *Sunday Mail*, Brisbane, 11 June 1950, p. 3.

'The Churches: Methodists Plan Missions in N G', *The Sydney Morning Herald*, 12 August 1950, p. 7.

'Prestige in India: Britain's Name Held in High Regard', *The West Australian* , Perth, WA, 22 November 1950, p. 17.

'Indians "Beginning to oust whites in Fiji"', *The West Australian*, Perth, 10 May 1951, p. 9.

'Methodist Crusade to Continue', *Northern Star*, Lismore, 6 March 1952, p. 8.

'Points from the Pulpit: Indian Church Gives Lead to the World', *Examiner*, Tasmania, 19 May 1952, p. 3.

Gribble, C F, 'Mission Work in New Guinea', *Sydney Morning Herald*, 15 November 1952, p. 2.

Tippett, A R, 'The Methodist Church in Fiji', *The Spectator*, 3 June 1953, p. 338.

'The New Challenge in Fiji', *The Spectator*, 17 March 1954, p. 10.

'Missions Have World Problem', *Courier Mail*, Brisbane, 22 May 1954, p. 6.

'Progress in Work of Missions', *The Advertiser*, Adelaide, 4 March 1953, p. 3.

Tippett, A, 'A Book is Being Printed', *The Spectator*, 27 October 1954, p. 7.

Gribble, C, '"No Greater Thing"', *The Spectator*, 10 August 1955, p. 1.

Raiwalui, A K, 'Fijian Slant on the Appeal', *The Spectator*, 10 August 1955, p. 1.

Amos, A W, '1855–1955', *The Spectator*, 10 August 1955, p. 4.

Carne, T C, 'Dudley Youth Club', *The Spectator*, 26 October 1955, p. 4.

Loy, A W, 'Overseas Missions: The Church in Fiji-India', 28 March 1956, *The Spectator*, p. 13.

'Overseas Missions: The Voice of the Younger Church', *The Spectator*, 16 May 1956, p. 13.

Wood, A H, 'Issues of Race and Peace at Lake Junaluska', *The Spectator*, 17 October 1956.

James, A, 'Overseas Missions Centenary Fund Appeal', *The Spectator*, 31 August 1955, p. 13.

Tippett, A R, MA, College Principal, Davuilevu, Fiji, 'What the Theological Student in Fiji Thinks', *The Spectator*, 13 January 1960, p. 14.

Robson, J R H, 'Fiji To-day: Problems Old and New', *The Spectator*, 13 April 1960, p. 17.

Fullerton, L D, 'Pacific Missionaries', *The Spectator*, 1 June 1960, p. 7.

Gribble, C F, 'The Older Pacific Churches', statement at the board of missions now in session in Sydney, *The Spectator*, 31 August 1960, p. 14.

'Report from Fiji', *The Spectator*, 23 August 1961, p. 14.

'Our Missionary Perspective', part two, *The Spectator*, 1 November 1961, p. 14.

Wright, C J, 'South Pacific Encounter', *The Spectator*, 29 November 1961, p. 13.

Published sources

Ali, A, 'Fijian Chiefs and Constitutional Change, 1874–1937', *Journal de la Societe des Oceanistes*, vol. 33, no. 54–55, 1977, pp. 55–64.

Anderson, B, *Imagined Communities: Reflections on the Origins and Spread of Nationalism*, London, Verso, 1991.

Andrews, C F, *India and the Pacific*, London, George Allen and Unwin Ltd, 1937.

Arno, A, 'Cobo and Tabua in Fiji: Two Forms of Cultural Currency in an Economy of Sentiment', *American Ethnologist*, vol. 32, no. 1, 2005, pp. 46–62.

Bain, A, 'A Protective Labour Policy? An Alternative Interpretation of Early Colonial Labour Policy', *The Journal of Pacific History*, vol. 23, no. 2, 1988, pp. 119–36.

Baledrokadroka, J, 'Fijian Ethno-nationalism', in J Fraenkel, S Firth and B V Lal (eds), *The 2006 Military Takeover in Fiji: A Coup to end all Coups*, Canberra, ANU E Press, 2009, pp. 415–8.

Ballantyne T, and A Burton (eds), *Moving Subjects: Gender, Mobility and Intimacy in an Age of Global Empire*, Illinois, University of Illinois, 2009.

Baleiwaqa, T, 'Setareki Akeai Tuilovoni and the Young People's Department of the Methodist Church in Fiji (1951–1957)', Bachelor of Divinity thesis, Pacific Theological College, 1987.

Baucom, I, *Out of Place: Englishness, Empire and the Locations of Identity*, Princeton, Princeton University Press, 1999.

Bellwood, P, J J Fox and D Tryon (eds), *The Austronesians: Historical and Comparative Perspectives*, Canberra, ANU E Press, 1995.

Bennett, J A, 'War, Emergency and the Environment: Fiji, 1939–1946', *Environment and History*, vol. 7, no. 3, 2001, pp. 255–87.

Bennett, J A, 'Meditation', *Journal of Pacific History*, vol. 48, no. 3, 2013, pp. 323–29.

Berndt, C, 'The Quest for Identity: The Case of the Australian Aborigines', *Oceania*, vol. 32, no. 1, 1961, pp. 16–33.

Bhabha, H, *Nation and Narration*, London, Routledge, 1990.

Birch, T, '"These children have been born in an abyss": Slum Photography in a Melbourne Suburb', *Australian Historical Studies*, vol. 123, 2004, pp. 1–15.

Bloch, M, *The Historian's Craft: Reflections on the Nature and Uses of History and the Techniques and Methods of Those Who Write It*, New York, Alfred A Knopf, 1953.

Bready, J W, *England: Before and After Wesley: The Evangelical Revival and Social Reform*, New York, Harper, 1938.

Breward, I, 'Wood, Alfred Harold (1896–1989)', *Australian Dictionary of Biography*, National Centre of Biography, The Australian National University, adb.anu.edu.au/biography/wood-alfred-harold-15624/text26824, accessed 4 May 2013.

Breward, I, *Dr Harold Wood: A Notable Methodist*, Preston, Australia, Uniting Academic Press, 2013.

Brison, K J, 'Imagining Modernity in Rural Fiji', *Ethnology*, vol. 42, no. 4, 2003, pp. 335–48.

Brookfield, H C, 'Fijian Farmers Each on his Own Land: The Triumph of Experience Over Hope', *Journal of Pacific History*, vol. 23, no. 1, 1988, pp. 15–35.

Burton, J W, 'Missions and Modernism: Christian Missions as Affected by Liberal Theology', *The Hibbert Journal*, vol. 7, 1908–1909.

Burton, J W, *Fiji of To-day*, London, 1910.

Burton, J W, *The Pacific Islands: A Missionary Survey*, London, World Dominion Press, 1930.

Burton, J W, *Modern Missions in the South Pacific*, Great Britain, Wm Carling and Co Ltd, 1949.

Burton, J W, *The Weaver's Shuttle: Memories and Reflections of an Octogenarian*, unpublished manuscript, n.d.

Bush, J E, 'Claiming a Christian State Where None Exists: Church and State in the Republic of Fiji', *Pacifica*, vol. 12, no. 1, 1999, pp. 55–68.

Bush, J E, 'Land and Communal Faith: Methodist Belief and Ritual in Fifi [sic]', *Studies in World Christianity*, vol. 6, no. 1, 2000, pp. 21–37.

Carne, T C, 'The Christ of the Indian Mind', Eighth Methodist Laymen's Memorial Lecture, Melbourne, 15 November 1927, Methodist Laymen's Missionary Movement, Victoria, digital.slv.vic.gov.au/view/action/singleViewer.do?dvs=1377806583753~29&locale=en_US&metadata_object_ratio=10&show_metadata=true&preferred_usage_type=VIEW_MAIN&frameId=1&usePid1=true&usePid2=true.

Cato, A C, 'A New Religious Cult in Fiji', *Oceania*, vol. 18, no. 2, 1947, pp. 146–56.

Cato, H, *The House on the Hill*, Melbourne, The Book Depot, 1947.

Chand, S, 'Ethnic Conflict, Income Inequality and Growth in Independent Fiji', State, Society and Governance in Melanesia discussion paper, vol. 97, no. 6, 1997, digitalcollections.anu.edu.au/bitstream/1885/40388/3/ssgm97-6.pdf, accessed 9 December 2013.

Chappell, D A, 'The Crisis of Bipolar Ethnicity on the Great Frontier: Nativist "Democracy" in Fiji, Malaysia, and New Caledonia', *Journal of World History*, 1990, pp. 171–98.

Close, K, 'Invisible Labourers: Cape Bedford Mission and the Paradox of Aboriginal Labourers in World War Two', Masters thesis, University of Melbourne, 2009.

Close-Barry, K, 'What's so Anti-Christian about Eequality?', *Republika*, October 2014, pp. 30–32, issuu.com/republikamag/docs/october_2014

Comaroff, J, and J Comaroff, *Of Revelation and Revolution: Christianity, Colonialism and Consciousness in South Africa*, vol. 1, Chicago, University of Chicago Press, 1991.

Comaroff, J, and J Comaroff, *Of Revelation and Revolution: The Dialectics of Modernity on a South African Frontier*, vol. 2, Chicago, University of Chicago Press, 1997.

Cooper, F, *Decolonisation and African Society: The Labor Question in French and British Africa*, Cambridge, Cambridge University Press, 1996.

Cooper, F, and A L Stoler (eds), *Tensions of Empire: Colonial Cultures in a Bourgeois World*, Berkeley, University of California Press, 1997.

Coulter, J W, *Fiji: Little India in the Pacific*, Illinois, Chicago, University of Chicago Press, 1942.

Couper, A D, 'Protest Movements and Proto-cooperatives in the Pacific Islands', *The Journal of the Polynesian* Society, vol. 77, no. 3, 1968, pp. 263–74.

Cowled, S, *Na Veisiko ki Maleya, Suva, Sa tabaki main na Vale ni Taba I vola ni Lotu Wesele*, 1954.

Cowlishaw, G, 'Colour, Culture and the Aboriginalists', *Man*, vol. 22, no. 2, 1987, pp. 221–37.

Cretton, V, 'Traditional Fijian Apology as a Political Strategy', *Oceania*, vol. 75, no. 4, 2005, pp. 403–17.

Cumpston, I M, 'Sir Arthur Gordon and the Introduction of Indians into the Pacific: The West Indian System in Fiji', *Pacific Historical Review*, vol. 25, no. 4, 1956, pp. 369–88.

Dalby, A, *Dictionary of Languages: The Definitive Reference to More Than 400 Languages*, London, Bloomsbury, 1999.

Darch, J H, *Missionary Imperialists? Missionaries, Government and the Growth of the British Empire in the Tropics, 1860–1885*, Colorado Springs, Paternoster, 2009.

Davey, C J, *The March of Methodism: The Story of the Methodist Missionary Work Overseas*, London, Epworth Press, 1951.

Degei, S B, 'The Challenge to Fijian Methodism: The vanua, Identity, Ethnicity and Change', Masters thesis, University of Waikato, 2007.

Doraisamy, T R, *The March of Methodism in Singapore and Malaysia, 1885–1980*, Singapore, Stanford Press, 1982.

Doss, G R, 'John R Mott, 1865–1955: Mission Leader Extraordinaire', *Journal of Applied Christian Leadership*, vol. 4, no. 1, 2010, pp. 72–81.

Douglas, B, and C Ballard (eds), *Foreign Bodies: Oceania and the Science of Race, 1750–1940*, Canberra, ANU E Press, 2008.

Dundon, C G, 'Raicakacaka: "Walking the road" From Colonial to Post-colonial Mission: The Life, Work and Thought of the Reverend Dr Alan Richard Tippett, Methodist Missionary in Fiji, Anthropologist and Missiologist, 1911–1988', PhD thesis, Australian Defence Force Academy, UNSW, 2000.

Elbourne, E, *Blood Ground: Colonialism, Missions and the Contest for Christianity in the Cape Colony and Britain, 1799–1853*, Canada, McGill Queen's University Press, 2002.

Elkin, A P, *Missionary Policy for Primitive Peoples*, Morpeth, NSW, St Johns College Press, 1934.

Elkin, A P, 'Civilised Aborigines and Native Culture', *Oceania*, vol. 6, no. 2, 1935, pp. 117–46.

Elkin, A P, 'Reconstruction and the Native Peoples of the South-West Pacific', *Mankind*, vol. 3, no. 5, 1943, pp. 133–35.

Emde, S, 'Feared Rumours and Rumours of Fear: The Politicisation of Ethnicity During the Fiji Coup in 2000', *Oceania: Relations in Multicultural Fiji: Transformations, Positionings and Articulations*, vol. 75, no. 4, 2005, pp. 387–402.

Eriksen, T H, *Small Places, Large Issues: An Introduction to Social and Cultural Anthropology*, third edition, New York, Pluto Press, 2010.

Eves, R, 'Colonialism, Corporeality and Character: Methodist Missions and the Refashioning of Bodies in the Pacific', *History and Anthropology*, vol. 10, no. 1, 1996, pp. 85–138.

Fabian, J, *Time and the Other: How Anthropology Makes its Object*, New York, Columbia University Press, 1983.

Fife, W, 'Creating the Moral Body: Missionaries and the Technology of Power in Early Papua New Guinea', *Ethnology*, vol. 40, no. 3, 2001, pp. 251–69.

Firth, S, and D Tarte, *20th Century Fiji: People Who Shaped this Nation*, Suva, USP Solutions, University of the South Pacific, 2001.

Forman, C, 'Tonga's Tortured Venture in Church Unity', *Journal of Pacific History*, vol. 13, no. 1, 1978, pp. 3–21.

Forman, C, *The Island Churches of the South Pacific: Emergence in the Twentieth Century*, Michigan, Orbis Books, 1982.

Forman, C W, 'Finding Our Own Voice: The Reinterpreting of Christianity by Oceanian Theologians', *International Bulletin of Missionary Research*, vol. 29, no. 3, 2005, pp. 115–22.

France, P, *The Charter of the Land: Custom and Colonization in Fiji*, Melbourne, Oxford University Press, 1969.

Frazer, J G, 'Preface' in B K Malinowski, *Argonauts of the Western Pacific: An Account of Native Enterprise and Adventure in the Archipelagoes of Melanesian New Guinea*, Long Grove IL, Waveland Press, 1984.

Fry, G, 'The South Pacific "experiment": Reflections on the Origins of Regional Identity', *Journal of Pacific History*, vol. 32, no. 2, 1997, pp. 180–202.

Gaitskell, D, 'Rethinking Gender Roles: The Field Experience of Women Missionaries in South Africa', in A Porter (ed.), *The Imperial Horizons of British Protestant Missions, 1880–1914*, Grand Rapids, Michigan, William B Eerdmans Publishing Company, 2003.

Gardner, H, *Gathering for God: George Brown in Oceania*, Dunedin, Otago University Press, 2006.

Gardner, H, 'The "faculty of faith": Evangelical Missionaries, Social Anthropologists, and the Claim for Human Unity in the 19th Century', in B Douglas and C Ballard (eds), *Foreign Bodies: Oceania and the Science of Race 1750–1940*, ANU E Press, 2008, pp. 259–82.

Gardner, H, 'The Culture Concept and the Theological Colleges', unpublished conference paper, Pacific History Association conference, Wellington, 2012.

Gardner, H, 'Defending Friends: Robert Codrington, George Sarawia, and Edward Wogale', in K Fullagar (ed.), *Atlantic World in the Antipodes: Effects and Transformations since the Eighteenth Century*, Newcastle Upon Tyne, England, Cambridge Scholars Publishing, 2012, pp. 146–65.

Gardner, H, 'Praying for Independence', *Journal of Pacific History*, vol. 28, no. 2, 2013, pp. 122–43.

Gardner, H, and C Waters, 'Decolonisation in Melanesia', *Journal of Pacific History*, vol. 48, no. 2, 2013, pp. 113–21.

Garrett, J, *Footsteps in the Sea: Christianity in Oceania to World War Two*, Suva, University of the South Pacific in conjunction with the World Council of Churches, 1992.

Garrett, J, *Where Nets Were Cast: Christianity in Oceania since World War Two*, Suva, Institute of Pacific Studies, University of the South Pacific in association with the World Council of Churches, 1997.

Gaunder, P, *Education and Race Relations in Fiji, 1835–1998*, Lautoka, Fiji, Universal Printing Press, 1999.

Gillion, K L, 'The Sources of Indian Emigration to Fiji', *Population Studies*, vol. 10, no. 2, 1956, pp. 139–57.

Gillion, K L, *The Fiji-Indians: Challenge to European Dominance, 1920–1946*, Canberra, Australian National University Press, 1977.

Gosden, C, and Y Marshall, 'The Cultural Biography of Objects', *World Archaeology*, vol. 31, no. 2, 1999, pp. 169–78.

Gravelle, K, *Fiji Times: A History of Fiji*, Fiji Times and Herald Ltd, 1979.

Gray, G, 'From Nomadism to Citizenship: A P Elkin and Aboriginal Advancement', in N Peterson and N Sanders (eds), *Citizenship and Indigenous Australians: Changing Conceptions and Possibilities*, Cambridge, Cambridge University Press, 1998, pp. 55–76.

Gray, G, '"You are … my anthropological children": A P Elkin, Ronald Berndt and Catherine Berndt, 1940–1956', *Aboriginal History*, vol. 29, 2005, pp. 77–106.

Gray, G, 'H Ian Hogbin: "Official adviser on native affairs"', in G Gray, D Munro and C Winter (eds), *Scholars at War: Australasian Social Scientists, 1939–1945*, Canberra, ANU E Press, 2012, pp. 73–93.

Green, N, 'Islam for the Indentured Indian: A Muslim Missionary in Colonial South Africa', *Bulletin of the School of Oriental and African Studies*, vol. 71, 2008, pp. 529–53.

Green, R H, *My Story: A Record of the Life and Work of Robert H Green*, Melbourne, 1978.

Gribble, C F, 'A New Voice for the South Pacific', *International Review of Missions*, vol. 39, no. 156, 1950, pp. 431–38.

Gribble, C F, 'Cecil Frank Gribble Interviewed by Diana Ritch [sound recording]', 1990–1991, TRC 2731.

Grimshaw, P, 'Missions, Colonialism and the Politics of Gender', in *Evangelists of Empire: Missionaries in Colonial History*, Melbourne, University of Melbourne Press, 2008, pp. 3–12.

Halse, C, 'The Reverend Ernest Gribble: Successful Missionary?', *Lectures in North Queensland History*, vol. 5, 1996, pp. 218–47.

Hanciles, J, *Euthanasia of a Mission: African Church Autonomy in a Colonial Context*, Wesport, Conn, Praeger, 2002.

Hanlon, D, 'Converting Pasts and Presents: Reflections on Histories of Missionary Enterprise in the Pacific', in B V Lal and P Hempenstall (eds), *Pacific Lives, Pacific Places: Changing Boundaries in Pacific History*, Canberra, Coombs Academic Publishing, 2001, pp. 143–54.

Harries, P, 'From the Alps to Africa: Swiss Missionaries and Anthropology', in H Tilley and R J Gordon, *Ordering Africa: Anthropology, European Imperialism, and the Politics of Knowledge*, Manchester, Manchester University Press, 2007.

Heartfield, J, '"The dark races against the light?" Official Reaction to the 1959 Fiji Riots', *Journal of Pacific History*, vol. 37, no. 1, 2002, pp. 75–86.

Heartfield, J, '"You are not a white woman!": Apolosi Nawai: The Fiji Produce Agency and the Trial of Stella Spencer in Fiji', *Journal of Pacific History*, vol. 38, no. 1, 2003, pp. 69–83.

Heath, I, 'Toward a Reassessment of Gordon in Fiji', *Journal of Pacific History*, vol. 9, no. 1, 1974, pp. 81–92.

Hilliard, D, *God's Gentlemen: A History of the Melanesian Mission, 1849–1942*, St Lucia, University of Queensland Press, 1978.

Hobsbawn, E, Nations and Nationalism Since 1780: *Programme, Myth, Reality*, Cambridge, Cambridge University Press, 1990.

Hogg, W R, *Ecumenical Foundations: A History of the International Missionary Council and its Nineteenth Century Background*, New York, Harper and Brothers, 1952.

Howard, A, *Hef Ran Ta (The Morning Star): A Biography of Wilson Inia, Rotuma's First Senator*, Suva, Institute of Pacific Studies, 1994.

Howe, R, 'The Australian Christian Movement and Women's Activism in the Asia-Pacific Region, 1890–1920s', *Australian Feminist Studies*, vol. 16, no. 36, 2001, pp. 211–32.

Jolly, M, 'Epilogue: Multicultural Relations in Fiji — Between Despair and Hope', Oceania, vol. 75, no. 4, *Relations in Multi-Cultural Fiji: Transformations, Positionings and Articulations*, 2005, pp. 418–30.

Kaplan, M, *Neither Cargo nor Cult: Ritual Politics and the Colonial Imagination in Fiji*, Durham, Duke University Press, 1995.

Kaplan, M, 'When 8.870 - 850 = 1: Discourses Against Democracy in Fiji, Past and Present', in D Gladney (ed.), *Making Majorities: Constituting the Nation in Japan, Korea, China, Malaysia, Fiji, Turkey, and the United States*, California, Stanford University Press, 1998, pp. 198–214.

Kaplan, M, and J Kelly, 'Rethinking Resistance: Dialogics of Disaffection in Colonial Fiji', *American Ethnologist*, vol. 21, no. 1, 1994, pp. 123–51.

Kaplan, M, and J Kelly, 'On Discourse and Power: Cults and Orientals', *American Ethnologist*, vol. 26, no. 4, 2000, pp. 843–65.

Kaplan, M, and J Kelly, *Represented Communities: Fiji and World Decolonization*, Chicago, University of Chicago Press, 2001.

Kelly, J, 'Fear of Culture: British Regulation of Indian Marriage in Post-indenture Fiji', *Ethnohistory*, vol. 36, no. 4, 1989, pp. 372–91.

Kelly, J, *The Politics of Virtue: Hinduism, Sexuality and Counter-Colonial Discourse in Fiji*, Chicago, University of Chicago Press, 1991.

Kelly, J, 'Threats to Difference in Colonial Fiji', *Cultural Anthropology*, vol. 10, no. 1, 1995, pp. 64–84.

Kelly, J, 'Aspiring to Minority and Other Tactics against Violence', in D Gladney (ed.), *Making Majorities: Constituting the Nation in Japan, Korea, China, Malaysia, Fiji, Turkey, and the United States*, California, Stanford University Press, 1998, pp. 173–97.

Kemp, A D, and R T Vinson, '"Poking holes in the sky": Professor James Thaele, American Negroes, and Modernity in 1920s Segregationist South Africa', *African Studies Review*, vol. 43, no. 1, special issue on the diaspora, 2000, pp. 141–59.

Knapman, B, 'Indigenous Involvement in the Cash Economy of Lau, Fiji, 1840–1946', *Journal of Pacific History*, vol. 11, no. 3, 1976, pp. 167–88.

Knapman, B, 'The "vakamisioneri" in Lau, Fiji: A Reply', *Journal of Pacific History*, vol. 13, no. 2, 1978, pp. 113–14.

Knapman, B, 'Capitalism's Economic Impact in Colonial Fiji, 1874–1939: Development or Underdevelopment?', *Journal of Pacific History*, vol. 20, no. 2, 1985, pp. 66–83.

Kraft, C H, and D D Priest, Jr., 'Who Was This Man? A Tribute to Alan R Tippett', *Missiology: An International Review*, vol. 17, no. 3, 1989, pp. 269–81.

Kuper, A, *The Reinvention of Primitive Society: Transformation of a Myth*, New York, Routledge, 2005.

Lal, B V, 'For King and Country: A Talk on the Pacific War in Fiji', in G M White (ed.), *Remembering the Pacific War*, occasional paper series 36, Honolulu, Hawai'i, Center for Pacific Islands Studies, School of Hawaiian, Asian, and Pacific Studies, University of Hawai'i at Mānoa, 1991, pp. 17–25.

Lal, B V, *Broken Waves: A History of the Fiji Islands in the Twentieth Century*, Honolulu, University of Hawai'i Press, 1992.

Lal, B V, 'Odyssey of Indenture: Fragmentation and Reconstruction in the Indian Diaspora', *Diaspora: A Journal of Transnational Studies*, vol. 5, no. 2, 1996, pp. 167–88.

Lal, B V (ed.), *Crossing the Kala Pani: A Documentary History of Indian Indenture in Fiji*, Canberra, Division of Pacific and Asian History, Research School of Pacific and Asian Studies, The Australian National University, Suva, Fiji, Fiji Museum, 1998.

Lal, B V, *Chalo Jahaji: A Journey Through Indenture in Fiji*, Division of Pacific and Asian History, The Australian National University and Fiji Museum, 2000.

Lal, B V, 'Bahut Julum: Reflections on the use of Fiji Hindi', *Fiji Studies: A Journal of Contemporary Fiji*, vol. 3, no. 1, 2005, pp. 153–58.

Lal, B V, *A Time Bomb Lies Buried: Fiji's Road to Independence, 1960–1970*, Canberra, ANU E Press, 2008.

Lal, B V, *A Vision for Change: A D Patel and the Politics of Fiji*, Canberra, ANU E Press, 2011.

Lal, B V, and B Shineberg, 'The Story of the Haunted Line: Totaram Sanadhya Recalls the Labour Lines in Fiji', *Journal of Pacific History*, vol. 26, no. 1, 1991, pp. 107–12.

Lambert, D, and A Lester, *Colonial Lives Across the British Empire*, Cambridge, Cambridge University Press, 2006.

Lane, J, 'Anchorage in Aboriginal affairs: A P Elkin on Religious Continuity and Civic Obligation', PhD thesis, University of Sydney, 2008.

Larson, E W, and R Aminzade, 'Nation-states Confront the Global: Discourses of Indigenous Rights in Fiji and Tanzania', *The Sociological Quarterly*, vol. 48, no. 4, 2007, pp. 801–31.

Leckie, J, 'Workers in Colonial Fiji: 1870–1970', in C Moore, J Leckie and D Munro, (eds), *Labour in the South Pacific*, Townsville, James Cook University, 1990.

Leerssen, J, 'Nationalism and the Cultivation of Culture', *Nations and Nationalism*, vol. 12, no. 4, 2006, pp. 559–78.

Lenwood, F, 'The International Missionary Council at Lake Mohonk, October 1921,' *International Review of Missions*, vol. 11, 1922, pp. 30–42.

Lester, A, 'Imperial Circuits and Networks: Geographies of the British Empire', *History Compass*, vol. 4, no. 1, 2006.

Lindenfield, D, and M Richardson (eds), *Beyond Conversion and Syncretism: Indigenous Encounters with Missionary Christianity, 1800–2000*, New York and Oxford, Berghahn Books, 2012.

Linnekin, J, and L Poyer (eds), *Cultural Identity and Ethnicity in the Pacific*, Honolulu, University of Hawai'i Press, 1990.

Lydon, J, '"Our sense of beauty": Visuality, Space and Gender on Victoria's Aboriginal Reserves, South-eastern Australia', *History and Anthropology*, vol. 16, no. 2, 2005, pp. 211–33.

Lyng, J, *Non-Britishers in Australia: Influence on Population and Progress*, Melbourne, Macmillan and Co with University of Melbourne Press, 1927.

Macnaught, T, 'Chiefly Civil Servants? Ambiguity in District Administration in the Preservation of the Fijian Way of Life, 1896–1940', *Journal of Pacific History*, vol. 9, 1974, pp. 3–20.

Macnaught, T, *The Fijian Colonial Experience: A Study of the Neotraditional Order Under British Colonial Rule Prior to World War II*, Canberra, ANU Press, Pacific Research Monograph Number 7, 1982.

Malinowski, B K, *Argonauts of the Western Pacific: An Account of Native Enterprise and Adventure in the Archipelagoes of Melanesian New Guinea*, Long Grove IL, Waveland Press, 1984.

Mamdani, M, 'Historicising Power and Responses to Power: Indirect Rule and its Reform', *Social Reform*, vol. 66, no. 3, 1999, pp. 859–86.

Mamdani, M, *When Victims Become Killers: Colonialism, Nativism, and the Genocide in Rwanda*, Princeton University Press, 2002.

Mamdani, M, *Define and Rule: The Native as Political Identity*, Cambridge, Massachusetts, Harvard University Press, 2012.

Manderson, L, and M Jolly, *Sites of Desire, Economies of Pleasure: Sexualities in Asia and the Pacific*, Chicago, University of Chicago Press, 1997.

Mathews, B, *Roads to the City of God: World Outlook from Jerusalem*, London, Edinburgh House Press, 1928.

Mausio, A, 'The "Fijian dilemma": The Revolving Door Syndrome in Ethnic Fijian Rural Development', *Fijian Studies*, vol. 5, no. 1, 2007, pp. 42–70.

McConvell, P, and H Gardner, 'The Descent of Morgan in Australia: Kinship Representation from the Australian Colonies', *Structure and Dynamics: eJournal of Anthropological and Related Sciences*, vol. 6, no. 1, 2013, pp. 1–23.

McGregor, R, 'From Old Testament to New: A P Elkin on Christian Conversion and Cultural Assimilation', *Journal of Religious History*, vol. 25, no. 1, 2001, pp. 39–55.

McGregor, R, 'Wards, Words and Citizens: AP Elkin and Paul Hasluck on Assimilation', *Oceania*, vol. 69, no. 4, 1999, pp. 243–59.

Mehta, U S, 'Liberal Strategies of Exclusion', in F Cooper and A L Stoler (eds), *Tensions of Empire: Colonial Cultures in a Bourgeois World*, Berkeley, University of California Press, 1997.

Miller, R J, 'Victory in the Constant Struggle: The Life and Times of Reverend Ramsey R H H Deoki', Honours thesis, Queen's College Library.

Moran, R, *Sex, Maiming and Murder: Seven Case Studies into the Reliability of Reverend E R B Gribble, Superintendent, Forrest River Mission 1913–1928, as a Witness of the Truth*, Bassendean WA, Access Press, 2002.

Morphy, H, 'Mutual Conversion?: The Methodist Church and the Yolnu, with particular reference to Yirrkala', *Humanities Research*, vol. 12, no. 1, 2005, pp. 41–53 epress.anu.edu.au/wp-content/uploads/2011/02/hrj-ch06.pdf, accessed 13 May 2013.

Mott, J R, *The Evangelization of the World in this Generation*, New York, Student Volunteer Movement for Foreign Missions, 1905.

Moynagh, M, 'Land Tenure in Fiji's Sugar Cane Districts Since the 1920s', *Journal of Pacific History*, vol. 13, no. 1, 1978, pp. 53–73.

Munro, D, 'The Making of Ai Matai: A Cautionary Tale in Fijian historiography and Publishing', *Pacific Studies*, vol. 20, no. 3, 1997, pp. 61–79.

Nanni, G, *The Colonization of Time: Ritual, Routine and Resistance in the British Empire*, Manchester, Manchester University Press, 2012.

Nawadra, T R, *Ai Matai – Malaya: 1st battalion, Fiji Infantry Regiment, Far East Land Forces, 1952–1956*, Suva, History and archives unit, Republic of Fiji Military Forces, 1995.

Nayacakalou, R, *Leadership in Fiji*, Oxford, University of the South Pacific in association with Oxford University Press, 1975.

Neill, S, *A History of Christian Missions*, London, Penguin, 1964.

Newbigin, L, *A Faith for this One World?*, London, SCM Press, 1961.

Newbury, C, '*Bose Vakaturaga*: Great Council of Chiefs, 1875–2000', *Pacific Studies*, vol. 29, nos 1 and 2, 2006, pp. 82–127.

Newbury, C, 'Chieftaincy in Transition', *Journal of Pacific History*, vol. 43, no. 2, 2008, pp. 167–87.

Nicole, R, *Disturbing History: Resistance in Early Colonial Fiji*, Honolulu, University of Hawai'i Press, 2011.

Norton, R, 'Culture and Identity in the South Pacific', *Man*, vol. 28, 1993, pp. 741–59.

Norton, R, 'Ethno-nationalism and the Constitutive Power of Cultural Politics: A Comparative Study of Sri Lanka and Fiji', *Journal of Asian and African Studies*, vol. 28, no. 3–4, 1993, pp. 180–97.

Norton, R, 'Chiefs for the Nation: Containing Ethnonationalism and Bridging the Ethnic Divide in Fiji', *Pacific Studies*, vol. 22, no. 1, 1999, pp. 21–50.

Norton, R, 'Accommodating Indigenous Privilege: Britain's Dilemma in Decolonising Fiji', *Journal of Pacific History*, vol. 37, no. 2, 2002, pp. 133–56.

Norton, R, 'A Preeminent Right to Political Rule: Indigenous Fijian Power and Multiethnic Nation Building', *The Round Table: The Commonwealth Journal of International Affairs*, vol. 101, no. 6, 2012, pp. 521–35.

O'Connor, T M, 'Thompson, Leslie Muir (1885–1975)', *Australian Dictionary of Biography*, National Center of Biography, The Australian National University, adb.anu.edu.au/biography/thompson-leslie-muir-11850/text21211, accessed 6 February 2013.

Ovendale, R, 'Macmillan and the Wind of Change in Africa, 1957–1960', *The Historical Journal*, vol. 38, no. 2, 1995, pp. 455–77.

Overton, J, 'A Fijian Peasantry: Galala and Villagers', *Oceania*, vol. 58, no. 3, 1988, pp. 193–211.

Overton, J, 'The Limits of Acculturation: Changing Land Tenure in Fiji', *Journal of Peasant Studies*, vol. 19, no. 2, 1992, pp. 326–42.

Paisley, F, 'Citizens of their World: Australian Feminism and Indigenous Rights in the International Context, 1920s and 1930s', *Feminist Review*, no. 58, 1998, pp. 66–84.

Pande, A, 'Indians and the Struggle for Power in Fiji', *Diaspora Studies*, vol. 3, no. 1, 2010, pp. 57–67.

Pels, P, 'Anthropology and Mission: Towards a Historical Analysis of Professional Identity', in R Bonsen, H Marks and J Miedema (eds), *The Ambiguity of Rapprochement: Reflections of Anthropologists on their Controversial Relationship with Missionaries*, Vondalstaat, Focaal, 1990.

Phelan, J, 'Robert Browning and Colonialism', *Journal of Victorian Literature*, vol. 8, no. 1, 2003, pp. 80–107.

Pickering-Bhagwan, M, 'A Historical Examination of the Indian Synod's Amalgamation into the Conference of the Methodist Church of Fiji and Rotuma', thejournalofaspiritualwonderer.blogspot.com.au/2013/05/a-historical-examination-of-indian.html.

Pitt Rivers, G H L, *The Clash of Culture and the Contact of Races*, New York, Negro Universities Press, 1927.

Proceedings of the Ecumenical Methodist Conference Held in City Road Chapel, London, September 1881, London, Wesleyan Conference Office, 1881.

Popke, E J, 'Managing Colonial Alterity: Narratives of Race, Space and Labor in Durban, 1870–1920', *Journal of Historical Geography*, vol. 29, no. 2, 2003, pp. 248–67.

Porter, A, '"Cultural imperialism" and Protestant Missionary Enterprise, 1780–1914', *Journal of Imperial and Commonwealth History*, vol. 25, no. 3, 1997, pp. 367–91.

Porter, A, *Religion Versus Empire? British Protestant Missionaries and Overseas Expansion, 1700–1914*, Manchester, Manchester University Press, 2004.

Ram, K, and M Jolly, *Maternities and Modernities: Colonial and Postcolonial Experiences in Asia and the Pacific*, Cambridge, Cambridge University Press, 1998.

Rasoqosoqo, L, 'Reverend Koroi Praises Reconciliation', *Fiji Sun*, 28 August 2014, fijisun.com.fj/2013/08/28/reverend-koroi-praises-reconciliation/.

Ratawa, P, *When the Spirit Says Move: An Autobiography*, Geelong, Printshop, 1996.

Ravuvu, A, *The Façade of Democracy: Fijian Struggles for Political Control, 1830–1987*, Suva, Fiji, Reader Publishing House, 1991.

Ravuvu, A D, *The Fijian Ethos*, Suva, Institute of Pacific Studies, University of the South Pacific, 1987.

Rensel, J, and M Rodman, *Home in the Islands: Housing and Social Change in the Pacific*, Honolulu, University of Hawai'i Press, 1997.

Riseman, N, 'Disrupting Assimilation: Soldiers, Missionaries and Aboriginal People in Arnhem Land During World War II', in A Barry, J Cruickshank, A Brown-May and P Grimshaw (eds), *Evangelists of Empire?: Missionaries in Colonial History*, www.msp.unimelb.edu.au/missions/index.php/missions/article/viewFile/20/22, accessed 13 May 2013.

Roberts, D L, *American Women in Mission: A Social History of their Thought and Practice*, Mercer University Press, 2005.

Rodman, M, *Houses Far from Home: British Colonial Space in the New Hebrides*, Honolulu, University of Hawai'i Press, 2001.

Russell, E W, 'Barnett, Frederick Oswald (1883–1972)', *Australian Dictionary of Biography*, National Centre of Biography, The Australian National University, adb.anu.edu.au/biography/barnett-frederick-oswald-5138/text8599, accessed 26 June 2013.

Russell, L, *Colonial Frontiers: Indigenous-European Encounters in Settler Societies*, Manchester, Manchester University Press, 2001.

Ryle, J, 'Roots of Land and Church: The Christian State Debate in Fiji', *International Journal for the Study of the Christian Church*, vol. 5, no. 1, 2005, pp. 58–75.

Ryle, J, *My God, My Land: Interwoven Paths of Christianity and Tradition in Fiji*, Farnham, Surrey, Ashgate, 2010.

Ryle, J, 'Burying the Past – Healing the Land: Ritualising Reconciliation in Fiji', in Y Fer (ed.), special issue, *Archives des Sciences Sociales des Religions: Changing Christianity in Oceania*, Janvier–Mars 2012, no. 157, pp. 89–111.

Samson, J, *Imperial Benevolence: Making British Authority in the Pacific Islands*, Honolulu, University of Hawai'i Press, 1998.

Samson, J, '"Race and Redemption": British Missions and Pacific Ethnography', in K Darian Smith, P Grimshaw, K Lindsey and S McIntyre (eds), *Exploring the British World: Identity, Cultural Production, Institutions*, Melbourne, Victoria, RMIT publishing, 2004, pp. 345–55.

Sanneh, L, *Translating the Message: The Missionary Impact on Culture*, Maryknoll, NY, Orbis Books, 2009.

Saunders, K, 'The Passing of Paternalism in Missions', *Journal of Religion*, vol. 2, no. 5, 1922, pp. 466–75.

Scarr, D, *More Pacific Island Portraits*, Canberra, Australian National University Press, 1978.

Scarr, D, *Ratu Sukuna: Soldier, Statesman, Man of Two Worlds*, London, Macmillan Education for the Ratu Sir Lala Sukuna biography committee, 1980.

Scarr, D, A *History of the Pacific Islands: Passages Through Tropical Time*, New York, Routledge, 2001.

Scott, E, 'Foreword', in J Lyng, *Non-Britishers in Australia: Influence on Population and Progress*, Melbourne, Macmillan and Co with University of Melbourne Press, 1927.

Schoonhaven, E J, 'Tambaram 1938', *International Review of Missions*, vol. 67, 1978, pp. 299–315.

Semple, R A, *Missionary Women: Gender, Professionalism and the Victorian Idea of Christian Mission,* Suffolk, The Boydell Press, 2003.

Sharma, U, and H Irvine, 'The Commodification of Labour: Accounting for Indentured Workers in Fijian Sugar Plantations, 1879–1920', www.apira2013.org/proceedings/pdfs/K028.pdf, accessed 6 March 2014.

Sidal, M, *Hannah Dudley: Hamari Maa: Honoured Mother, Educator, and Missioner to the Indentured Indians in Fiji, 1864–1931*, Suva, Fiji, Pacific Theological College Press, 1997.

Skinner, R, and A Lester, 'Humanitarianism and Empire: New Research Agendas', *The Journal of Imperial and Commonwealth History*, vol. 40, no. 5, 2012, pp. 729–47.

Smith, W T, 'An Appraisal of Thomas Coke's Africa mission, 1796–1811', *Church History*, vol. 40, no. 3, 1971, pp. 306–16.

Snyder, L L, 'The Idea of Racialism: Its Meaning and History', in E Cashmore and J Jennings (eds), *Racisms: Essential Readings*, Thousand Oaks, California, London, 2001.

Sohmer, S H, 'Idealism and Pragmatism in Colonial Fiji: Sir Arthur Gordon's Native Rule Policy and the Introduction of Indian Contract Labour', *Hawaiian Journal of History*, vol. 18, 1984, pp. 140–55.

Stanley, B, *The Bible and the Flag: Protestant Missions and British Imperialism in the Nineteenth and Twentieth Centuries*, Leicester, England, Apollos, 1990.

Stanley, B, 'The Church of the Three Selves: A Perspective from the World Missionary Conference, Edinburgh, 1910', *Journal of Imperial and Commonwealth History,* vol. 36, no. 3, 2008, pp. 435–51.

Stanley, B, *The World Missionary Conference, Edinburgh 1910*, Grand Rapids, Eerdmans, 2009.

Stocking, G, *Race, Culture and Evolution: Essays in the History of Anthropology*, London, Collier-Macmillan Limited, 1968.

Stocking, G W, *After Tylor: British Social Anthropology, 1888–1951*, London, Anthlone, 1996.

Stoler, A L, 'Rethinking Colonial Categories', *Comparative Studies in Society and History*, vol. 31, no. 1, January 1989, pp. 134–61.

Stoler, A L, *Race and the Education of Desire: Foucault's History of Sexuality*, Durham, Duke University Press, 1995.

Stoler, A L, 'Sexual Affronts and Racial Frontiers: European Identities and the Cultural Politics of Exclusion in Colonial Southeast Asia', in A Brah and A Coombes (eds), *Hybridity and its Discontents: Politics, Science, Culture*, London, Routledge, 2000.

Stoler, A L, *Carnal Knowledge and Imperial Power: Race and the Intimate in Colonial Rule*, Berkeley and Los Angeles, University of California Press, 2002.

Suchet, S, '"Totally Wild"?: Colonising Discourses, Indigenous Knowledges and Managing Wildlife', *Australian Geographer*, vol. 33, no. 2, 2002, pp. 141–57.

Sullivan, S, *Revealing Whiteness: The Unconscious Habits of Racial Privilege*, Bloomington, Illinois, Indiana University Press, 2006.

Susu, I K, 'The Centennial Anniversary of the Davuilevu Theological College (1908–2008)', in *Light on the Hill: To Commemorate the 100 years of Davuilevu Methodist Theological College, 1908–2008*, Suva, Davuilevu Theological College, 2008.

Tarte, D, Fiji: *A Place to Call Home*, ANU Press, 2014.

Teaiwa, T, 'An Analysis of the Current Political Crisis in Fiji', in B V Lal and M Pretes (eds), *Coup: Reflections on the Political Crisis in Fiji*, Canberra, ANU E Press, 2008.

Telfer, D, *Of Love and Privilege*, Fullarton, South Australia, Colin Telfer, 2009.

Thomas, N, *Out of Time: History and Evolution in Anthropological Discourse*, Michigan, University of Michigan Press, 1989.

Thomas, N, 'Partial Texts: Representation, Colonialism and Agency in Pacific History', *Journal of Pacific History*, vol. 25, no. 2, 1990, pp. 139–58.

Thomas, N, 'Sanitation and Seeing: The Creation of State Power in Early Colonial Fiji', *Comparative Studies in Society and History*, vol. 32, no. 1, 1990, pp. 149–70.

Thomas, N, 'The Inversion of Tradition', *American Ethnologist*, vol. 19, no. 2, 1992, pp. 213–32.

Thomas, N, *Colonialism's Culture: Anthropology, Travel and Government*, Melbourne, Melbourne University Press, 1994.

Thomas, N, 'Exchange Systems, Political Dynamics, and Colonial Transformations in Nineteenth Century Oceania', in P Bellwood, J J Fox and D Tryon (eds), *The Austronesians: Historical and Comparative Perspectives*, Canberra, ANU E Press, 1995.

Thompson, E W, *The Call of India: A Study in Conditions, Methods and Opportunities of Missionary Work Among Hindus*, London, The Wesleyan Methodist Missionary Society, Bishopsgate, 1912.

Thornley, A, 'The Methodist Mission and the Indians in Fiji, 1900 to 1920', Masters thesis, University of Auckland, 1973.

Thornley, A, 'The Methodist Mission and Fiji's Indians: 1879–1920', *The New Zealand Journal of History*, vol. 8, no. 1, 1974, pp. 137–53.

Thornley, A, 'The "vakamisioneri" in Lau, Fiji: Some Comments', *Journal of Pacific History*, vol. 12, no. 2, 1977, pp. 107–12.

Thornley, A, 'Fijian Methodism: 1874–1945: The Emergence of a National Church', PhD thesis, The Australian National University, 1979.

Thornley, A, 'Custom, Change and Conflict: Fijian Wesleyan Ministers, 1835–1945', in R J May and H Nelson (eds), *Melanesia: Beyond Diversity*, Canberra, Research School of Pacific Studies, The Australian National University, 1982.

Thornley, A, 'Fijians in the Methodist Ministry: The First Hundred Years, 1848–1945', in A Thornley and T Vulaono (eds), *Mai kea ki vei? Stories of Methodism in Fiji and Rotuma*, proceedings of the Fiji Methodist history conference, Davuilevu, 10–13 October 1995, Fiji Methodist Church Press, 1996.

Thornley, A, '"Through a glass darkly": Ownership of Fijian Methodism, 1850–80', in P Herda (ed.), *Vision and Reality in Pacific Religion*, Canberra, Pandanus Books, 2005, pp. 132–53.

Tippett, A, *Oral Tradition and Ethno-history: The Transmission of Information and Social Values in Early Christian Fiji, 1835–1905*, Canberra, St Marks Library, 1980.

Tippett, A R, *The Christian (Fiji 1835–67)*, Auckland, Institute Printing and Publishing Society, 1954.

Tomlinson, M, 'Sacred Soil in Kadavu, Fiji', *Oceania*, vol. 72, no. 4, 2002, pp. 237–57.

Tomlinson, M, *In God's Image: The Metaculture of Fijian Christianity*, Berkeley, University of California Press, 2009.

Tomlinson, M, 'Passports to Eternity: Whale's Teeth and Transcendence in Fijian Methodism', in L Manderson, W Smith and M Tomlinson (eds), *Flows of Faith: Religious Reach and Community in Asia and the Pacific*, Melbourne, Springer, 2012, pp. 215–31.

Toren, C, 'Making the Present, Revealing the Past: The Mutability and Continuity of Tradition as Process', *Man*, New Series, vol. 23, no. 4, 1988, pp. 696–717.

Toren, C, Mind, *Materiality and History: Explorations in Fijian Ethnography*, London, Routledge, 1999.

Toren, C, 'Becoming a Christian in Fiji: An Ethnographic Study of Ontology', *Journal of the Royal Anthropological Institute*, vol. 10, no. 1, 2003, pp. 709–27.

Tschoegi, A E, *Foreign Banks in the Pacific: Some History and Policy Issues*, d1c25a6gwz7q5e.cloudfront.net/papers/1096.pdf, accessed 25 January 2014.

Turner, J W, 'Blessed to Give and Receive: Ceremonial Exchange in Fiji', *Ethnography*, vol. 26, no. 3, 1987, pp. 209–19.

Tuwere, I S, *Vanua: Towards a Fijian Theology of Place*, Suva, Fiji, Institute of Pacific Studies, University of The South Pacific, 2002.

Tylor, E B, *Primitive Culture: Researches into the Development of Mythology, Philosophy, Religion, Art, and Custom*, vol. 2, London, John Murray, 1871.

Vedalankar, P N, and M Somera, *Arya Samaj and Indians Abroad*, Durban, South Africa, Sarvadeshik Arya Pratinidhi Sabha, 1975.

Veracini, L, '"Emphatically not a white man's colony": Settler Colonialism and the Construction of Colonial Fiji', *Journal of Pacific History*, vol. 43, no. 2, 2008, pp. 189–205.

Veracini, L, *Settler Colonialism: A Theoretical Overview*, Houndmills, Palgrave Macmillan, 2010.

Voigt-Graf, C, 'Transnationalism and the Indo-Fijian Diaspora: The Relationship of Indo-Fijians to India and its People', *Journal of Intercultural Studies*, vol. 29, no. 1, 2008, pp. 81–109.

Wainwright, G, *Lesslie Newbigin: A Theological Life*, Cary, NC, USA, Oxford University Press, 2000.

Wallace, L, 'A House is not a Home: Gender, Space and Marquesan Encounter, 1833–34', *Journal of Pacific History*, vol. 40, no. 3, December 2005, pp. 265–88.

Walls, A, 'Foreword: A Salute to Lamin Sanneh' in A E Akinade (ed.), *New Day: Essays on World Christianity in Honor of Lamin Sanneh*, New York, P Lang, 2010.

Ward, G, 'Internal Migration in Fiji', *Journal of the Polynesian Society*, vol. 70, no. 3, 1961, pp. 257–71.

Washington, B T, *Working With the Hands: Being a Sequel to 'Up From Slavery', Covering the Author's Experiences in Industrial Training at Tuskegee*, New York, Doubleday Page and Company, 1904.

Washington, B T, *Up From Slavery: An Autobiography*, London, Oxford University Press, 1945.

Washington, B T, *The Story of My Life and Work*, New York, Cosimo, 2007.

Webb, T, 'Tribal Organisation in Eastern Arnhem Land', *Oceania*, vol. 3, no. 4, 1933, pp. 406–11.

Webb, T, *Spears to Spades*, Sydney, Department of Overseas Mission, 1938.

Weir, C, 'The Work of Mission: Race, Labour and Christian Humanitarianism in the South-west Pacific, 1870–1930', PhD thesis, The Australian National University, 2003.

Weir, C, 'An Accidental Biographer? On Encountering, Yet Again, the Ideas and Actions of J W Burton', in B V Lal and V Luker (eds), *Telling Pacific Lives: Prisms of Process*, Canberra, ANU E Press, 2008, pp. 215–25.

Wells, E, *Reward and Punishment in Arnhem Land, 1962–1963*, Canberra, Australian Institute of Aboriginal Studies, 1982.

West, M R, *The Education of Booker T Washington: American Democracy and the Idea of Race Relations*, New York, Columbia University Press, 2006.

Wetherell, D, *Charles Abel and the Kwato Mission of Papua New Guinea 1891–1975*, Melbourne, Melbourne University Press, 1996.

White, C, 'Affirmative Action and Education in Fiji: Legitimation, Contestation and Colonial Discourse', *Harvard Educational Review*, vol. 71, no. 2, 2001, pp. 240–68.

White, C M, 'Minority Status as a Contested Terrain: Defining the Parameters of Subordinate Status in Post-independent Fiji Discourse', *Social Identities: Journal for the Study of Race, Nation and Culture*, vol. 8, no. 1, 2002, pp. 11–43.

Williams, P, *The Ideal of the Self-Governing Church: A Study in Victorian Missionary Strategy*, Leiden, E J Brill, 1990.

Wise, T, *A P Elkin: The Self-made Anthropologist*, Sydney, George Allen and Unwin, 1985.

Wolfe, P, 'Land, Labour, and Difference: Elementary Structures of Race', *The American Historical Review*, vol. 106, no. 3, 2001, pp. 866–905.

Wood, A H, *Overseas Missions of the Australian Methodist Church: Tonga and Samoa*, vol. 1, Melbourne, Aldersgate Press, 1975.

Wood, A H, *Overseas Missions of the Australian Methodist Church: Fiji*, vol. 2, Melbourne, Aldersgate Press, 1978.

Wood, A H, *Overseas Missions of the Australian Methodist Church: Fiji-Indian and Rotuma*‚ vol. 3, Aldersgate Press, Melbourne, 1978.

Worrall, H, 'A Racial Riddle: The Clash of Alien Races in the Pacific', *Life*, 1 August 1912, pp. 137–42.

Zorn, J, 'Changes in the World of Mission and Ecumenism, 1947–1963', *International Review of Mission*, vol. 88, no. 350, 1999, pp. 279–90.

17695338R00142

Printed in Poland
by Amazon Fulfillment
Poland Sp. z o.o., Wrocław